Reclaiming the Tomboy

Reclaiming the Tomboy

The Body, Representation, and Identity

Edited by Erica Joan Dymond, Jennifer Harrison, and Holly Wells

LEXINGTON BOOKS
Lanham • Boulder • New York • London

Published by Lexington Books
An imprint of The Rowman & Littlefield Publishing Group, Inc.
4501 Forbes Boulevard, Suite 200, Lanham, Maryland 20706
www.rowman.com

86-90 Paul Street, London, EC2A 4NE

British Library Cataloguing in Publication Information Available

Library of Congress Cataloging-in-Publication Data

Names: Dymond, Erica Joan, editor.
Title: Reclaiming the tomboy : the body, representation, and identity / edited by Erica Joan Dymond, Jennifer Harrison, and Holly Wells.
Description: Lanham, Maryland : Lexington Books, [2022] | Includes bibliographical references and index. | Summary: "With the tomboy figure currently operating in a liminal space between extinction and resurgence, this collection is an unabashed celebration of her rebellious, independent, and pioneering spirit. Reclaiming the Tomboy: The Body, Identity, and Representation pays tribute to tomboys of the past, present, and (hopefully) future"— Provided by publisher.
Identifiers: LCCN 2022014847 (print) | LCCN 2022014848 (ebook) | ISBN 9781793622945 (cloth) | ISBN 9781793622969 (paper) | ISBN 9781793622952 (ebook)
Subjects: LCSH: Gender identity. | Tomboys.
Classification: LCC HQ1075 .R426 2022 (print) | LCC HQ1075 (ebook) | DDC 305.3—dc23/eng/20220516
LC record available at https://lccn.loc.gov/2022014847
LC ebook record available at https://lccn.loc.gov/2022014848

Contents

Acknowledgments vii

Introduction 1

PART I: A RETROSPECTIVE: THE TOMBOY IN HISTORY 13

Chapter 1: Rise of the Marketplace Tomboy 15
Renée M. Sentilles

Chapter 2: The Momboy: Maternal Tomboys on Stage 31
Lynn Deboeck

PART II: THE WRITTEN WORD: THE TOMBOY IN LITERATURE 55

Chapter 3: Queer Epistemologies of the Tomboy in Stacey Waite's *Butch Geography* 57
CE Mackenzie

Chapter 4: Reclaiming Female Power in Postcolonial Africa: The Tomboy in Tsitsi Dangarembga's *Nervous Conditions* 73
Tatiana Prorokova-Konrad

Chapter 5: Tomboy Ethos in Children's Non-Fiction 91
Jennifer Harrison

PART III: THE SMALL SCREEN: THE TOMBOY ON TELEVISION 107

Chapter 6: "Whoever I Want to Be": Tomboy and/as Femme Fatale in Marvel's *Agent Carter* 109
Cara McClintock-Walsh

Chapter 7: Tomboys, *Annedroids*, and the New Normal 135
Rebecca Feasey

Chapter 8: Misnomers and Contemporizations: An Examination of the Tomboy Figure in the Duffer Brothers' *Stranger Things* 159
Erica Joan Dymond

PART IV: THE VIRTUAL WORLD: THE TOMBOY IN VIDEO GAMES AND ON THE INTERNET 185

Chapter 9: *Beyond Good and Evil* … and Gender and Humanism? Exploring Jade as a Posthuman Protagonist 187
Poppy Wilde

Chapter 10: How #Tomboy Instagram Reclaims the Tomboy from White, Middle-Class Straight Women 209
Holly M. Wells

Index 233

About the Editors 243

About the Contributors 245

Acknowledgments

Erica Joan Dymond: I would like to thank my parents, Eric D. Dymond and Joan A. Dymond, who gifted me both dresses and pants, let me play in the woods as well as with Care Bears, who paid for my skateboard as well as my watercolors, and allowed me to indulge in countless hours of "violent" video games as well as flower tending. Thank you for never replacing my ripped-up jeans, beloved *Castlevania*, or coveted Stephen King books with something "gender appropriate." Thank you for letting me be my own type of tomboy. And thank you to my brother, Jason B. Dymond, who taught me how to beat the tough bosses in *Mario*, rode Space Mountain alongside me, and watched the entire *Stranger Things* series with me . . . again. You are the best. Finally, I would like to extend a thank you to Roland M. Nguyen who taught me to be an efficient rogue in WoW, introduced me to *Hunter X Hunter*, and didn't laugh when I crashed my Hoverboard. You are a glorious sounding board, friend, and partner.

Jennifer Harrison: I would like to thank my two awesome co-editors, who worked so hard to keep this project going despite the huge upheavals caused by the pandemic.

Holly Wells: Not sure "thank you" is the right phrase, but a shout-out to my mom, may she rest in peace, for calling me "Hal" when I went through my childhood transgender phase (yes, I wanted to be a boy); thanks also to my husband, Jaryl, for never expecting me to perform femininity because I'm terrible at it; to my birth mother, Roberta, for being a superb role model of adult tomboyhood at 75; and to my sons, Stefan and Julian, for educating me on the appropriate modern lingo for all things, but especially things LGBTQ+ related.

Introduction

HALF A MILLENNIUM OF TOMBOYS AND A TWENTY-FIRST CENTURY CONTROVERSY

The word "tomboy" is first noted in 1556 as a way to describe boys who are "extra-boisterous." Here, the first part of the word, "tom-," derives from the twelfth century, Middle English variant of the word meaning "boy-type" (as observed in words such as "*tom*cat," "*tom*fool," "*tom* turkey," etc.) (Davis 2020, 17). Not until the 1590s does the term evolve to refer to a "wild, romping girl, [a] girl who acts like a spirited boy" (King 2017). This definition, for the most part, remains stable from here, as reflected in the Oxford English Dictionary's current definition (i.e., non-obsolete definition) of "tomboy" as "a girl or young woman who acts or dresses in what is considered to be a boyish way, esp. one who likes rough or energetic activities conventionally more associated with boys" ("Tomboy" n.d.).

While the tomboy figure, as we know her, has existed since the late sixteenth century, she begins to gain genuine prominence in the first half of the 1800s. By the late 1880s, this figure is ubiquitous in the United States. What distinguishes these adult tomboys from their predecessors is their purpose. Many are among the middle-and upper-class women fighting for gender equality—specifically, the right to vote. At this point, the tomboy figure becomes closely tied to first-wave feminism, an association that continues into the early twentieth century (King 2017).

Tomboyism as an expression of feminism is also seen in the literature of 1800s. Here, the tomboy figure begins to appear in popular American novels. Perhaps unsurprisingly, this figure is most frequently found in the work of feminist authors such as Elizabeth Stuart Phelps and Louisa May Alcott. In fact, in *Tomboys: A Literary and Cultural History*, scholar Michelle Ann Abate declares that it is "the appeal of the topsy turvy tomboy that propelled

Little Women to instant success" (2008, IX–X). As a result of Alcott's Jo March, by the late 1800s the tomboy becomes iconic.

Throughout the early 1900s, the tomboy continues to experience popularity in both real life and the arts. Further, in the 1950s, tomboy fashion becomes the new "cool" as exemplified by the carefree style of the much beloved Audrey Hepburn. A tomboy in her adolescence, Hepburn, with her signature black capri pants, inspires many to copy her style (Gitlin 2009, 4). Those pants become so inextricably linked to her tomboy persona that she continues to wear them both on and off screen throughout her life (Caughran 2016, 65). It is little wonder why *Elle* magazine's Natasha Harding declares her "The Ultimate Tomboy Style-Muse" (2018).

No discussion of tomboys in Hollywood would be complete without mentioning Mary Tyler Moore. Her insistence on wearing capri pants on the *Dick Van Dyke Show* (1961–1966) led to a legendary battle with CBS in which the network's executives "made Carl Reiner promise not to let [Moore] wear pants in more than one scene [per episode]" (Desta 2017). Desta quotes Moore as saying:

> We went along with that for about three episodes, and then finally, I was just wearing the pants. We got the absolution of men everywhere and women kind of breathed a sigh of relief, too, and said, 'Hey, that's right. That's what we wear.'

Moore's point is that women were not vacuuming their homes while wearing high heels and frilly dresses with crinolines. Thus, even though everyday women are not able to wear pants in public without social repercussions until the 1960s, Audrey Hepburn and Mary Tyler Moore's tomboy fashion (along with that of early pants-adopters like Marlene Dietrich and Katherine Hepburn) helps to normalize them (Snodgrass 2015, 591–2).

Following the passing of Title IX in 1972, there is a surge of tomboy representation in the arts, particularly on television and in film. *Film Comment*'s Sheila O'Malley states, "One of the unique aspects of the 1970s tomboy is how the formerly subversive went mainstream. Tomboyishness was the dominant model for little-girlhood for a brief glorious season. Promoted by Disney, no less!" (2019). On television, Mary Ellen Walton's character on the long-running family drama *The Waltons* (1972–1981) and Laura Ingalls Wilder's character (based on the memoirs of the famed settler/pioneer and real-life tomboy) on the award-winning family drama *Little House on the Prairie* (1974–1982) capture viewers' hearts. From here, the tomboy figure soon appears in the characters of Jo Polniaczek on the popular sitcom *The Facts of Life* (1979–1988), the title character on the smash-hit sitcom *Punky Brewster* (1984–1988, 2021–present), and the character of Darlene Conner on the mega-hit sitcom *Roseanne* (1988–1997, 2018). As Lisa Selin Davis notes, "[these TV] tomboys were often accepted and even celebrated for their non-conforming way" (2020, 73). Underscored by each of these unforgettable characters is the fact that playing baseball, enjoying fishing, riding motorcycles, and drawing comic books are not activities exclusive to boys and men. Essentially, these tomboys, on screens all over America and the world, open a greater dialogue about gender.

Meanwhile, on the big screen, tomboys occupy the same space. Whether it is Amanda Whurlitzer in *The Bad News Bears* (1976), Annabel Andrews in *Freaky Friday* (1976), or Watts in *Some Kind of Wonderful* (1987), each character breaks the boundaries created by perceptions of gender. And, in the world of film, this trend continues through the 1990s and into the early 2000s. Tomboy characters like Vada Sultenfuss in *My Girl* (1991), Kit Keller in *A League of Their Own* (1992), Jules in *Bend it Like Beckham* (2002), Maggie Fitzgerald in *Million Dollar Baby* (2004), and the title character in *Juno* (2007) show girls/young women as capable critical thinkers and athletes. Every one of these films is a box-office success in its own right, but the tomboy character of each remains the subject of discussion to this day.

Of course, conspicuous by her absence is the tomboy of color. Michelle Ann Abate argues that up to the 1990s, Hollywood tomboys are associated with "various forms of nonwhiteness" (2008, 221); however, tomboys of color are essentially invisible in popular culture during this period. In Chapter 10 of this collection, contributor Holly Wells touches upon the absence of nonwhite representations of tomboyhood in two image-heavy books about tomboys and how tomboys of color are (re)claiming their place in the discussion.

As the tomboy continues onscreen, her real-life role comes under scrutiny. In the 2010s, as gender barriers for girls and women continue to deteriorate, the centuries-old "tomboy" designation begins to provoke social confusion and unease. In 2013, in response to such concerns, The University of New Hampshire offers a "Bias-Free Language Guide" to its students. In this publication, the authors relegate "tomboy" to the "problematic/outdated" category with the preferred terminology being "children who are gender nonconforming" or "children who are gender variant" (Meltzer 2015). In 2015, the guide is brought to the public's full attention. Ridiculed in the media, the "Bias-Free Language Guide" is disowned by The University of New Hampshire, which claims its contents are the unauthorized product of staff and students. The university's president, Mark Huddleston, states:

> I want to make it absolutely clear that the views expressed in this guide are NOT the policy of the University of New Hampshire . . . The only UNH policy on speech is that it is free and unfettered on our campuses. It is ironic that what was probably a well-meaning effort to be 'sensitive' proves offensive to many people, myself included. (Associated Press of Concord New Hampshire 2015)

Nonetheless, the concern over "tomboy" (among other words) comes to the fore. In the heated reception to this guide, both sides of the debate become clear.

While the "Bias-Free Language Guide" is denounced by and divorced from its own school, the war on the "tomboy" designation is just beginning. Shortly following the negative publicity surrounding the "Bias-Free Language Guide," *The New York Times* publishes Marisa Melzer's "Where Have All the Tomboys Gone?" (2015). In this piece, Melzer references the now infamous guide and alludes to its imprudent suggestions. However, in the spirit of detente, she looks at our evolving world and gently suggests that "it is possible in all of this, while embracing the new gender-neutral bathrooms and zero tolerance for bullying, to feel a whiff of nostalgia for tomboyhood" (Melzer 2015). Via comments from writers, editors, directors, and other artists, Melzer's piece presents a balanced account of both the importance of the rebellious tomboy figure and the worry of her being antiquated. The equitable nature of this article proves to be rare in an historical moment that seems predicated on reaction.

Perhaps the least measured among the barrage of articles is Amanda Bradley's 2017 "No More Tomboys!" (The exclamation mark seems an early indicator that the article will not be objective). Published in the *Huffington Post*, this piece assumes the perspective of a self-professed full-time mother who is concerned for the future of her daughter. The article boldly opens with, "I'm on a new crusade against the word Tomboy. If I get my way, I'll cut it out of every dictionary" and continues to state:

> Every time someone calls [my] [d]aughter a tomboy, I wince twice. Once because it tells girls that it's cool to be boyish, but not to be girlish, and a second time because there is no parallel positive (or even neutral) phrase for boys who step out of their traditional gender profile. The nearest we have today is 'metrosexual,' and imagine saying that about an eleven-year-old! (Bradley 2017).

The piece concludes with the bolded "#NoMoreTomboys" on a separate line (Bradley 2017). Bradley's piece seems to dismiss the vibrant history and purpose of tomboyism simply because the author's interpretation of the word *as it applies to her child* makes her bristle. While the author's lack of detachment and avoidance of this figure's social benefits may disqualify her writing from true consideration, her sentiment is one some well-intended, anxious parents share. However, the suggested alternative terminology to "tomboy" and approach to tomboyism provokes equal concern in parents.

While this call for change comes from a place of concern, the consequences prove unfortunate. Those who identify as tomboys are referred to in terms reserved for those who identify as transgender, and the tomboy's gender identity erroneously falls into question. In "My Daughter Is Not Transgender. She's a Tomboy," a 2017 piece for *The New York Times*, Lisa Selin Davis expresses joy that those who identify as transgender are gaining much-deserved and long-overdue recognition, but also offers consternation that girls/young women who pursue masculine-coded hobbies and those who prefer a masculine-coded aesthetic are told by authority figures to question their gender identity. Here, the author writes:

> My daughter wears track pants and T-shirts. She has shaggy short hair (the look she requested from the hairdresser was "Luke Skywalker in Episode IV"). Most, but not all, of her friends are boys. She is sporty and strong, incredibly sweet, and a girl. And yet she is asked by the pediatrician, by her teachers, by people who have known her for many years, if she feels like, or wants to be called, or wants to be, a boy. In many ways, this is wonderful: It shows a much-needed sensitivity to gender nonconformity and transgender issues. It is considerate of adults to ask her—in the beginning. But when they continue to question her gender identity—and are skeptical of her response—the message they send is that a girl cannot look and act like her and still be a girl. (Davis 2017)

Davis concludes with the admonition that "while celebrating the diversity of sexual and gender identities, we also need to celebrate tomboys and other girls who fall outside the narrow confines of gender roles. Don't tell them that they're not girls" (2017). Here, the author strongly insists that the term "tomboy" is a unique, necessary word. While Davis's piece is one based in personal experience (like Bradley's piece), it is also a plea for inclusivity . . . not a reduction of choice.

While Lisa Selin Davis's article asks for a preservation of the "tomboy" designation, this request largely seems disregarded. In 2019, the Girl Scouts of the United States of America posts an article titled "It's Time to Stop Calling Her a Tomboy" on their official website. Here, they denounce the word "tomboy" for "misgendering girls as boys" as well as implying that certain activities and careers are confined to boys/men (2019). The piece concludes by stating:

> These gender labels can cause her to second guess her interests and what she opens herself up to in the near term—and what she sees as possible for herself in the future. It's time to stop calling girls tomboys and just let girls be girls—in all the wonderful, varied ways that's possible. (2019)

It may seem counterintuitive that the Girl Scouts would make such a statement considering that at their inception "critics worried about girls becoming 'tomboys' who would reject the more socially acceptable roles for women in the domestic sphere—homemaker, wife, mother" (Winkle et al. 2019).

However, since the Girl Scouts have always had to push against social convention (of what girls/young women should and should not do), it also makes sense that they would want to oppose a term they perceive as a potentially outdated or restrictive. Other writers will address this issue as well.

In mid–2019, *The Washington Post* features an article by Lynne Stahl. Here, the author foregrounds the ongoing debate and even references the discussion opened by Lisa Selin Davis's "My Daughter Is Not Transgender. She's a Tomboy." This critical examination synthesizes the achievements of the tomboy figure as well as the arguments against the word. Most importantly, the author discusses the need for the "tomboy" designation, explaining that it is a celebration of girls/young women who refuse to conform to expectations: "Beyond resisting gender norms, tomboys give us a way to see the complex dynamics that shape our expression and perception of identity. And even if the word 'tomboy' is reaching its own ending, the tomboy's refusal to conform keeps its power still" (Stahl 2019). While Stahl may (reluctantly) view the tomboy designation as fading into disuse, others see a potential rise in popularity.

In 2020, Lisa Selin Davis's article, "Bring Back the Tomboys," boasts of accomplishments from new-school tomboys like Billie Eilish and proposes:

> Let's bring the tomboy back, without taming her. Let's have feminine boys and masculine girls amid the varied depictions of gender identities and presentations. In today's world of exponentially expanding media, and exponentially expanding understanding of the complexity of gender, we have room for all of them. (Davis 2020)

In this same year Davis also publishes *Tomboy: The Surprising History and Future of Girls Who Dare to Be Different*. She comments on the unexpected resurgence of the word (or, perhaps more accurately, its refusal to die): "No matter how many times it's pronounced dead, it springs back to life" (2020, 326). Later, she adds, "To me, focusing on the word 'tomboy' is missing the point. It's not just that the word is improperly gendered. It's that childhood is overly gendered" (2020, 332). The book earns high praise in a review by *The New York Times*' Lisa Damour (2020). Undoubtedly, there is strong support for not only preserving but lauding the "tomboy" designation.

Even amidst this nearly decade-long debate, the tomboy figure continues to flourish in the arts, especially on television. Characters like *Stranger Things*' Max Mayfield, *Last Man Standing*'s Eve Baxter, *Gravity Falls*' Wendy Corduroy, *Game of Thrones*' Arya Stark, *Orange Is the New Black*'s Poussey Washington, *The Walking Dead*'s Maggie Greene, *The Marvelous Mrs. Maisel*'s Susie Myerson and even *The Good Place*'s Eleanor Shellstrop all represent the tomboy figure. All are prominent in the popular culture world.

Ultimately, as this controversy continues, this collection serves to pay homage to the tomboy. It is a celebration of her role in history, the arts, and real life. Until the day when sexism no longer exists, the tomboy is a needed figure. She provides opportunity for exploration. She offers a buffer from judgment. She is life preserver.

#LongLivetheTomboy

A RETROSPECTIVE: THE TOMBOY IN HISTORY

The first part of this collection examines the history of the tomboy in real-life, literature, and on-stage. In Chapter 1, Renée Sentilles investigates the tomboy figure at the turn of the century. Through an exploration of different representations of tomboys throughout history, Sentilles argues that the early use of the term "tomboy" as a rebuke coexisted with the emergence of a commercial "marketplace tomboy," born in the rise of consumerism in the late nineteenth century. Understanding early commercial uses of the term helps to explain why it remains such a powerful yet ambiguous way of understanding youthful female gender performance. Girls constructed tomboy selves both independently and in response to popular representations in ways that clarify the admirable traits and the forbidden lines within female masculinity.

This collection then moves to Lynn Deboeck's exploration of the tomboy as she appears on stage in the role of mother or "momboy." In Chapter 2, Deboeck examines the assumption that a woman loses access to the tomboy designation once she reproduces (the argument being that since there is now tangible evidence of her womanhood, it is assumed that a mother cannot operate in this seemingly ambiguous area). The author uses the world of theater to prove the existence of the momboy and elucidate her role. Deboeck employs three plays, spanning over one hundred years, as case studies. Not all roles are laudable (such is the case with Bertolt Brecht's Mother Courage) but all illuminate this transgressive figure and society's response to it. Critically, these stage representations were disregarded as wild, fictional exaggerations by the patriarchy. It is this precise dismissal that allowed for these momboy figures to promote their progressive message and spur social change.

THE WRITTEN WORD: THE TOMBOY IN LITERATURE

The second part of this collection examines the tomboy as she appears in an array of literature. In Chapter 3, CE Mackenzie begins this section by explicating the poetry of Stacey Waite. Mackenzie unpacks the varied appearances and experiences of the tomboy throughout Waites's *Butch Geography*. Here the tomboy is presented in strained terms. The external world is threatening . . . poised to harm, humiliate, and denigrate the tomboy. Still, as Mackenzie discovers, amidst this pain, there is strength. Waites's tomboys resists capitulating to prescribed gender norms, pushing back while preserving themselves. While the tomboy's life is fraught with anxiety and struggle, there is also a modicum of hope that a life of thriving is near.

In Chapter 4, Tatiana Prorokova-Konrad brings readers to postcolonial Rhodesia (Zimbabwe) where she explores the employment of the tomboy figure in Tsitsi Dangarembga's *Nervous Conditions*. As depicted throughout the novel, Rhodesian women live in servitude to men. Their own hopes and desires are extinguished by a patriarchal system. However, Dangarembga presents the tomboy as a type of "loophole." Not without peril, this figure is (potentially and grudgingly) permitted opportunities otherwise denied to the women of this country. In the novel, cousins Tambu and Nyasha believe their tomboy spirit will lead them to a more rewarding and multifaceted life. However, their willful, independent behavior is derided and perceived as a threat to masculinity. Their tomboy identification, though having the potential to benefit the young women, makes them the target of violence. In Tsitsi Dangarembga's *Nervous Conditions*, the dangers of being a tomboy are real . . . as real as the rewards.

In Chapter 5, Jennifer Harrison concludes this part of the collection by exploring representations of the tomboy figure in picture books for young readers. She examines where this figure can be found, how she is portrayed, and what value she serves. While Harrison gauges physical markers like hair and clothing, she also looks toward depictions of intellectual curiosity. For instance, the tomboy child actively engaging in STEM might hold more significance than one watering flowers. Harrison also decodes more subtle aspects of these illustrations. She explicates, for instance, posture as depicted in these picture books, viewing a stylishly attired child peering into a bin on tip toes as having all the hallmarks of "cuteness" but lacking in the tomboy spirit. Her study ranges from books on gardening/homesteading to those on anatomy/physiology.

THE SMALL SCREEN: THE TOMBOY ON TELEVISION

The third part of this collection examines the tomboy as presented in contemporary television. From the superhero genre to children's programing to science-fiction/fantasy, the tomboy figure is still very much present in this medium. In Chapter 6, Cara McClintock-Walsh explores the Marvel Cinematic Universe (MCU) films and television shows, illustrating how two strong female characters—Peggy Carter (hero) and Whitney Frost (villain)—exemplify the ethos of the tomboy. Agent Carter uses her tomboy identity both to gain access to the military and to operate outside of its official channels. Carter is, for McClintock-Walsh, a "tomboy untamed," who maneuvers and manipulates the sexist system in which she works. Meanwhile, Whitney Frost represents the femme fatale who channels her tomboy youth to gain power and mete revenge on the patriarchy. In both cases, early involvement in tomboyism provides these characters with an abiding strategy of female defiance throughout their lives.

In Chapter 7, Rebecca Feasey then continues this study with her analysis of the Canadian live-action series *Annedroids*. For parents who are concerned about the otherness of the term "tomboy," Feasey assures readers that this show portrays tomboyism as a way of being a girl, a "new normal," as opposed to a brief phase that passes with maturity. While tomboyism is often connected to athletics, the author discusses how this show prizes STEM instead. Here, Anne is depicted as using her tomboyism to cultivate a future career in the competitive, prestigious field of robotics. Feasey, thus, demonstrates how Anne's future benefits from her tomboy adventures as a child/young woman.

In Chapter 8, Erica Joan Dymond then concludes this section with her examination of the Netflix original series *Stranger Things*. Here, public and media perception of Eleven as a tomboy is dismantled and examined. Through a close reading of select scenes, Eleven is explained as gender conforming—in spite of her external presentation (which reads very closely to that of the tomboy figure). The same lens is then applied to the character of Max Mayfield. In this case, a close reading shows her as embodying the tomboy spirit. Max's new-school tomboy style is dissected and explored, showing how her hybrid nature makes her a rare type of tomboy: one who is surrounded by admirers rather than a lone figure. In examining Max's character, Dymond also addresses how Max's "aging-out" of tomboyism should not be regarded as a betrayal but as a natural transition for many young (often heterosexual) tomboys.

THE VIRTUAL WORLD: THE TOMBOY IN VIDEO GAMES AND ON THE INTERNET

The final part of this collection explores the tomboy as she appears in the virtual world. Here, in Chapter 9, Poppy Wilde analyzes the figure of the tomboy through the main character, Jade, from the 2003 videogame *Beyond Good and Evil*. Wilde explores Jade as a posthuman protagonist whose blurring of the lines between many different categories (human/nonhuman, human/animal, maternal/warrior, and so on) opens a space for non-normative "tomboy" gender performance.

This part concludes with a piece that brings the collection to this very moment in time. In Chapter 10, Holly Wells, aware that the tomboy of American history is overwhelmingly white, middle-class, and cisgender, presents an alternative tomboy: a social media denizen who identifies as #tomboy and proudly wears her/their #tomboystyle for the world to see. These tomboys are white, Asian, brown, and Black; they present with makeup or without it; are somewhat feminine, androgynous, or masculine presenting; they wear their hair long, shoulder-length, short, or in various natural African styles; they are straight, but more often LGBTQ+; and they belong to every class imaginable, all around the world.

In totality, this collection shows the tomboy as diverse, innovative, transgressive, and strong. As much as she is presented as being in danger, she is also admired and actively building her own opportunities. At the turn of the century, she resisted identifying as a tomboy, fearful of the negative connotations attached to that complex label. At the beginning of a new millennium, she embraces this designation, posting her "selfies" on Instagram as an announcement of being, as a celebration of who she is. Certainly, if social media is any indication of her viability, it would seem the tomboy is here to stay.

BIBLIOGRAPHY

Abate, Michelle Ann. 2008. *Tomboys: A Literary and Cultural History*. Philadelphia: Temple University Press.

Associated Press of Concord, New Hampshire. 2015. "New Hampshire School Officials Distance Selves from 'Bias-Free Language Guide.'" *The Guardian*. July 29, 2015. https://www.theguardian.com/us-news/2015/jul/29/university-of-new-hampshire-bias-free-language-guide.

Bradley, Amanda. 2017. "No More Tomboys!" *HuffPost*. January 29, 2017. https://www.huffpost.com/entry/no-more-tomboys_b_588dd3d8e4b06364bb1e26bb.

Caughran, Mary. 2015. "Capri Pants." In *Clothing and Fashion: American Fashion from Head to Toe*, edited by José F. Blanco et al., 65. Santa Barbara: ABC-CLIO.

Davis, Lisa Selin. 2020. "Bring Back the Tomboys." *The New York Times*. February 11, 2020. https://www.nytimes.com/2020/02/11/opinion/tomboys-culture.html.

———. 2017. "My Daughter Is Not Transgender. She's a Tomboy." *The New York Times*. April 18, 2017. https://www.nytimes.com/2017/04/18/opinion/my-daughter-is-not-transgender-shes-a-tomboy.html.

———. 2020. *Tomboy: The Surprising History and Future of Girls Who Dare to Be Different*. New York: Hachette.

Desta, Yohana. 2017. "How Mary Tyler Moore Subverted TV Sexism with a Pair of Capris." *Vanity Fair.* January 25, 2017. https://www.vanityfair.com/hollywood/2017/01/mary-tyler-moore-pants

The Girls Scouts of the United States of America. 2019. "It's Time to Stop Calling her a Tomboy." https://www.girlscouts.org/en/raising-girls/happy-and-healthy/happy/what-is-a-tomboy.html.

Gitlin, Martin. 2009. *Audrey Hepburn: A Biography*. Westport: Greenwood.

Harding, Natasha. 2018. "Audrey Hepburn Is the Ultimate Tomboy Style Muse." *Elle* (Australia). July 19, 2018. https://www.elle.com.au/fashion/audrey-hepburn-tomboy-style-18085.

King, Elizabeth. 2017. "A Short History of the Tomboy." *The Atlantic*. January 5, 2017. https://www.theatlantic.com/health/archive/2017/01/tomboy/512258/.

Melzer, Marisa. 2015. "Where Have All the Tomboys Gone?" *The New York Times*. October 13, 2015. https://www.nytimes.com/2015/10/15/fashion/where-have-all-the-tomboys-gone.html.

O'Malley, Sheila. 2019. "Present Tense: Tomboys." *Film Comment*. November 21, 2019. https://www.filmcomment.com/blog/present-tense-tomboys/.

Snodgrass, Mary Ellen. 2015. "Trousers." In *World Clothing and Fashion: An Encyclopedia of History, Culture, and Social Influence*, edited by Mary Ellen Snodgrass, 590–592. New York: Routledge.

Stahl, Lynne. 2019. "'Tomboy' is anachronistic. But the concept still has something to teach us." *The Washington Post*. June 28, 2019. https://www.washingtonpost.com/outlook/tomboy-is-anachronistic-but-the-concept-still-has-something-to-teach-us/2019/06/28/b295375a-96ae-11e9-8d0a-5edd7e2025b1_story.html.

"Tomboy, nd." *OED Online*. Oxford University Press. https://www.oed.com/view/Entry/203097.

Winkle, Tom, Amanda B. Moniz, and Amelia Grabowski. 2019. "A Scout by Any Other Name." *Smithsonian National Museum of American History*. March 12, 2019. https://americanhistory.si.edu/blog/scout.

PART I

A RETROSPECTIVE: THE TOMBOY IN HISTORY

Chapter 1

Rise of the Marketplace Tomboy

Renée M. Sentilles

When writer and critic Jeannette Gilder published her memoir in 1901, she titled it *Autobiography of a Tomboy* because she knew that "tomboy" would sell the book. By the turn of the century, the tomboy character that had first taken off as a literary figure in America's postbellum years had become a full-blown marketplace character. The word "tomboy" was now selling everything from fabric to canned goods, and the tomboy character had become the reigning girl protagonist in entertainment culture (Sentilles 2018, 149). Yet Gilder expressed discomfort with the term she had used to lure readers, noting: "I never quite understood why a girl who climbed trees, clung to the tail-end of carts, and otherwise deported herself as a well-conditioned girl would, was called a tomboy. It always seemed to me that, if she was anything she should be, it was a tomgirl" (Gilder 1901, 287). All of her life, Gilder had been proud of her physicality and sense of fun, and she saw herself as a particularly lively girl, not any kind of boy. As a girl, she had tried to shrug off the term but found it frustrating when adults brandished it as a weapon: "I did not care what they called me, so long as they let me alone; but that they were loath to do. My relations and friends of the family predicted all sorts of dreadful ends for me, and talked in my presence about the awful fate awaiting whistling girls and crowing hens" (Gilder 1901, 287). Thus, with her title and her opening, Gilder used the tomboy label against the wishes of her childhood self, for whom it had felt more like a limitation than a liberation.

Between Gilder's girlhood in the 1860s and the launching of her memoir, the tomboy had shifted from a queer figure of cultural resistance to a mainstream icon. Gilder was right about the allure of "tomboy" in the title of memoir; the book was so commercially successful that she quickly published a sequel, *The Tomboy at Work* (1904). The trajectory she traced within these two texts was familiar to American audiences who, by the 1880s, were already familiar with the trope of feisty girls growing into great women thanks to a slew of biographies of public female figures, from actresses to reformers.

Yet, "tomboy" remained a challenging term. This essay argues that the earlier sense of the term as a rebuke coexisted with the emergence of what I am calling a commercial "marketplace tomboy," born in in the rise of consumerism in the late nineteenth century. In this period, tomboys in retrospect became a way of explaining the singularity of independent women. Despite a growing affection for tomboy biographical and literary heroines, however, girls of the post-bellum and Progressive periods (1865–1920) rarely used the term to describe themselves and repudiated it when adults applied to them. Every now and then, a letter would make it into a newspaper, such as that of an unnamed fourteen-year-old girl who proclaimed in the 1887 Louisville *Courier-Journal*: "I'm healthy, like fun and boys (in fact I like boys better than girls). I am called a 'Tom Boy' at home, and think the name suits me." But she quickly followed the claiming of the term with a complaint about the way the adults used it to try to curtail her freedoms, stating, "If I go climbing out on the chicken coop mamma says 'You ought to be ashamed of yourself, a great big 15-year-old girl, thinking about beaux, to be climbing about like a boy'" ("Trials of a Girl of Fourteen" 1887, 17).

The marketplace tomboy arose from industries hoping to sell such girls products, not in response to real girls struggling against the confinement imposed by femininity and maturation. Although adults still scolded girls for flouting gender conventions, the celebration of marketplace tomboys simultaneously suggested that society was better served by independent-minded girls who questioned the outdated status quo (Abate 2008; Sentilles 2018; Kitch 2001). Famous women—such as writers, actresses, scientists—began claiming the characteristics associated with tomboys, but not the term itself. Juvenile fiction and "great woman biography" naturalized the ambitions and life trajectories of public women even as the term remained controversial.

At the turn of the twentieth century, publishers, retailers, and clothing designers embracing the power of the tomboy moniker to sell everything from novels to newspapers also changed the cultural function of the cultural figure. With her supposedly modern zest for physicality and play, she became a way of repackaging the past as more strictly defined by the gender binary. According to diaries, memoirs, and letters, young women had always climbed trees, hunted, fished, and played pranks, but the selling of the tomboy erased that past and amplified an image of Victorian passivity (McLeod 1994, 6–13; Sentilles 2018). Thus, the celebration of tomboys became as much about drawing a line between the past and the present as it was about girls claiming new freedoms.

My use of "marketplace tomboy" stems from journalist Andi Zeisler's analysis of late twentieth-century marketplace feminism. Zeisler asserts that through decontextualization and depoliticization, consumer culture is able to embrace explicit forms of resistance—such as feminism—and turn them into mainstream cultural products that can be used in opposing ways (Zeisler 2016, xii). Likewise, through the marketplace, tomboys became a staggeringly popular iteration of free-spirited girlhood, even as rougher tomboys often found themselves sidelined by the culture surrounding them.

The central message of the marketplace tomboy was that Victorian gender norms were passing out of fashion and giving way to healthy girls with a public voice. Some things truly were changing: the bicycle craze of the 1880s and sports like basketball, which took off in the early 1890s, meant that girls were embracing physical play in unprecedented ways. But at the same time, this narrative presented a miscasting of past girlhoods, and particularly rural ones. The celebration of ambition was new, and the fact that girls could travel all over independently on bicycles created a profound internal shift in many female psyches, but physical freedoms and rowdy play were not new. As Anne Scout McLeod's research in diaries has shown, throughout the nineteenth century, girls spent hours sledding, playing pranks, hunting, fishing, tree-climbing, and engaging in all of the other typical rural pastimes that late nineteenth-century authors turned into the hallmarks of tomboy identity (McLeod 1994, 6–9). Indeed, it is arguable that many girls at the end of the nineteenth century enjoyed *fewer* physical freedoms than their earlier counterparts, because so many more grew up in urban environments where they were more closely observed by elders. But appearing as singular—which is to say, different from the conventional (and implicitly boring) girls around her—the marketplace tomboy served as a figure of cultural resistance even as she became acceptably mainstream.

This mainstream world of popular culture was dominated by white writers and publishers, and for the most part, they ignored the existence of girls of color altogether. Michelle Ann Abate demonstrates that Topsy, one of the most memorable characters in Harriet Beecher Stowe's *Uncle Tom's Cabin* (1851), may have served as an inspiration for Jo March of Louisa May Alcott's *Little Women* (1868), arguably the most significant tomboy heroine (Abate 2008, 33–47). As a historian, I find that assertion fascinating because Topsy was arguably the *only* black girl character known to most white readers until well into the twentieth century and an internationally recognized figure. African American authors such as Harriet Jacobs, Harriet Wilson, F. E. W. Harper, and Charles Chestnutt, as well as short story writers contributing to black papers such as the *Baltimore Afro-American*, *Chicago Defender*, and, a bit later, *The Crisis*, posited adolescent female protagonists, but none of them could claim the cultural power of Topsy. But even if Alcott did borrow heavily from Topsy, as Abate suggests, Jo March's whiteness put her in a different position. One of the reasons that papers like *The Crisis* regularly celebrated black female athletes without ever calling them tomboys, as was common in the white mainstream press by the 1880s, was because the femininity that allowed a girl to outgrow her boyishness was treated as a white privilege.[1]

Even while supposedly refuting femininity, marketplace tomboys reinforced the centering of femininity within white womanhood. Nearly every tomboy tale from the late nineteenth century through the early twentieth century ends with the tomboy transformed through marriage (Sentilles 2018, 43–5; Abate 2008, 21; O'Brien, "Tomboyism," 354). But that formulaic tale only worked because the tomboy's femininity was understood by the (white) mainstream audience as a sign of immaturity rather than a lack of respectability.

But as always, it is up to individual readers to identify with characters, and Barbara Sicherman has found ample evidence of African American (and immigrant) girls identifying with Jo March (Sicherman 2010, 29–31). To say that the mainstream press assumed that the tomboy was white does not mean that plenty of girls of color failed to find relief in her rebellion against propriety. After all, as writers such as Jacobs and Harper have asserted, and multiple scholars of black girlhood attest, girls of color have historically lived under tremendous social pressure to perform femininity and respectability (Wright 2016, 19–20; Simmons 2015, 4–5).

Many rebellious, white, middle-class girls repudiated the term if they felt it was used against them, but none did so more emphatically and eloquently than Minnie Thomas, who would grow up to be M. Carey Thomas, president of Bryn Mawr College. In 1871, Thomas began a new diary on which she penciled in tall letters on the cover: "The Journal Kept by Jo March." Clearly identifying with the tomboy heroine of Louisa May Alcott's 1868 novel *Little Women*, one might expect Thomas to proudly call herself a tomboy. She certainly *acted* like tomboys found in fiction: playing pranks and vocally objecting to female dress and oppressive femininity. But Thomas had clearly been scolded with the term and instead of owning it, rejected it: "Girls can never have any fun. They can't play or else everybody thinks they're tomboys, and I haven't had one nice game since I came home, and I am nearly fifteen, and each year I have less fun" (Carey Diary, October 1, 1871). Thomas saw the label tomboy—even if it was often used to describe her beloved heroine Jo March—as an oppressive rhetorical device and rejected it as a false description.

And yet with the rise of marketplace tomboys, the tomboy label so detested by Minnie Thomas also worked well in explaining her development into M. Carey Thomas. The iconoclastic M. Carey Thomas came from tomboy Minnie, who rejected female oppression. She was living proof of the tomboy trope.

Even as girls like Thomas were struggling against the label—arguing essentially that what she was doing was normal for a girl, rather than suggestive of boyish identity—the larger public was embracing tomboy girls as the natural origin of uncommon women. In periodic and book-length treatments alike, female pioneers in medicine, literature, entertainment, reform, and, of course, athletics, were often depicted as scrappy, outdoor-loving girls who grew naturally from ignoring the gender norms of childhood to circumventing them in adulthood.

Ironically, it was Thomas's beloved Jo March who motivated publishers to turn the tomboy into a marketplace trope. Alcott's *Little Women* broke ground in cultural resistance in myriad ways that continue to make the book widely read. Alcott began the book reluctantly, and only because her family needed the income. When publisher Thomas Niles reached out to her to write a book for girls rivalling the newly popular adventure books for boys, she acquiesced out of need rather than conviction. Niles was essentially turning over the cultural sofa cushions in search of unclaimed coins; middle-class girls had money but no effective market designed to part them from their pennies.

Alcott famously wrote in her private journal, "Never liked girls or knew many, except my sister; but our queer plays and experiences may prove interesting, though I doubt it" (Wadsworth 2006, 48). It turned out that their "queer" ways of play were far more normal than anything that had thitherto appeared in print. Most importantly, Alcott—a dedicated spinster and ambitious writer who filled journals expressing frustration over her own character flaws—wrote Jo March as a fictionalized version of herself. As feminist scholar Judith Fetterly notes, *Little Women* is "built on a paradox; the figure who most resists the pressure to become a little woman is the most attractive" (Fetterly 1979, 379). A century after its publication, book critic Elizabeth Janeway observed: "This Victorian tract, sentimental and preachy, was written by a secret rebel against the order of the world and woman's place in it and all the girls who ever read it know it" (Janeway 1968, 42). Indeed, it became such a phenomenon that the newspapers began keeping track of the numbers sold, and by the time of Alcott's death in 1888, the book had sold over 200,000 copies in the United States alone (Sicherman 2010, 14).

"Tomboy" had actually been in use for centuries, but the American marketplace narrowed its meaning to address only girls and young women. Abate notes that its sudden shift to femininity might be attributable to the work of women and girls during the Civil War, when they routinely broke gender norms in service of fighting or survival (Abate 2008, 25). By the final decades of the century, the term remained a scold, but the spirit of the tomboy was grafted onto a national movement promoting physical health in child-raising

(Sentilles 2018, 104–12). With the international love affair with Jo March, the emerging tomboy figure functioned mostly as a quintessentially American form of cultural resistance—asserting that girls raised in a nation cultivating independence naturally enjoyed many of the same activities as boys and to do so was a sign of good health—but also as cultural entrenchment, because the term itself reinforced that these girls borrowed such freedoms from boys and would outgrow them.

Tomboys had become iconic American girls within popular culture by the 1880s, both because they were useful characters for attracting juvenile dollars and because their ambiguity proved to be useful as industrialization, urbanization, and incorporation began changing expectations for young women. In all tenses—past or present—resistance is central to tomboy identity. If a girl was scolded in the present tense for "acting like a tomboy," it was because she was resisting the pressures of femininity that come with both sex and age. If an adult memoirist recalled joyous days of tomboy freedom, she was emphasizing her life-long independent spirit. If she was an actress, athlete, reformer, or publicly celebrated woman, her publicist was highlighting her long-standing singularity. And yet, the more tomboys were used as symbols of resistance and freedom, the more tomboy behavior became consigned to youth and acceptably packaged. The cooption of the term reinforces a dynamic noted by feminist theorist Susan Bordo: even when cultural resistance becomes popular, it is not on "equal footing with forms that are culturally entrenched" (Bordo 1993, 29). Tomboys became a beloved form of resistance against an entrenched belief that women and men are opposites by both nature and divine design. The development of marketplace tomboys used the implicit resistance embodied by tomboys to shore up culturally entrenched gender norms, and it did so mainly by celebrating great women as former tomboys, marketing beloved fictional characters capable of adapting to norms upon maturity, and selling tomboy associations as modern. A major part of making the tomboy marketable was using her to disconnect modern girls from Victorian norms, and yet many of those norms persisted in a more liberated guise.

With her fictional doppelganger, Alcott was able to challenge the conventional tomboy tale already common in popular fiction. Until Jo, the main point of tomboy heroines appearing in publications like *Godey's Lady's Book* was to reinforce the importance of femininity and the transformative power of love and marriage. In story after story, love for a good man transformed the spirited but untutored girl into awkward but adorable femininity, thus reinforcing all of the gender norms while also giving a nod to spirited girls. These tropes would, of course, persist long past the challenges posed by Jo March, but Alcott's character gave the tomboy unheard of depth beyond her role in romance. Other than appearing in romantic short stories, the only earlier tomboys whose principal role strayed from serving as a romantic heroine was Gypsy Breynton, the twelve-year-old title heroine of the Sunday School series by Elizabeth Stuart Phelps, beginning in 1866. One could argue that irrepressible Capitola Black, of E. D. E. N. Southworth's 1859 serialized novel *The Hidden Hand*, was as much of a tomboy as a romantic heroine, but she was tamed by love in the tradition of tomboy tales. Historian Daniel E. Cohen has also found serialized short stories by Winnie Woodfern (Mary Gibson) appearing in northeastern story papers in the 1850s with central heroines who follow their public ambitions and display preferences such as wearing their hair short and smoking cheroots that would have been understood as a sign of manliness at the time (Cohen 2012, 10–1). But most tomboy characters before Jo March were not in the service of female liberation but rather in asserting that tomboys grow up and embrace femininity when the right man comes along.

Jo upset the conventional narrative by refusing to marry the obvious love interest, much to the dismay of Alcott's readers, and instead passionately pursuing nondomestic ambitions. She also defied the common depiction of tomboys as tree-climbing hoydens, beautiful under their smudged faces and torn hems, by creating a tomboy character whose appearance gets almost no attention at all. Most importantly, Jo herself does not place any value on beauty; the external is of less interest to her than the possibilities of her internal self. Finally, in Jo, readers had a three-dimensional girl: headstrong, jolly, well-meaning, ambitious, and capable of both great sensitivity and callous disregard. Readers of all ages, genders, races, classes, and ethnicities read *Little Women*, transforming it into one of the best-selling novels of the century (Sicherman 2010, 27–31). Over and over, readers proclaimed seeing authenticity in Alcott's depictions of the March sisters, and particularly Jo. Readers recognized themselves in her (Sicherman 2010; Sentilles 2018, 59–60).

Passion for Jo March also proved to have a longevity that addresses why the tomboy character became and has remained beloved. Writer Cynthia Ozick wrote in 1982 of reading *Little Women* "a thousand, ten thousand times" because "we identify in the end not so much with the Jo of the book as with 'some Jo of the future,' the independent woman she failed to become" (Ozick 1982, 24). In other words, as represented by Jo, the tomboy is a promise that girls will have more opportunities than girls did in the past. And, after Jo, what sets the tomboy apart is not simply her inept approach to all things feminine, but her confidence that conformity is not important. Twentieth-century French feminist Simone de Beauvoir later wrote that as a young girl, "I identified myself passionately with Jo, the intellectual . . . Jo was superior to her sisters, who were either more virtuous or more beautiful than she, because of her passion for knowledge and the vigor of her thinking; her superiority was as outstanding as that of certain adults, and guaranteed that she would have an unusual life: she was marked by fate" (Sicherman 2010, 28). The rebellion of Jo's tomboy identity is not simply against social expectations for girls in terms of dress and decorum, but also against the idea that girls should care more about pleasing others than following their own moral compass and pursuing their intellectual ambitions.

Yet Jo March's authenticity is also what made the character a major element in the creation of the marketplace tomboy. She is a clear example of the tomboy as a figure of cultural resistance who nevertheless ends up supporting cultural norms—not because she was a sell-out to conventional marriage, like most tomboy heroines, but because she successfully sold rebellion. Jo's inability to match up with the cultural ideal for girls—being plain, ambitious, intellectual, and often "cross"—dovetailed with her charisma as a vivid character, passionately devoted to her family, full of fun and interesting ideas. Jo, in a word, is *interesting*; not a trope or a cliché, but a mess of contradictions and good intentions. Jo March brought dimension to the tomboy character—and in the process, to American girls themselves—and a market grew in her wake.

Tomboys became newly and enormously popular after *Little Women*, and publishers began earnestly pursuing manuscripts about girls, but those versions of the tomboy tended to be more appreciative of femininity than Jo March. Few of the many authors who attempted to capitalize on the success of *Little Women* came close to making a tomboy character nearly as complex, but they nevertheless reinforced the notion of the tomboy as a singularly American girl. Indeed, eventually girls with tomboy-like independence mixed with innate femininity became the central heroines of the series novels, like *The Campfire Girls*, *The Girls of Central High*, and, eventually, *Nancy Drew,* that would come to dominate the juvenile publishing market for nearly a century (Sentilles 2018, 149–60).

One of the clearest indicators of the growing popularity of the marketplace tomboy is the massive proliferation of tomboy stories that filled story papers and periodicals throughout the Progressive period. Although stories with tomboy-like heroines had appeared in periodical fiction from as early as the 1830s, the heroine actually labeled "tomboy" did not become ubiquitous until after the Civil War. The titles of these stories are obvious and interchangeable, usually along the lines of "The Tomboy" (1867), "What Came of a Tomboy" (1872), and "Reddy: A Tomboy" (1885). In nearly all of them, the tomboy captures the interest of a male onlooker who is beguiled by her pure spirit but disquieted by her demeanor. Once she, in turn, falls in love with him, the purity of her spirit remains even as she embraces the positive aspects of femininity, such as modesty and the desire to follow rather than lead.

But alongside these fictional portrayals came a slew of articles about real women, from celebrities, athletes, and society women, to pioneers in education, medicine, and reform, who showed their independence early as tomboy girls. Unlike the tomboy tales of popular fiction, the biographical tomboy rarely married, and she did not confine herself to the domestic but rather embraced her independence to work toward change in the wider world.

Harriet Hosmer, America's first internationally celebrated female sculptor, proved to be a perfect pathbreaker for the phenomenon of the marketplace tomboy. Indeed, when nine-year-old Gilder ran across Hosmer's first biographical sketch in a New Jersey local paper, she immediately resolved to follow in her footsteps (Gilder 1901, 183). That 1858 biographic article circulated the country for six months, capturing the public's imagination with adventures that claimed that Hosmer's tomboy characteristics were rooted in the pursuit of physical health, and that her professional success was rooted in that tomboy girlhood. The story goes that after losing four of his five children and his wife to consumption, Hosmer's physician father concluded that ladylike cultural norms would prove deadly to his remaining daughter. He gave her "a horse, dog, gun and boat," and insisted that she live "an outdoor life" ("Anecdote of Harriet Hosmer" 1858, 157). Although her biographer, Katie Culkin, suggests that within Watertown, Hosmer was quite notorious even as a girl, the papers reported stories of her childhood with unfettered zest (Culkin 2010, 9). This story of loss and triumph essentially rationalized why it was acceptable for Hosmer to transgress gender norms: she was raised to do so by a father who was a well-known doctor, for reasons of health. In other words, none of her behaviors were spurred by her own need to challenge convention, even if that was the end result.

Hosmer also embodied a cleaned-up version of the dime novel heroine who was also growing in popularity and largely regarded as a "western tomboy" (Haebegger 1982, 177–81). With "pistols in her belt" and "prepared to take the life of anyone who interfered with her," Hosmer was not only a product of health culture but also the manifest destiny of westward expansion ("Harriet Hosmer" 1858, 147). According to the 1858 article, twenty-year-old Hosmer moved to St. Louis to attend Missouri Medical College and perfect her understanding of human anatomy in order to hone her art skills. Hosmer considered holiday breaks an ideal time to travel up and down the Mississippi River, initially with a friend and then on her own. Her adventures were colorful: traveling down a lead mine in a bucket, bringing home a peace pipe she had shared with Native Americans at St. Andrews Falls in Wisconsin, and having an Iowa bluff named after her for winning a footrace (Culkin 2010, 9, 19).

Then tomboy Hosmer conquered the world, which is what made her tomboy roots important to Americans advocating modern opportunities for women. After briefly returning home to Massachusetts to sculpt a bust of Hesper, a nymph from Greek mythology, she took a daguerreotype of the work and brought it with her to seek instruction in Rome. There, Hosmer gained artistic credibility while socializing with many of the most famous entertainers, artists, and writers of the period. Indeed, she enjoyed a romantic relationship with America's most famous actress of the period, Charlotte Cushman, though papers only reported them as friends (Culkin 2010, 18–20). She lived a glamorous, self-driven life according to her many biographical sketches, and it all began with a girlhood that sidestepped feminine retirement in favor of living a life that embraced what were widely regarded as freedoms of boyhood.

It is also telling that Hosmer's life story largely disappeared from public culture until the 1880s, when she suddenly reemerged as a cultural icon. The impact of Hosmer on the full development of marketplace tomboys suggests that the 1880s—over a decade after the end of the war, when office jobs were opening up for young, unmarried women, nursing and teaching were developing as respectable female professions, and women were becoming an increasing public presence—is when tomboyism in retrospect became a way of explaining the singularity of independent women. During this period, most newspaper articles touched lightly on Hosmer's accomplishments as a sculptor and focused instead on her rough and tumble girlhood. Pieces such as "Anecdote of Harriet Hosmer," which appeared in several newspapers in the summer of 1888, retell her tomboy days: "many were the pranks this wild young colt played; swimming the broad stream, riding bareback, shooting, rowing and fishing" ("Anecdote" 1888, 3). Hosmer's girlhood predilection for adventure was not depicted as a curious anomaly, but as support for a movement to portray tomboy girlhoods as a central characteristic of publicly successful women. Her generational peers, such as Alcott, Elizabeth Cady Stanton, and Frances Willardhad silvered into respectability, and American publishers and newspapers sold their tomboy girlhoods with equal fervor.

The first major compilation of great American women biographies appeared in 1883 and has been reprinted sporadically until 2016: *Our Famous Women: Comprising the Lives and Deeds of Famous American Women,* written by twenty female authors who were widely known at the time. It was a compilation consciously produced for modern times, as explained in the preface: "Probably no aspect of our time is more significant of progress than the ever-growing discussion of the place and duties of women in the social state . . . All over the land, women are conscious of a ferment and disturbance of thought which is the prophecy of better things. Everywhere they are asking, 'What can *I* do to hasten the New Day?'" (Stowe et al. 1884, v).

Well, one thing they could clearly do, according to sketch after sketch, was celebrate rather than squelch the independent spirit of their ambitious daughters. All sixteen sketches are rife with terms like "rebel," "rebellious," "vigorous," "animal spirits" (which meant "innate liveliness"), "strong," "ambitious," and "independent"—all of which were terms associated with tomboys. The book rarely uses the term tomboy (and when they did, they spelled it "tom-boy," which was common usage into the twentieth century), but does expand how these remarkable young women saw themselves not as failed boys but as girls embracing a full range of human expression. Some, like Harriet Beecher Stowe's sketch of her beloved older sister, Catherine Beecher, reassert femininity alongside more conventionally masculine traits, essentially laying claim to women's equal need for civic engagement and action (Stowe 1884, 77–8). Others, like Lucy Larcom, writing about Red Cross founder Clara Barton, play up the well-established tomboy trope of being close to nature. Indeed, Barton sounds somewhat like Hosmer, "going through wild snow-drifts or summer sunshine two miles to school, playing on the hillsides, wading in the brooks, or scampering across her father's fields on any untamed pony she could find" (Larcom in Stowe 1884, 95).

But perhaps the most astonishing is the sketch that gave almost Amazon-like traits to the "Doctors Blackwell"—Elizabeth and Emily, respectively, the first and third women to earn medical degrees in the United States, who established The Women's Medical College in New York City in 1868. Here Lucia Gilbert Runkle credits their mother's attitude, stating "[t]he wise mother was not frightened at the name of tom-boy, nor disturbed by the cheerful din of the host of children who 'rampaged' through the passages between lesson hours." Runkle tells the story of a visitor to the Blackwell's childhood home, asserting the physical weakness of women, only to be rebuked by a brother who claimed that "when Elizabeth chooses she is more than a match for the rest of us at wrestling or lifting, and carries us about as she likes" (Runkle in Stowe 1884, 135–7). When the visitor expressed disbelief, Elizabeth supposedly picked him up and carried him around the room. Clearly, the characters featured in *Our Famous Women* were not typical, but author after author suggests that their success lay in healthy girlhoods at odds with the supposedly passive Victorian girlhood that the book explicitly wished to leave behind.

The book begins with a sketch of Alcott who was, at that moment, arguably the most famous person appearing in the compilation, as her outpouring on books on adolescent youth lay at the center of a major new publishing market. She was widely considered America's tomboy herself, due in no small part to her editor's efforts to blur her identity with that of Jo March. One of the most compelling marketing devices of both Alcott, as a figure, and the books about the March family, which now included *Little Men* and *Jo's Boys*, was this deliberate conflation of writer and heroine. Simply put, even though Alcott succumbed to a market demand to have her heroine marry at the end, with the success of the fictionalization of her own self and family life, Alcott lived out Jo's dreams. Indeed, the conflation has remained so compelling that the most recent feature films (1994, 2019) based on *Little Women* change the ending of the story, so that Jo March publishes *Little Women*, rather than Alcott.[2] If

Jo capitulated to marriage, Alcott did not, and that made for a wonderfully complex and satisfying close to the story.

In the sketch written by fellow novelist Louise Chandler Mouton, Alcott lays claim to what gender scholar Jack Halberstam would later go on to describe as "female masculinity," an innate sense of masculinity in herself: "I am more than half-persuaded that I am a man's soul, put by some freak of nature into a woman's body" (Moulton in Stowe 1884, 49). When Mouton asks why she thinks of herself that way, Alcott astonishingly suggests an attraction to other women. "'Well, for one thing,' Alcott answers with laughter in her eyes, 'because I have fallen in love in my life with so many pretty girls, and never once the least little bit with any man'" (Moulton in Stowe 1884, 49). To be clear, falling in love with other girls was to some extent a common and even expected phenomenon for middle-class girls of the period (Sentilles 2018, 171). It was unusual, however, for Alcott to equate romantic attraction with gender identity.

Even as they celebrate the achievements of their subjects, however, the sketches reinforce that the transition from a free tomboy life to adult womanhood was often devastating. Kate Sanborn makes the adolescent despair of Frances Willard central to her self-identity by including a central passage from her diary:

> This is my seventeenth birthday and the oath of my martyrdom. Mother insists that I shall have my hair done up woman fashion, and my dress made to trail like hers. She says she shall never forgive herself for letting me run wild so long. We had a great time over it all, and here I sit like another Sampson shorn of my strength. That figure won't do though, for the greatest trouble with me is I shall never be shorn again; my back-hair is twisted up like a corkscrew. I carry eighteen hairpins; my head aches; my feet are entangled in the skirt of my new gown. I can never jump over a fence again so long as I live. As for chasing the sheep down in the shady pasture it's out of the question, and to climb to my eagles'-nest seat in the big burr-oak would ruin this new frock beyond repair. Altogether, I recognize the fact that my occupation is gone. (Sanborn in Stowe 1884, 698–9)

In most of these sketches and memoirs, the authors repeat the message: tomboys make the most admirable grown women, but the transition to womanhood is painful, and the young woman takes to the required path with a sense of loss.

Although tomboy-infused biographical sketches appeared in newspapers and story papers long before *Our Famous Women*, they increased in number after its commercial success, and it would not be a stretch to say that claiming a tomboy girlhood became typical for famous women. It also became common to assure readers that a tomboy girlhood led to a rich, womanly life, and not a masculine woman. In 1887, for example, in her autobiography, writer and activist Jessie Benton Freemont proudly declared, "I was called 'Tom-boy,' and never had an untorn dress . . . So I understood boy-nature and knew that . . . the natural outcome and strength and will and courage and fun would come out all right when it settled into working channels" (Fremont 1887, 317). Likewise, legendary actress Charlotte Cushman enters James Parton's *Daughters of Genius* (1888), declaring "I was born a tomboy." But Parton hastens to explain of the actress who gained international fame by her serious performances of male characters that tomboy meant "she was a vigorous, strong-limbed courageous girl, who might have been the mother of heroes if it had not been her fortune to be a heroine herself" (Parton 1888).

In the real world, tomboys had become so representative of American spunk and individualism that California sent a statue of a tomboy to represent the state in the 1893 Chicago World's Fair. The description of the young woman upon whom the statue was modeled is a telling celebration of sexually charged beauty and a disdain for society's dictates:

> A girl from Pasadena, with the decidedly plebeian name of Katy Brown, the daughter of a poor railroad employee, was chosen. She is said to be so shapely that she will out-Venus the Venus of Milo and have a face as perfect and as spiritually beautiful as Raphael's Madonna. Katy is said to be a hoydenish, romping girl who has played with her brothers until she is almost like one of them in manner. She is only 16 but has the development of a woman of twenty . . . She is tall, and large, or she would not be so typical of California. Her beautiful face is covered with a mass of waving curling hair, that never has known what it is to be tied in fashionable knots. ("Statue" 1893, 9)

This was a tomboy who was more about repudiating fashionable culture than challenging gender norms. Indeed, the sexually charged physical description of Katy Brown eclipses the assertion that she is almost like a boy in manners. This is a tomboy to suit the male gaze, not the one made popular by Alcott, of a young woman comfortable in her innate sense of self.

Despite the popularity of the marketplace tomboy, *Harper's Bizarre* published an article in 1898 that proved so immensely popular that it was reprinted in newspapers nationwide for several months: "The Passing of the Tomboy." The author asserts that the "tomboy is an antiquarian's word. Women who were little girls twenty years ago know how potent of a reproach it used to be when it was still in vogue in the homes of the land" ("Passing" 1898, 64). The author notes that descriptions of Hosmer's childhood were met with "some complacency" because she proved so immensely talented and "open air exercise was known to be good for high strung girls of exceptional endowments" ("Passing" 1898, 64). In other words, the tomboy girlhoods of great women were okay because they were exceptional from the beginning.

The irony of the 1898 article is that if one searches for "tomboy" and "tom-boy" in databases of old newspapers, magazines, and fiction, and reads memoirs from the turn of the century, the frequency of its use increases in the 1880s and continues to climb to the present day. The author is incorrect about the term becoming passé; tomboy was not an antiquated term, but rather one that had gained new meaning as physicality, ambition, and self-assertion in young women gained traction. The creation of the marketplace tomboy, alongside the older version of reproach, meant that the term was still used, but to suggest that nonconformity and rebellion was in fact the most common trait of American girls. As the author notes, when silver-haired grandmothers recounted their tomboy girlhoods, the pranks, games, and adventures that their memories are on par with popular images of American girlhood.

One of the reasons we find girls disavowing the term "tomboy" and older women looking back upon the term fondly in the late nineteenth century is the emergence of the marketplace tomboy alongside the term of reproach. Much like contemporary feminists have sought to reclaim and transform pejorative terms, "tomboy" continued to operate on both tracks: one suggesting that playful, intellectual, or physical behavior was aberrant and inappropriate in girls and another that such behaviors were not only natural but a mark of the greater female individuality that so many contemporaries celebrated as indicative of modernity. "Tomboy" became a way of separating girls of the past from girls of the present, but as a term that shows no sign of going away, it also serves to reinforce the intractability of gender roles.

NOTES

1. I have not been able to find evidence of tomboys in African American written culture until 1923, when Ruth Arnett, a youth organizer, declared that the African American community should raise girls as tomboys for health reasons (Jackson 1923, 12). Tomboys of color did not become ubiquitous, or a source of pride in the black community, until the late second half of the twentieth century.

2. See films *Little Women*: 1994 and 2019.

BIBLIOGRAPHY

N. A. 1888. "Anecdote of Harriet Hosmer." *Patriot* (Harrisburg, PA). July 27, 1888.

N. A. 1898. "The Passing of the Tomboy." *Harper's Bizarre* 31 (32). August 6, 1898.
N. A. 1893. "Statue of a Tomboy Will Be at the Fair for California." *Daily Inter Ocean* (Chicago, IL). January 26, 1893.
N. A. 1887. "Trials of a Girl of Fourteen." *Courier-Journal* (Louisville, KY). October 2, 1887.
N. A. 1867. "The Tom-Boy." *Pittsfield Sun* (Pittsfield, MA). May 23, 1867.
N. A. 1872. "What Came of a Tomboy." *Cincinnati Daily Enquirer* (Cincinnati, OH). November 25, 1872.
Abate, Michelle Ann. 2008. *Tomboys: A Literary and Cultural History*. Philadelphia, PA: Temple University Press.
Alcott, Louisa May. 1989. *The Journals of Louisa May Alcott*. Boston: Little Brown, and Company.
———. (1868–1869) 2004. *Little Women.* New York: Penguin Press.
Bordo, Susan. 1993. *Unbearable Weight: Feminism, Western Culture, and the Body*. Berkeley: University of California Press.
Carey, Thomas M. 1982. Diary, October 1, 1871, vol. 10, real 1, frame 469. *Papers of M. Carey Thomas in the Bryn Mawr College Archives*, ed. Lucy Fisher West. 217 reels; Woodbridge, CT: Research Publications International.
Chas, W. Chase. 1885. "Reddy, The Tomboy." *Rocky Mountain News* (Denver, CO). December 3, 1885.
Cohen, Daniel E. 2015. "Introduction." *'Hero Strong' and Other Stories: Tales of Girlhood Ambition, Female Masculinity, and Women's Worldly Achievement in Antebellum America*, edited by Mary F. W. Gibson, 1–61. Knoxville, TN: University of Tennessee Press. 35.
Culkin, Kate. 2010. *Harriet Hosmer: A Cultural Biography*. Amherst: University of Massachusetts Press.
Fetterly, Judith. 1979. "Alcott's Civil War." *Feminist Studies* 5 (2): 379.
Fremont, Jessie Benton. 1887. *Souvenirs of My Time*. Boston: D. Lothrop.
Gilder, Jeannette L. 1901. *The Autobiography of a Tomboy*. New York: Doubleday, Page & Co.
Haebegger, Alfred. 1982. *Gender, Fantasy, and Realism in American Literature.* New York: Columbia University Press.
Jackson, A. L. 1923. "The Onlooker," *Chicago Defender*, September 1, 1923.
Janeway, Elizabeth. 1968. "Meg, Jo, Beth, Amy, and Louisa," *The New York Times Book Review*, September 29, 1968.
Kitch, Carolyn L. 2001. *The Girl on the Magazine Cover: The Origins of Visual Stereotypes in American Mass Media*. Chapel Hill: University of North Carolina Press.
McLeod, Anne Scout. 1994. *American Girlhood: Essays on Children's Literature of the Nineteenth and Twentieth Centuries.* Athens: University of Georgia Press.
O'Brien, Sharon. 1979. "Tomboyism and Adolescent Conflict: Three Nineteenth-Century Case Studies." In *Woman's Being, Woman's Place: Female Identity and Vocation in American History*, edited by Mary Kelly, 351–72. Boston: G. K. Hall and Co.

Ozick, Cynthia. 1982. "The Making of a Writer." *The New York Times Book Review*. January 31, 1982.

Parton, James. 1888. *Daughters of Genius: A Series of Sketches of Authors, Artists, Reformers, and Heroines.* Philadelphia: Hubbard Brothers.

Sentilles, Renée. 2018. *American Tomboys: 1850–1915.* Amherst: University of Massachusetts Press.

Sicherman, Barbara. 2010. *Well-Read Lives: How Books Inspired a Generation of American Women*. Chapel Hill: University of North Carolina Press.

Simmons, LaKisha Michelle. 2015. *Crescent City Girls: The Lives of Young Black Women in Segregated New Orleans.* Chapel Hill: University of North Carolina Press.

Stowe, Harriet Beecher et al. 1884. *Our Famous Women: Comprising the Lives and Deeds of Famous American Women Who Have Distinguished Themselves in Literature, Science, Art, Music, and the Drama, Or Are Famous as Heroines, Patriots, Orators, Educators, Physicians, Philanthropists, Etc.* Hartford, CT: A. D. Worthington & Co.

Wadsworth, Sarah. 2006. *In the Company of Books: Literature and Its "Classes" in Nineteenth-Century America*. Amherst: University of Massachusetts Press.

Wright, Nazera Sadiq. 2016. *Black Girlhood in the Nineteenth Century*. Urbana: University of Illinois Press.

Zeisler, Andi. 2016. *We Were Feminists Once: From Riot Girrl to Covergirl, the Buying and Selling of a Political Movement*. New York: Public Affairs.

Chapter 2

The Momboy: Maternal Tomboys on Stage

Lynn Deboeck

In the past two centuries, the treatment of girls acting like boys in American literature clearly illustrates how the tomboy construct is equated with youthfulness, freedom, and a relinquishing of responsibility that is "intrinsically queer" (Sentilles 2018, 16–7). Renée Sentilles, author of *American Tomboys: 1850–1915*, explains that for the tomboy, "[a]mbiguity was central to her appeal and acceptable because it was rooted in a youth that would inevitably pass" (5). Characters such as Pricilla Tomboy from the 1790 musical *The Romp* engaged with youthful, female leads who challenged social norms for young women of the era (Lloyd 1788; Sentilles 2018, 6). Between the American Revolution and the Reconstruction Era of the mid-nineteenth century, gender roles were being constructed in a burgeoning nation. These roles supported the "separate spheres" ideology. In this context, the tomboy played an integral part in how girls and young women could identify and resist the imposed roles. The potential for such resistance had two parts: the creation of tomboy characters and their stories, and the consumption of those characters' stories. Despite the fact that societal pressures in the late eighteenth and early nineteenth centuries rarely allowed young girls and women access to the masculine freedoms fictional tomboys were allowed, the reality that the characters were created and consumed meant that seeds were sown. New possibilities were born and were in direct contrast to the gendered structures of the day. Over time, tomboy depictions increasingly included more fierce, independent, and determined young women who specifically challenged the social mores surrounding marriage and sex by avoiding them. This then leads to today, where a certain amount of "latitude in the performance of girlhood" is afforded to girls, demonstrating what is now "a rare example in which the gender deck is stacked in their favor" (Damour 2020, 1).

The earliest usage of the term "tomboy," which referred to unruly boys, was in 1556 (Sentilles 2018, 6). Licentious women had started to earn the label by the end of the sixteenth century, and over the next two and a half centuries, more tomboy references were directed at girls and young women, although the characteristic of promiscuousness seems to have been largely dropped (Sentilles 2018, 5).The tomboy is defined by current tomboy scholars (Renée Sentilles and Michelle Abate being among the most prominent) as a female-identifying person who engages in behavior typically associated with masculine persons. The cognitive dissonance present when confronting a gender contradiction like the tomboy results from the expectation of a particular, socially sanctioned femininity while viewing masculine performance from that same body (Bailey et al. 2002, 333). But the tomboy shows her face so often that audiences and readers are quite adept at accepting any contradiction she poses.

The tomboy moniker has not been associated with a mother character despite the tendency to force compulsory femininity (and its requisite gender roles) into the space of mother performance. Mothers have additional, unwritten rules governing their performance and restricting their access, particularly to patriarchal power and masculine dominance. One example is the role of perpetually kind, docile nurturer. While not all mother characters fall into this stereotype, it is a part of the foundation of the maternal gender role (defined in contrast to the paternal role of strict disciplinarian) that restricts the mother's performance. As such, it is difficult for people to see masculinity present in a maternal body since it is typically associated with less yielding personalities. What makes motherhood such a contradictory state when combined with tomboyhood is the fact that the meta-narratives of motherhood have largely been under male control. This was particularly true in the Victorian era. Patriarchal dominance extended to include how mothers should be and how they should be understood. Patrice DiQuinzio, in her feminist assessment of the paradox of mothering, addresses this notion by looking at the history of motherhood's construction by men, highlighting that "[g]iven the hegemony of individualism and essential motherhood, mothers' (and women's) identities, situations, and experiences themselves are contradictorily over-determined" (1999, 243). Nevertheless, mothers' experiences, particularly in the Victorian era when the tomboy was born, mirrored those of youth who wished to resist their restrictive childhoods. The difference is that boys, presumably, had better luck with this. Girls were given a period as tomboys to refuse the inevitable yoke of marriage and motherhood, but once those institutions fell upon them, they were caught in a new form of restriction, under the rule of a husband. What evolved alongside the tomboy in the late nineteenth century, at least in the imaginary, was a second tomboyhood that occurred within the space of maternity.

The dramatic portrayal of mothers enjoys a long tradition, though sometimes facets of mother characters have been overlooked in an effort to focus on either the plight of the mother's offspring or her failures with respect to her maternity.[1] Traditional images of motherhood, however, have been and are now being challenged and altered to reveal "mothers as humans who redefine their own 'motherness,' speak with their own voices, articulate their own experiences, and thereby alter the longstanding cultural myths and practices of the patriarchal mother" (Osnes and Andes 2010, i–ii). In effect, mother characters are starting to be revisited to see just how defiant they have always been toward gendered limitations. The measures and tactics used by mother characters to achieve their objectives have evolved to be wide-ranging and inventive. Not limited to seduction and murder, mothers too can manipulate their own gendered reception. Given the bodily realities of motherhood and the finite understanding of gendered associations regarding the body, manipulation of gender is rarely considered for a mother character. How can someone be perceived as masculine if she have/will/could breastfeed? The case study examples here show that maternity is not a barrier to other gender expression. Maternity lures the unsuspecting audience members into a sense of security, of knowing who and what they are seeing. So much is assumed about a mother in a story, including what she wants and how she might get it. This security-of-assumption has often hidden what I term the "momboy" from view.

The discourse on tomboys includes definitions that range from boyish girls (Bailey et al. 2002, 334) to feminists (Craig and LaCroix 2011, 451); from androgynous individuals to lesbians (Bailey and Zucker 1995, 44). Renée Sentilles looks at figures in literature she terms "proto-tomboys" who exhibit tomboy behavior but are not granted the title (Sentilles 2018, 17). I understand and use the term "tomboy" here to refer less to presentation, orientation, or political persuasion, and more to the power being wielded. Tomboys wield masculine power. Sometimes this takes the form of a subversive power-grab. At other times, it is a fully sanctioned loan. Regardless, the tomboy is involved in usurping power that society does not normally give girls/young women and utilizing it for her own means, most typically to preserve what freedom she can for as long as possible. The momboy, in a similar way, assumes masculine power. This can take the form of displacing the father figure, but it also can have little or nothing to do with the parental status of the momboy, instead involving simply the use of the masculine toolbox to serve her own ends.

The maternal status of the momboy is the main contradiction through which we must dig to uncover the parallels between her and the tomboy.

Even though it troubles our understanding to encounter one or more of these "non-normative" gendered bodies, the tomboy has become a relatively positive idea. For the past century and a half, tomboys have maintained an ever-presence in our cultural consciousness (see, e.g., Abate 2008; Sentilles 2018; Stockton 2009). From early figures such as Elizabeth Stuart Phelps's *Gypsy Breynton* (Phelps 1866–1867) to the inexorable Jo March, the tomboy had made her indelible mark on our social landscape by the mid-nineteenth century. The Victorian era continued to usher in new ideas about girls, women, and femininity through a tomboy trope that challenged, though it did not altogether break, the norms of female subjugation. The twentieth century saw the tomboy exhibited in *Little House on the Prairie,* as well as in a plethora of media and advertisements using masculinized women to promote the need for women in the workforce during World War II (Abate 2008). The most famous of these was, of course, the Rosie the Riveter campaign, but the movement also included recruitment for the Women's Army Corps and the Navy, with calls to "release a man to fight at sea."

With posters and advertisements depicting young girls pining for such an experience, novels started being published that brought to life what an exciting time a tomboy could have.

Harper Lee, famous author of *To Kill a Mockingbird*, "left a great deal of work to readers' imaginations in regard to the question of whether or not Scout would outgrow her gender nonconformity in adulthood" (Proehl 2018, 111). Hers was a different approach since most novels quite clearly laid out an end point in marriage. Harper's choice reflected a new ambiguity on the horizon—that of perpetual tomboyhood. The combination of how these tomboy figures have been created, consumed, and analyzed has truncated their very existence. Notwithstanding the question of Scout's gender nonconformity, the tomboy's existence has consistently been understood to end with marriage and motherhood. Yet, what are we to do, then, with the mother characters who performed masculinity in the same way as tomboys?

In theatrical depictions, tomboys and, more broadly, the masculinization of women, have been used as tools in farces and agitprop plays, as well as in dark comedy. Perhaps the most common theatrical reference to the masculinization of women was "breeches roles," wherein a female character would don male clothing and pretend to be a man. Breeches roles began in earnest during the latter half of the seventeenth century and were largely used within the plot of the play to help a woman navigate public spaces from which she would normally be excluded. The practice has been acknowledged by scholars as an act "deliberately traversing meaningful boundaries," specifically with gendered clothing (Berlanstein 1996, 338). The convention then began to be used more frequently as a sexualizing feature, highlighting the shape of

Figure 2.1 "Enlist in the Waves release a man to fight at sea."

a woman's leg in the snug breeches and tights normally worn by men. Despite the objectification, the female characters enjoyed extra freedoms as men.

Maternal characters who enact performances similar to tomboys have largely been underexplored and ignored because of the assumption that tomboys are, or should be, prepubescent. The tomboy label has rarely, if ever,

Figure 2.2 "This artwork became the basis for a recruiting poster with the phrase 'Wish I Could Join Too!'" John Falter, "Little Sister With a Picture of a Wave." 1944. Painting, Oil on Canvas, 36 x 27 in.

been applied to a reproductive person. This means that no one was looking for her. The evolution of the New Woman ideal of the late-nineteenth century affected girls and their choices by showing them independent women many wished to emulate.[2] Despite some of the public's general distaste for the New Woman and her sensibilities, the tomboy was a subjectivity girls could and did inhabit to game the system of gendered expectations (Abate 2008, 51). However, in this era tomboy behavior was still limited to childless young women. Mothers and tomboys could not coexist in one person because mothers display physical evidence of their sexuality and a particular load of gendered responsibility is applied to them with regard to the care of their children. The tomboy, in her asexual status, exhibits the freedom that men can feel well into adulthood. However, that freedom was inevitably curtailed in Victorian tomboy literature at the moment the young woman became a wife (and subsequently, it was assumed, would become a mother). I pose a challenge to the definition of "tomboy," not to include more specifications, but to focus on the two most important. I argue that the sexual, marital, or parental status of the tomboy is less important than firstly, the grasp for male intellectual independence and secondly, the pursuit of power conferred to the patriarchy. Both of these we see abundantly in mother characters.

In this chapter, I look at three plays as case studies that each illustrate the momboy and her similarity to the tomboy. More specifically, I will demonstrate the cyclical nature of the mother-character in her constant social relegation to powerlessness, from which she uses tomboy tactics to free herself. Essentially, the momboy has the potential to be a forever-tomboy, never completely breaking free and attaining full power, but also not shifting to a new, socially sanctioned gender role. The plays include an anti-suffrage parlor drama entitled *The Spirit of Seventy-Six, or The Coming Woman, a Prophetic Drama* (Curtis 1868), which depicts Mrs. Wigfall executing male dominance as a judge and paternal-mother once she achieves the right to vote, Bertolt Brecht's *Mother Courage and Her Children* ([1939] 1991), wherein the title character utilizes her masculine wiles as a "con-man" to make a profit during the Thirty Years' War, and Paula Vogel's *And Baby Makes Seven* (1984), which features a pregnant woman, Anna, engaging in a game wherein she pretends to be a boy named Cecil. These plays demonstrate the very real existence of the momboy—not only because of their gender role transgressions, but due to their maternal ones as well.

THEORETICAL FRAMEWORK: AT THE INTERSECTION OF FEMINIST, QUEER, AND LITERARY THEORY

Stories—written, oral, and performed—have, in large part, shaped generations of boys and girls in their performances of boyhood and girlhood. In fact, the practice of storytelling forces a particular gender performance by presuming a "proper" or "correct" philosophy of gender. In contrast to the actual development of that philosophy, storytelling can be static in its creation. As feminist scholar Florentien Verhage, taking her lead from Gloria Anzaldúa, explores what she calls "the philosophy of the in-between, or a marginal philosophy," she shows how the *act* of bringing into being philosophically has to acknowledge the different, marginal worlds that are being inhabited (2016, 147). Stories do not have to acknowledge these worlds in the same way because they operate inside social laws that do not often concern themselves with philosophies of being or identity, assuming them to be fixed in order to carry the story. Resisting the performance of womanhood and shrugging off the feminine label with appearances, motivations, stories, and behaviors is work that pushes past social mores and hopes to make a mark on philosophies of being. The plays put forth here (written in 1868, 1939, and 1984) show mothers dressing in masculine clothing, drawing motivation from selfish desires (rather than selfless nurturing), and acting in accordance with a stereotypical white man's role in the public sphere. These mothers always existed, but the forms in which they were allowed to exist have evolved to include primarily satire, from political agitprop performance to mainstream dramas and comedies. In each form, they are represented determining their own fates. I suggest that amid these stories, a new type of subjectivity exists that has gone under-examined, which queers both mothers and the notion of the tomboy itself—the "momboy."

Literary interpretations of feminine and masculine behavior have contributed to the socially constructed gender binary. In other words, we understand specific behaviors to fall under those two designations, and analysis of gendered characters tends to reinforce those associations. A performance of masculinity means something specific because it is associated with men (typically white men) and their position in society. A queer reading of mothers offers a new understanding of her potential for masculine performance. The momboy is a mother character who exhibits masculine behavior in order to enjoy control over her life or a situation. Much like the tomboy, the momboy wields masculinity as a means to access independence and control that is often withheld from her based on her status as a woman. A main difference is that the momboy is also resisting additional societal pressures and oppressions based on her maternal status. Some of these include the assumption that she should put her children's welfare and wishes above her own and the assumption that motherhood is her main reason for existence. Tomboys have the luxury of operating independently, the only drive to care for others coming from her own choice. Mothers are compelled not only to care for their offspring, but also to desire to do so. What makes the momboy-tomboy connection paradoxical is the fact that motherhood is a part (along with marriage) of what supposedly extinguishes the tomboy's existence. The momboy is the double-contradiction of a female character who clearly demonstrates her reproductive status and role by virtue of being outwardly maternal, but who also exhibits masculine tendencies and freedoms presumed to be outside of the female grasp. As such, my exploration of momboys in dramatic literature contributes to the scholarship surrounding mothers and feminine persons, expanding the narratives that have historically restricted them. Once acknowledged, there is hope for other resistant subjectivities to be uncovered as well.

The wider understanding of tomboys evolved over time to gain acceptance—and even currency—in particular situations. For example, literature and gender scholar Michelle Abate discusses how the growing nationalism sparked by turn-of-the-twentieth-century immigration catapulted tomboyhood into a favorable light because it showed girls exhibiting their "American-ness" through their male-ness (2008, 73). However, motherhood has typically been understood to be one of the last great bastions to contain and preserve a femininity rooted in patriarchal dominance. This makes motherhood the last place one would look to find a tomboy, which is exactly why the *momboy* has been hidden for so long. The surprise at encountering her makes necessary waves, which in turn can create change for mothers, much in the same way the tomboy has expanded what gender performance is available to girls. The tomboy aesthetic and associated (sometimes considered androgynous) mannerisms provide an avenue of acceptance to the female character who, while taboo in general culture, has been sanctioned by audiences much like breeches roles, because of the infallible logic that made her a fad and a curiosity to begin with. Tomboys are *allowed to be* contradictory—in fact, that is their purpose. Momboys, though not yet granted this right, are contradictory all the same.

The age and fecundity-status line, which seemed hard and unquestionable to Victorian audiences and readers, is a part of what has hidden momboy evolution from immediate view. The point of marriage drew a bold, Victorian dividing line that separated what came before (youth, tomboyhood) from what came after (maturity, motherhood). *Little Women*'s Jo March exemplified this division with her marriage to Professor Bhaer (Alcott 1868). Louisa May Alcott's quintessential tomboy character initially resisted the trope of ending her tomboyhood by not marrying Laurie, the handsome suitor. However, she still acquiesced to the final stage of womanhood that would put an end to her quest for independence and self-sufficiency (Sentilles 2018, 54–7). The plays used here are an effort to reveal how this firm line was thwarted by mother characters. The tomboy served as a transitional figure (from youth to adulthood) as the United States adopted a new modern girl archetype. The momboy served, and continues to serve, as a defiant figure, challenging the status quo. Momboys demonstrate how reproductive women characters can continue to hold on to their own subjectivities and autonomy longer, if not indefinitely. In essence, momboys effectively complete the promise tomboys fall short on by ignoring the reproductive demarcation line that has been used to rob women of their independence. The momboy uses obvious tomboy tactics in her drive to acquire the same independence and power held by men.

MOMBOY CASE STUDY 1: ANTI-SUFFRAGE PARLOR DRAMA

Some of the most notable masculine performances by maternal women were in media, images, and messages (including drama) depicting women's escape from the oppression of their gender role duties (including housekeeping and maternal ones) during the suffrage era.

Ariana Randolph Wormeley Curtis wrote *The Spirit of Seventy-Six, or The Coming Woman, A Prophetic Drama* (1868) in an effort to expound upon what many anti-suffragists were arguing would happen to "the fairer sex" if they indeed obtained the right to vote; namely, that they would become aggressive and man-like. In this parlor drama, the main female character, Judge Susan Wigfall, explains the woman's quest for suffrage in exaggerated language: "A hundred years ago it was thought a fine thing for a few

Figure 2.3 "The new woman–wash day."

American men to throw off the British Tyrant's yoke—but that was a trifling achievement, compared to the new Revolution, in which twenty millions of ladies have thrown off all restraint, and now plant their victorious feet on the neck of the Male Oppressor!" (Curtis 1868, 30). Though not the only example of a masculinized woman in the play, Judge Wigfall is a maternal figure as well, which makes her transgression all the more conspicuous.

The Spirit of Seventy-Six was a commentary on the role of women and men in society, and was "received at every representation with great laughter and applause by large and fashionable audiences" (Classified Ad 1868). Set in Boston in 1876, it tells the story of Thomas Carberry, a businessman who has been living in China for the past ten years without any connection to the happenings in America. He has just returned to his hometown of Boston and finds, much to his astonishment, and eventually chagrin, that women have obtained the right to vote in his absence and have voted themselves into every executive office in the city. He learns from one woman he meets (Victorine, the Judge's daughter) that not only are women working in positions previously held by men, but they have taken the social and romantic roles of men as well. Women are expected to ask men to dance at parties, woo them, and propose to them. Victorine's mother, Judge Susan Wigfall—known simply as "the Judge"—takes her masculine role quite seriously and is known to wear her judge's robes everywhere she goes and to push her opinion as law in every situation. She is able to exercise her judge's rights because women are now in the roles that matter in the public sphere, whereas, according to a newspaper review of the production, "[t]he members of that degenerate sex, on the other hand, are nursery maids and rock the cradle when the babies (who are all female, for even infants scorn the masculine gender) cry" (Hale 1868). In her literary attempts to disparage masculine women, Curtis additionally highlights the hypocrisy and ridiculous behavior of men, emphasizing the fact that the men do, in fact, have power that women do not, and that they do not always employ it well.

As the play progresses, we learn that the Judge wishes her daughter to follow in her footsteps and go into law. However, Victorine resists this fatherly urging from her mother in the following scene:

> JUDGE. [. . .] You don't deserve to be my daughter,—and the end of it will be, you'll have to marry,—you are not fit for anything better!
>
> VICTORINE. I don't want anything better!
>
> JUDGE. Because you have never risen above the level of girls before the Revolution. I give you up, and I shall centre all my hopes upon your sister Portia,—a child of great promise,—who *cries* for Cruise's Digest.
>
> VICTORINE. Hurrah! then I need n't be a lawyer, after all! (Curtis 1868, 40)

Despite her disapproval of marriage on the whole, the Judge concludes that Victorine must have another way of being provided for, and suggests that she propose to Carberry. This proposal is understood to be a necessity and not for sentimental reasons, as the Judge asserts that "love is as obsolete as a line-of-battle ship" and that "[w]ives *rule* their husbands" (Curtis 1868, 42). Victorine is too nervous and embarrassed to propose, however, and so the Judge asserts that Carberry will soon be "snatched up" by some other woman. In fact, Carberry is found to be a desirable husband by two other women, in addition to Victorine. The first is Miss Griffin, who, wishing to benefit her political causes with his wealth, proposes soon after meeting him. The second suitor is Mrs. Badger, an assessor of the internal revenue whom Carberry meets briefly at the train station at the beginning of the play. She is a widow of seven years who blackmails him over an unfairly billed tax so that he will agree to marry her. Carberry tells Victorine that Miss Griffin (her aunt) wishes to wed him but that he is really in love with her, and he asks for her hand on the spot, saying, "I came home with the idea of marrying some nice pretty little wife, such as they used to have,—who would make much of me, and give me good dinners, and look pretty at the head of the table,—which is all a man wants in a wife" (Curtis 1868, 52). This scene is interrupted by Miss Griffin, brandishing two pistols and declaring him a traitor because she believes him to be violating their engagement, claiming that "[b]reach of Promise is a capital crime!" (Curtis 1868, 66). In the middle of the ensuing duel, the Judge enters and arrests both parties for disturbing the peace. At the point of sentencing them each to a twenty-year prison term, Mr. Wigfall exaggerates his show of support for his wife's sentence, and she ends up letting them off just to spite her husband. She completes her judgment by giving Victorine permission to marry Carberry. The play ends with both Griffin and Badger denouncing men entirely and the Judge addressing the audience as a jury and charging them to "find [them]selves for or against the defendant, MAN" (Curtis 1868, 73).

Judge Wigfall, as the prominent momboy figure, is useful in her tomboy function of representing resistance to imposed gender roles in a way that has already been sanctioned by readers. In other words, since the tomboy has been accepted as "allowed" to move in society like a man (with agency and autonomy), the momboy can do some of the same work for mothers by making the social commentary that the demarcation of motherhood is arbitrary when it comes to such agency and autonomy. After all, it is the Judge who moves the plot forward and she determines not only her daughter's fate, but the fate of everyone else in the story. Particularly within a farce, which means the performance of woman-as-man is taking place in the context of woman-can't-be-man, use of the momboy in *The Spirit of Seventy-Six* is thrown into greater relief. Victorine, being the youngest and not yet married, most closely aligns herself with the tomboy ideal of the day in which the play was written. She, thus, represents what everyone already knows. However, Victorine's lack of masculine power, due to her reticence to take on more masculine endeavors such as studying law, affords her little mobility in the story. She is instead moved by others. It takes the Judge (the momboy) to push the action forward with her own masculine power. The satirical nature of *The Spirit of Seventy-Six* allows it to represent older, masculine women's tomboy-like aspirations even more clearly because they have been given all the power. Curtis was not just taking a stance on women's suffrage with this piece, but she was highlighting the disparities and oppressions for both of the acknowledged sexes. The fact that obtaining male power in such a way as represented in the script was not realistic for women of the period, and therefore treated as a joke, underscores the way that all tomboys have been situated in literature: as non-representative of reality, and therefore effective for resistance. Characters who are not representative of the current reality are effective at resistance because they are frequently and unwisely dismissed by the powers they are trying to resist. Dismissed as nonsense, these characters are allowed to be present to entertain, when in fact (unbeknownst to the patriarchal powers) they are representing a reality for which many wish to fight. Tomboys have been such a force. Incorporated into young women's literature the way they were and mediated by the male-dominated publishing world to stay in their parameters of adolescent pre-marriage, it would seem they were not seen as a threat to the status quo. And yet, tomboys rocked the boat largely because they were underestimated in this way. Momboys do the same.

Sentilles writes about the rise in popularity of the tomboy during the Victorian age (when *The Spirit of Seventy-Six* was published), when girls were allowed and even encouraged to "adopt male freedoms" for a time (Sentilles 2018, 7). Sentilles also explains that the evolution of fictional tomboy stories played a big role in the social construction of (typically white) girls/young women who were expected to gladly give up their youthful, tomboy freedoms for the sake of marriage, motherhood, and wifely duties. Motherhood for these same, white, middle-class women was in many ways like a second childhood. With a new man in charge of her, and responsibilities that restricted her, the maturing, feminine wife and mother was yet again thrust into an existence from which she might understandably wish to escape, even just temporarily. Tomboyhood provides that for girls/young women, and momboy-hood does so for reproductive women. Prior to her enfranchisement, according to the context given in the play, the Judge was relegated to caring for her family, without any control over or power within the household. She then acquires new "male freedoms," which she is not so quick to relinquish. This fictional story (just as other, earlier tomboy stories), "serve[s] as a playful assertion that, like boys, girls have a right to 'be' irrespective of what they will 'become'" (Sentilles 2018, 21). The tomboy and momboy tactics are used to acquire what the girl/woman has a right to, despite what she has been or eventually will be. In other words, girls can be independent and influential when they are young, despite the fact that later they *may* marry or have children. In the same way, the Judge has the right to be powerful, despite her having been subservient in marriage and motherhood in the past. As the tomboy retains power *prior to* a change in her future life, the influence and power work bi-directionally for the momboy. No matter what she has been or will become, she is entitled to the autonomy that has historically only been given to men. The Judge is able to pursue an intellectual career, she has direct say in what kind of future her daughter can have and she is able to open and publicly disagree with her husband if she chooses.

The Judge's story mirrors many of the tomboy stories in its silly, fictitious, and short-lived treatment. In the same way that early audiences of tomboy stories grinned at and humored those characters, firmly understanding that this was not reality, so too the Judge's existence in a farcical play is meant as a literary tool. Rather than represent reality, the play is intended to make a misogynous point about women being out of their element in masculine roles, be enjoyable, and end. The Judge wrestles with the same issue that tomboys have confronted from the beginning: their inevitable demise. They exist in a liminal space and time, with the threat of impending adulthood (tomboy) or a re-suppression into submissive femininity (momboy) on the horizon, ready to rob them of their agency. Perhaps the saddest part of this expected departure is the fact that tomboys and momboys do not leave because the girl or woman no longer needs or wants their agency—they leave because the stories within which they live are dependent on their ephemerality. Tomboy dramas are written with the tomboy aging out at the end into marriage and motherhood. Momboy ones depend upon her either reverting back to a character with less autonomy (underscoring the masculine power and agency being usurped) or completing the story on an unsustainable note (i.e., with a tongue-in-cheek commentary that she will continue to wield her powers, when it is obvious this would be highly unlikely to happen in real life). Despite Curtis's own position regarding women's suffrage, she chose to end her play with the latter approach. In lieu of reverting back to women in a more submissive position, she extended the story to imagine a future where a woman could stand and dispense judgment, even on man.

MOMBOY CASE STUDY 2: BRECHTIAN EPIC DRAMA

Moving into the twentieth century, the tomboy found herself rising in popularity, described as being "everywhere, dovetailing with both women's suffrage and first-wave feminism," and as such were being used for particular political and social functions separate from just adolescent entertainment (King 2017). Momboys followed a similar trajectory, using their unique position in the social landscape to manipulate story and theme as well as make larger commentary on what was happening at the time—most notably, as a reaction to war. In the late 1930s and early 1940s, Germany watched, participated, and, in some cases, resisted as the Third Reich took a firm hold of their country and began to advance its ideology across the borders. In addition, global effects from the Great Depression affected how the tomboy's tale changed to "present tomboyish young girls as capable, productive and industrious [. . .] as both feminine and heterosexually appealing" (Abate 2008, 140). This was, of course, the perfect preparation for the necessary transition that would occur in the war to come when women would be entering the workforce to replace men, and then swiftly back home again once the men returned.

Bertolt Brecht's famous play, *Mother Courage and Her Children* (written in 1939), is often touted as one of the stronger condemnations of Nazism and other authoritarian regimes. The play follows Canteen Anna (also called Anna Fierling or "Mother Courage"), a con-woman who is endeavoring to profit from the Thirty Years' War. We see her through twelve years of this war, finding ways to make a living for herself and, at times, to support her children. Brecht's intentions for portraying Mother Courage were as a character to criticize. She adopts a masculine role in her efforts to sell items to the soldiers. Rather than nurturing or selfless gestures, often associated or conflated with mother figures, this character deliberately cons and blackmails others to get things for herself, often neglecting or harming her own children.

The play begins in the midst of war, with officers openly bewailing the need for more soldiers to enlist. Mother Courage enters, with wares to sell to the soldiers, and as one officer distracts her with a sale, another signs up one of her sons (Eilif) to fight in the war. Her other two children (both from different fathers than Eilif's, though none that Mother Courage married) subsequently get pressured into roles in the war, and Mother Courage, instead of exhibiting motherly worry or pride in her children, chastises them for not putting themselves first always. Her other son (Swiss Cheese) is killed, and when presented with his body, Mother Courage denies she knows him in an effort to save herself. She then refuses an offer of marriage, preferring not to lose control of her life and destiny. After this, her daughter (Kattrin) is raped and disfigured by a soldier, which leads Mother Courage to curse the war, but still work to support it by selling much-needed merchandise to the armies. Eilif, after murdering a peasant and stealing his animals for himself, is executed, but Mother Courage does not learn about this. She proceeds to abandon Kattrin with a peasant family, only for her daughter to be shot by soldiers who invade the village. The play ends with Mother Courage having the peasants bury her daughter's body and pulling her wagon of wares to, presumably, start selling again.

From the initial performances of *Mother Courage and Her Children*, audiences' perceptions of its protagonist were decidedly different from Brecht's own designs for them. Their reactions were empathetic toward Mother Courage rather than critical. Brecht "found it important to make a few more changes [. . .] where attempts were made to obstruct any inclination in the audience to identify with Mother Courage" (Thomson 1997, 22). However, he remained quite disconcerted after hearing the reviews and sentimental audience response toward another production at the Deutsches Theatre in 1949. He returned to Berlin in 1951 to personally direct the play in order to elicit what he felt was the proper response. To Brecht's way of thinking, as long as the production followed his theoretical framework for what he termed "epic theatre," the audience would be compelled to view Mother Courage critically rather than empathetically (*Brecht on Stage*). However, the audience of his production was also swayed by emotion (connecting to Mother

Courage with empathy) rather than intellect or logic (being convinced by reason that her actions were objectively worthy of reproach). Two reasons for this reaction are the assumption of selfless care associated with maternity as well as motherhood being connected to a weaker femininity. Brecht chose to use a mother instead of a father, assuming her transgressions would be more easily critiqued, when in fact, she was viewed as a damsel in distress. What Mother Courage used in her story, though, was not helpless femininity, but autonomous, aggressive masculinity. In essence, she used momboy tactics to create agency for herself, all the while with the audience bias toward forgiving maternal figures protecting her from criticism of her aggressive approach.

One example of Courage's masculine aggression is when she sings the "Song of Grand Capitulation." Brecht weaved a number of songs into his play along with theatrical conventions such as noted placards that denoted what was to come in the next scene, eliminating suspense and the suspension of disbelief. Both of these practices were meant to condemn war by pushing the audience's attention out of the story and form and on to the specific actions and perspectives of the character, which he intended to mark as deplorable. In the "Song of Grand Capitulation," Mother Courage sings:

> Back when I was young, I was brought to realise
> What a very special person I must be
> (Not just any old cottager's daughter, what with my looks
> and my talents and my urge towards Higher Things)
> And insisted that my soup should have no hairs in it.
> No one makes a sucker out of me!
> (All or nothing, only the best is good enough, each man for himself, nobody's telling *me* what to do.) (Brecht 1939, 41–2)

This song, with specific reference to "each man for himself" and the assertion of independent will that was not commonly afforded to women in the same way, as well as the choices she makes to neglect and abandon her children in favor of making a sale or saving her own business, all afford her a masculine presence. Her momboy characterization reads in direct contrast to how a mother (and in fact, a woman) was expected to perform, which is perhaps most clearly articulated in Hitler's criticism of equal rights between men and women as "draw[ing] women into realms of society where they are inferior." According to his ideology (which was pervasive in Germany at the time of Brecht's play), "[t]he woman has her own battlefield. With every child that she brings into the world, she fights her battle for the nation" ("Llewellyn, Southey, and Thompson 2020").

Every written and performative choice Brecht made for Mother Courage was to demonstrate how her actions are indisputably unforgivable. In *Brecht in Practice: Theatre, Theory and Performance*, David Barnett et al. note that *Mother Courage* is one of many plays by Brecht wherein his methodology is blatantly activist. As they assert, "[i]f the Brechtian method is to have any meaning, it has to be understood as enabling a radical insight into the way society and its citizens work with a view to changing both of them" (Barnett et al. 2014, 3). However, many of Mother Courage's actions, disgraceful though they are, are not often viewed critically as right or wrong, moral or immoral (by masculine definitions). They are seen as un/motherly. Motherliness is granted an entirely different category that denotes negativity outside of the general morality scales because only a mother can commit such a crime as being unmotherly and motherly morality is only applied to women. Given the fact that men and their actions have historically been taken as universal representations in literature and media, it is feasible that a man performing the role of Mother Courage would be judged on the basis of morality. Having a momboy in this situation—a mother wielding masculine power to acquire autonomy and agency—is not judged on morality because once again, she does not represent reality. In the same way that a woman could not be seen realistically as the Judge, Mother Courage and her choices were not seen as possible and therefore not critiqued according to actual moral codes. The expectation is that no mother would neglect her own children. However, it is more difficult for an audience to maintain such disbelief in the momboy for as long as they can indulge a tomboy. This is likely because of the level of control society feels it holds over the young as well as the level of threat contained in a maternal figure who transgresses outside her given role. Therefore, a maternal figure acting in such a way is ridiculous because it *cannot* continue and could never be true in the same way that, no doubt, audiences of early tomboy literature did not believe masculine girls would ever maintain agency in reality past marriage.

Given the popularity of tomboy stories and dramas, readers and audiences appear to have humored these adolescent tomboys, happily allowing them to transgress norms, likely because there was a clear end point in sight (Sentilles 2018, 5). Marriage and motherhood were the expected transition back to normalcy, where women would once again fulfill their expected social roles. Early tomboys were expected to "willingly and lovingly choose her domestic cage, a requirement that would end the arc of the stereotypical 'tomboy tale' later in the century" (Sentilles 2018, 29). But as tomboys evolved in the mid-and late-twentieth century to resist other things outside of compulsory femininity, so did momboys evolve to examine other ways to resist the limitations put upon mothers. Some of these ways include taking a dominant position regarding their own sexuality (a move frequently seen as masculine, given mainstream heterosexual hierarchies), challenging the nuclear family structure (which implicitly supports masculinity through elevating the patriarchal head of the household), pursuing public spheres of influence in employment and social influence, and defying maternal archetypes entirely by abandoning, neglecting, or abusing offspring.

MOMBOY CASE STUDY 3: FEMINIST COMEDY-DRAMA

As a final example, I offer Paula Vogel's *And Baby Makes Seven* as a play that makes some very strong choices with regard to combining the maternal and tomboy aesthetics. The momboy character in this play confronts more contemporary assumptions about motherhood involving singular maternal devotion and heteronormativity. Vogel displays a pregnant subject as a sexual being with desires who wrestles with maternal ambiguity while also enjoying power and agency in her life. Realistic representation of pregnancy was slim during the 1980s (when Vogel's play made its debut) due to several simultaneous occurrences. Second wave feminists were firmly rejecting compulsory motherhood (Chodorow 1978). There was also a strong backlash against this opinion that reinforced women's place in the privacy of the home (Schlafly 1981). In addition, the representation and higher visibility of abortion politics were redirecting attention to moral concerns about choice (Flowers 2018). And emerging third wave feminists were placing the focus away from female reproduction and onto other issues of inequality within (among many other things) sexuality, class, and race (hooks 1984). Paula Vogel's *And Baby Makes Seven*, published in 1984, was both a product of and contributed to the political climate surrounding reproductive rights in this era.

The main character, Anna, is pregnant. She lives in a house with Peter and Ruth. Peter is the biological father of the baby, but Anna is romantically involved with Ruth. In addition to living together, the three of them engage in a frequent game of make believe in which Anna and Ruth pretend to be three little boys (Cecil, Henri, and Orphan) who are their "imaginary" children.[3] Peter feels that they should rid the house of these personae before the baby is born. Ruth thinks there needs to be a storyline for this to happen, so she proposes that they construct scenarios to kill off each of the boys. Anna, Ruth, and Peter agree to this and carry out the plan. After the boys are gone and the baby is born, there is a palpable sense of loss and banality to their family life. So, Peter invents a ruse to bring the imaginary boys back. The play ends with a family tableau, including the imaginary boys.

Intriguingly, *And Baby Makes Seven* both engages with and defies normative understandings of maternity and boyhood. Compared to other plays that include a reproductive female, Vogel is fairly thorough in her treatment of Anna—and this can be connected to her momboy characterization. Even though Vogel wrought a play that is more comprehensive in its treatment of the reproductive female experience, she counters the notion that to do so inevitably means writing a play *about* pregnancy—or even about a maternal woman. Vogel weaves a story about sexuality, family, power dynamics, fantasy, and morality that happens to include the stages of a pregnancy and birth in a character who adopts masculine traits. Anna's reproductive agency is a part of the power-grab she makes in the household. Though a woman and pregnant, she is the "man of the house," resisting those that would control how she experiences pregnancy and making choices in how home life will be established. Examples of this include choosing when and how things are purchased for the home as well as with whom she allows to share her bed and when. Perhaps the most important example of leadership in the home is how she takes charge of the plan to get rid of the imaginary boys.

Clearly, Vogel makes deliberate efforts to afford Anna control in *And Baby Makes Seven*, which contribute to her patriarchal presence in the household and therefore extend her tomboy grab for "male freedoms" past when she pretends to be Cecil. Considered from a patriarchal perspective to be the most "uncontrollable" body on stage, Anna is the character with the most power and influence in the story. The juxtaposition of a boy—Cecil—being played by a pregnant body challenges the audience to expand and question how they read the pregnant belly and how to interpret the emotions (particularly when framing them as "masculine" emotions) displayed by that body. Having a pregnant character in the role of Cecil also provides a visual of an ever-present motivation. Anna/Cecil's belly continuously reminds us of the adults' decision to get rid of the other children before the baby comes. Anna is the one who is orchestrating most of the murder scenarios and, since she is a part of the story, she in effect serves as some sort of mob boss (a masculine-coded caricature). When Anna plays Cecil, she has a way to "get out of her own skin" by *becoming* a boy, while still always maintaining her maternal status throughout the play. This has the effect of pushing back on the assumed double standard applied to men and women regarding pregnancy (i.e., that the man alone has the powers of escape), allowing the reproductive woman a means of escape, albeit temporarily.

In this play, Ruth also plays a momboy—though her maternal status is less defined since she is not biologically connected to the child Anna carries, but is expected to take on a parental role once the baby is born. She plays Henri (a French boy) and Orphan (a boy raised by wolves), who both grant her moments to step outside of herself and to a place where she can assert her momboy, masculine claim on the child to be born and adopt animalistic behavior deemed highly unfeminine. An example of the former is in Act 2, Scene 10, when Ruth decides to claim paternity rights by going, as Henri, to visit Anna late at night and threatening her that "he" will tell Peter who the actual father of the baby is:

> HENRI. Peter still thinks he is the father to your child. You have led him to think so.
>
> ANNA. He most certainly is! I should know. Why are you—
>
> HENRI. I have reason to think otherwise. We both have reason to think otherwise.
>
> ANNA. I don't know what you are talking about—
>
> HENRI. You will hear me out. I have learned a lot in your country. I know how to count up to nine. In English.
>
> ANNA. What are you implying?
>
> HENRI. That I am the father to your child.
>
> ANNA. Whoa. Time out, Ruthie. We agreed never to—
>
> HENRI. It was late in November. All the leaves had fallen. Ruse was out of town. We had seen that film which had made you so sad.
>
> ANNA. (*Starting to understand.*) Are we feeling a little bit jealous?
>
> HENRI. I will always treasure that night. My "education sentimentale." And no one has to know. (Vogel 1984, 32)[4]

Henri is an extension of Ruth, and the fact that both are played by the same body creates a separate plane of existence where taboo desires—such as wishing to be the father of the child, or showing particular erotic curiosity (which Henri does for Peter in earlier scenes)—can have a place.

In addition to the obvious dissonance offered by Anna's pregnant body playing Cecil, Vogel gives the imaginary boys their own reaction to the pregnancy (one of disdain), which gives Anna moments to resist the pregnancy and its incumbent responsibility with maternal ambiguity, thereby exercising a will that is much more masculine. In fact, it is by using a momboy character that Vogel manages to highlight the mother-to-be without losing the woman-that-is, which the hard marriage/motherhood line tended to do in the Victorian era. The assumption that maternity subsumes femininity is analogous to how young women's marriages in the Victorian era subsumed their young lives. As such, use of the tomboy aesthetic actually makes the maternal aspects easier to see. By fleshing out a character with masculine influence, the pregnancy and maternal status is thrown into greater relief, giving the audience some food for thought regarding how society treats maternity writ large, since it can be seen as a separate entity, apart from the woman.

Female subjectivity is often rejected when representing visible pregnancy by reducing the pregnant woman to an out-of-control belly at the mercy of men and stereotypes. Vogel refuses to limit Anna with stereotypical behavior by making her a momboy. One place this is seen is in Vogel's delay to display Anna exhibiting tension or anxiety. Bypassing the cliché of the "hysterical" pregnant stereotype, Vogel allows the audience time to understand the reasons behind Anna's stress, empowering her with masculine control and ownership of her feelings. Vogel waits until Scene 8 to give a more distraught depiction of the pregnant subject—in fact, a performance of masculine anger in which Anna demands respect from Ruth and Peter, ending her lengthy diatribe with, "You can both suck my imaginary dick!" (Vogel 1984, 28). After this moment, both Ruth and Peter are cowed. This is also just before they witness her giving birth and voice their disbelief in how Anna was able to accomplish such a feat. The anger Anna exhibited was of a masculine form in the way in which it controlled the people around her and was not easily mollified or ignored. It also offered a show of strength before a parallel physical show of strength of giving birth.

In the last scene in which we see Anna pregnant, we watch her make a pivotal decision with regard to what her postpartum world will look like. It is Cecil's death scene. Cecil decides he wants to die like Julius Caesar. Peter holds out a sword and Cecil runs into it, impaling himself. Before doing so though, there are stage directions that explain how Anna and Peter arrange the sword explicitly so as to avoid the belly and enter under one of Anna's arms. The choice of death method and the act of arranging the sword make the audience aware that it is the pregnancy that helps put Cecil's destiny in Anna's control. She decides which child she will save, and with the force of her own weight against a weapon, extinguishes the other. Rather than understood as infanticide, this is a masculine suicide and justified killing of a threat to family. Much can be said about the phallic symbolism of the sword in this execution. Not only does it not-so-subtly underscore Peter's insemination of Anna, but in arranging the sword specifically in the scene, Anna takes the phallic power for herself. In addition, Anna/Cecil's choice to reenact Caesar's slaying, but essentially make it a suicide, usurps masculine power over the scenario.

CONCLUSION

As many scholars have helped us to understand, the tomboy is "not simply a girl who cared little for feminine pursuits, but a girl who actively pursued an independent life of the mind" (Sentilles 2018, 60). Such a life has historically been coupled to the masculine gender (and whiteness) by virtue of his privilege, which has (for longer than women, anyway) allowed him to navigate both intellectual and physical spheres without much, if any, resistance. In other words, the momboy I have outlined is not simply a mother who shirks from maternal pursuits, but one who actively chooses to engage her mind in such a way that clearly demonstrates her independence as a thinking creature. While society now acknowledges that mothers are thinking creatures, there is still a stronger association between patriarchal and masculine power and an independent mind. And it is with this engagement of her own mind that the mother demonstrates her autonomy from particular, limiting associations. All of the examples offered here reveal figments or fictional realities because that is one of the few ways in which women in the reproductive stage of their lives can find power. The same can be said of how tomboys, in their relatively powerless childhood status, can reach for power beyond themselves. What is more, the manner in which these variations on tomboys are depicted serves dramatic purposes that reflect real-world negotiations today. After all, "by now, a thirst for adventure and a desire for independence isn't solely reserved for the 'spirited boy' or the 'wild romping girl'" (Khinda 2013), and therefore the definition and usage of the tomboy or momboy should continue to be expanded to encompass all subjectivities who long for such freedoms.

NOTES

1. Classically, the good and bad mother archetypes have been, and continue to be, used heavily in drama. This creates a world where the mother fills a stock-character need in a piece as either a villainess or saint, but rarely ever anything in between. In addition, this theatrical treatment results in mother characters without subjectivities of their own.

2. Sentilles's work on tomboys explains how the character served as a transition figure when the New Woman and New Girl archetypes were being formed. In addition, a variety of fields have reckoned with the changing tides of motherhood. In particular, feminist and work historians have detailed the prevalent changes, the patterns in these changes, and how the role, today, continues to evolve. One such source of this information is: Jodi Vandenberg-Daves. 2014. *Modern Motherhood: An American History*. (New Brunswick, NJ: Rutgers University Press, 2014).

3. In other words, the two women signal to each other that they are playing the game by starting to act like one of the three boys. Anna plays Cecil and Ruth plays both Orphan and Henri. In improvisational style, the other woman in the scene picks up on what is happening, either responding to the "boy" as herself or pretending to be one of the other boys and adding to the game in that way.

4. Henri pronounces Ruth's name "Ruse" because Henri's character is supposed to have a French accent. He is based on the main boy character in the French film, *Le Ballon Rouge*. The use of such a heavily masculine-coded form, such as French film, adds to the commentary of who can wield masculine power.

BIBLIOGRAPHY

Abate, Michelle. 2008. *Tomboys: A Literary and Cultural History.* Philadelphia: Temple University Press.

Alcott, Louisa May. 1968. *Little Women.* Boston: Roberts Brothers.

Bailey, J. Michael, Kathleen T. Bechtold, and Sheri A. Berenbaum. 2002. "Who are Tomboys and Why Should We Study Them?" *Archives of Sexual Behavior* 31 (4): 333–41.

Bailey, J., and K. Zucker. 1995. "Childhood Sex-Typed Behavior and Sexual Orientation: A Conceptual Analysis and Qualitative Review." *Developmental Psychology* 31 (1): 43–55.

Barnett, D., E. Brater, and M. Taylor-Batty. 2014. *Brecht in Practice: Theatre, Theory and Performance*. New York: Bloomsbury Publishing.

Berlanstein, Lenard. 1996. "Breeches and Breaches: Cross-Dress Theatre and the Culture of Gender Ambiguity in Modern France." *Comparative Studies in Society and History* 38 (2): 338–69.

Brecht, Bertolt. 1939. *Mother Courage and Her Children* (Trans. Eric Bentley). New York: Grove Press.

Brecht on Stage. 1989. Directed by Richard Bessel. VHS. London: BBC-TV for Open University Educational Enterprises Ltd.

Chodorow, Nancy. 1978. *The Reproduction of Mothering: Psychoanalysis and the Sociology of Gender*. Los Angeles: University of California Press.

Classified Advertisement for Selwyn's Theatre. 1868. *Boston Daily Advertiser,* Issue 105, Col. A, May 2, 1868.

Craig, Traci, and Jessica LaCroix. 2011. "Tomboy as Protective Identity." *Journal of Lesbian* Studies 15 (4): 450–65.

Curtis, Ariana Randolph Wormeley. 1868. *The Spirit of Seventy-Six or The Coming Woman, a Prophetic Drama*. Boston: Little, Brown, and Company.

Damour, Lisa. 2020. "'Tomboy' Looks at Gender Roles and Role-Playing, Through the Ages." *The New York Times*. October 7, 2020. https://www.nytimes.com/2020/10/07/books/review/lisa-selin-davis-tomboy.html.

DiQuinzio, Patrice. 1999. *The Impossibility of Motherhood: Feminism, Individualism, and the Problem of Mothering*. New York: Routledge.

Flowers, Prudence. 2018. *The Right-to-Life Movement, the Reagan Administration, and the Politics of Abortion.* London: Palgrave MacMillan.

Hale, Nathan. 1868. "The Spirit of Seventy-Six." *Boston Daily Advertiser,* Issue 74, Col. B, March 26, 1868.

hooks, bell. 1984. *Feminist Theory: From Margin to Center*. Boston: South End Press.

Khinda, Navneet. 2013. "Deconstructing the 'Tomboy.'" *The Wanderer.* August 26, 2013. https://thewandereronline.com/deconstructing-the-tomboy-by-navneet-khinda/.

King, Elizabeth. 2017. "A Short History of the Tomboy." *The Atlantic*. January 5, 2017. https://www.theatlantic.com/health/archive/2017/01/tomboy/512258/.

Llewellyn, Jennifer, Jim Southey, and Steve Thompson. 2020. "Women in Nazi Germany." *Alpha History*, August 2, 2020. https://alphahistory.com/nazigermany/women-in-nazi-germany/.

Lloyd, T. A. 1788. *The Romp. A Musical Entertainment. In Two Acts. Altered from Love in the City, by Mr. Bickerstaff. As Now Performed at the Theatre-Royal in Drury-Lane*. London & Dublin: Printed for Messrs. Gilbert, Wilkinson, M'donnell Colles, Walker, Perrin, Chamberlaine, Byrne, Sleater, Jones, Burnet Moore, and Dornin.

Osnes, Beth and A. Andes. 2010. "Introduction." In *Essays and Scripts on How Mothers are Portrayed in the Theatre: A Neglected Frontier of Feminist Scholarship*, edited by Beth Osnes and Anna Andes, i–ii. Lewiston, NY: The Edwin Mellen Press.

Phelps, Elizabeth Stuart. 1894. *Gypsy Breynton Series*. New York City: Dodd Mead & Company.

Proehl, Kristen. 2018. *Battling Girlhood: Sympathy, Social Justice, and the Tomboy Figure in American Literature*. New York: Routledge.

Sentilles, Renée. 2018. *American Tomboys: 1850–1915*. Boston: University of Massachusetts Press.

Schlafly, Phyllis. 1981. *The Power of the Christian Woman*. Cincinnati, OH: Standard Pub.

Stockton, Kathryn Bond. 2009. *The Queer Child, or Growing Sideways in the Twentieth Century*. Durham, NC: Duke University Press.

Thomson, Peter. 1997. *Brecht: Mother Courage and Her Children*. New York: Cambridge University Press.

Vandenberg-Daves, Jodi. 2014. *Modern Motherhood: An American History*. New Brunswick: Rutgers University Press.

Verhage, Florentien. 2016. "Philosophy Comes to Life: Elaborating an Idea of Feminist Philosophy." In *Feminist Philosophies of Life,* edited by Hasana Sharp and Chloe Taylor, 147–62. Chicago: McGill-Queen's University Press.

Vogel, Paula. 1984. *And Baby Makes Seven*. New York: Dramatists Play Service, Inc.

PART II

THE WRITTEN WORD: THE TOMBOY IN LITERATURE

Chapter 3

Queer Epistemologies of the Tomboy in Stacey Waite's *Butch Geography*

CE Mackenzie

"When the neighborhood kids realize you are not a boy, / run—head-tucked, arm-pumping, leg-burning run," Stacey Waite advises in their[1] poem "For Tomboys." "Run from the burning field / run away // from them circling you in the wooded pines, their fingers arrows in your pounding chest. Run now. For your life. Run" (2013, 59). Waite organizes "For Tomboys" into couplets, a traditionally lyrical form of poetry known for its elegiac tone and its material, temporal focus. The repeating, reiterating "run" thereby heightens the poem's affective reverberations—the tomboy is both physical and feeling, present and fleeting. And Waite's poem does run, forcefully down the page toward these final lines, this cry to flee both pine forests and open fields, before ending in its own stuttered punctuation. Significantly, Waite does not urge the tomboy to hedge or clarify—that is, to explain themselves through apology or straight logics—but to run, away from danger and yet toward no definable destination. Throughout *Butch Geography*, Stacey Waite positions the tomboy in a world that demands constant gendered legibility, that organizes its epistemological projects around and through the human, from which it exhorts meaning. Waite's speakers are young queers aging both into and out of tomboy identification, slipping into and away from the taxonomic forces of a gendering world, forced to make meaning. But in these moments, Waite's tomboys resist. Indeed, readers follow Waite to insist on the tomboy as more than allegory for transgression—a (capitalist) move that relegates the queer to a political and theoretical object—but to also signal epistemological possibility through acts of interruption and delay. Waite encourages readers to think through the possibilities of the tomboy, beyond its conventional function as organizing meaning through deviance, which protects the binary even under the optics of criticizing it.

The tomboy—even as, and especially as, they age out of the label—reveals ways of surviving beyond the political hold and in the face of totalizing taxonomic forces. Waite's tomboy, specifically, requires readers to pose questions of genre and theory, as queer embodiment undergoes coercion in an array of spaces—physical, but also within the problems of language and epistemology. That is, as one strains against the limitations and failures of language, and as epistemological habits are coerced by the capitalist "will to know," questions arise. Is there any genre, written or embodied, that resists teleological ends, that refuses contained meaning? How does one explore landscapes without destinations in mind? How does one withstand, or even subvert, a capitalist[2] model predicated on the commodification of the self, a model that reinforces itself through tropes of overcoming and aspirational striving? When queer and trans subjects are configured as ciphers of meaning for dominant understandings of gender, their embodied misalignment is also insisted upon and aspirational models of gender expression are reified. Further, those subjects are trapped into figures of meaning that must then be scripted as both legible and productive (Heaney 2017, 6). How then does the tomboy both refuse signification and offer epistemological alternatives to productive, legible, and age-coherent figurations of normative gender? And how does the tomboy inspire imaginaries that confront the "regime of the human," especially as readers understand them in Waite's poetry (Muñoz 2015, 209)?

Butch Geography navigates these questions, simultaneously withholding closure while illuminating epistemological potentiality. Indeed, this analysis elevates a queer episteme marked by non-teleological ways of knowing. That is, knowledge that relinquishes fixed ends and finished products. In particular, the poetic topographies of *Butch Geography* are explored with specific attention to the tomboy envisaged in Waite's serial pieces, "Dear Gender" and "On the Occasion of Being Mistaken For." These poems reveal the tomboy's precarity as they age out of the label's "appropriate" range and into an opacity that renders them vulnerable. But rather than cast the tomboy as dire (tragedy is often a specter haunting the queer), Waite subverts this trope. The tomboy (and the queer) is fraught but not tragic. "Gender, I want you to turn me to chain / I want to bleed you out without dying" (2013, 62). Because these poems enact echo, reiterating across the pages of *Butch Geography*, meaning travels through circuits of delay and deferral. And within the folds of these repetitions, and through a voice marked by instability, queer ways of knowing bloom. And perhaps most significantly, by focusing on the temporal and material, Waite preempts the reader from investing in platitudes of *becoming* and undermines aspirational models of queerness, both of which fall within epistemologies of capital. Finally, through their formal enactments (epistolary and repeating) Waite refuses genres that imitate state power, that hegemonic demand for product, outcome, and legibility. Their poems and the rest of *Butch Geography* map desire against cartographical force (as the book's title implies), through which they point toward meaning that interrupts rather than aspires.

DEFINING THE TOMBOY AND MAPPING QUEER EPISTEMOLOGIES

Traditionally clocked as a young, white girl resisting her Sunday dress with skinned knees and a flat chest, the tomboy's aesthetic is what consistently defines (while containing) their figuration. Clad in basketball shorts and topless, the tomboy is told to put a shirt on, to make friends with girls in their grade. And with puberty imminent, the tomboy is also imbued with temporality. "It is in the context of female adolescence that the tomboy instincts of millions of girls are remodeled into compliant forms of femininity," writes Jack Halberstam (1998, 6). While it is worth preserving the argument that the tomboy's chronology does undergo certain pressures in adolescence, Halberstam's own definition requires an extension beyond gendering, beyond the instinct of a girl forced to comply. The idea of the tomboy—the tomboy imaginary—should expand beyond mere aesthetic affectation to instead envisage this figure *not* as a cipher for meaning but as disrupting and redirecting meaning. Kathryn Bond Stockton explains how the queer child "grows toward a question mark," and "whose identity is a deferral," which serves to demote aspirational models of gender, that is, models predicated on transition from something approximate to something authentic (2009 3, 11). Under the "demand for recognition within the circle of humanity," write Dana Luciano and Mel Chen, queer and trans subjects are forced to comply with the narrative of becoming or aspiring (2015, 184). They are coerced into rhetorics of authentication in order to produce meaning that can be coherently consumed by cis, hetero, and white logic. Despite Halberstam's limitations, his borrowing of Eve Sedgewick's term "nonce taxonomies" may prove helpful, as "classifications of desire, physicality, and subjectivity that attempt to intervene in hegemonic processes of naming and defining" (1998, 8). Indeed, Waite's "For Tomboys" counsels those who may be exposed as "not a boy," which according to cis-logics would translate that exposure to mean, not a boy and therefore a girl. However, Waite never suggests a gender other than "not a boy," and even then this is equivocal. Readers do not know if the tomboys are girls. And readers do not need to know; they know only that tomboys must run.

Such will to know, such epistemological force, maintains colonial roots in hegemonic projects, wherein meaning circulates through functions of power (Foucault 1978, 11). Against which, queer ways of knowing seek alternative modes of interruption and restraint. By tracing queer epistemological resistance, Waite's work can be positioned within an interminable project of queer knowing. But first it is helpful to imagine the queer epistemological genealogy as constellatory rather than linear; that is, as an archive that privileges collage—the assembling of strange parts to designate or signal a whole—it also diminishes comprehensivity and estranges teleological satiation. This analysis focalizes not only a queer imaginary that reckons with fragmentations, but also illuminates the slow collapsing of fixed knowledges, and the categories by which they are contained, within queer epistemological activities. Indeed, one could designate the movements of the queer episteme as *roaming*, a traverse of wild topographies (with cartographical nods toward Waite). The drive toward clarity, definition, and demarcation folds in on itself as one realizes there is no end to desire—epistemological or embodied—it is endless, and yet sends one on their way.

Michel Foucault's *The History of Sexuality: An Introduction, Volume 1* offers a crucial scaffold for examining discursive sexual knowing and what often motivates it—delineation and management. To first frame queer consciousness through Foucault is to emphasize the prominence of power and its demand for coherence within sexual expression and experience. That is, one cannot contour queer epistemological genealogies without placing at the fore "the will to know." Foucault writes, "One had to speak of it as a thing to be not simply condemned or tolerated but managed, inserted into systems of utility, regulated for the greater good of all, made to function according to an optimum" (1978, 24). Sexual knowledge, Foucault offers, becomes contingent on truth and definition and protected under the aegis of truth-seeking: "They constructed around and apropos of sex an immense apparatus for producing truth . . . the truth of sex became something fundamental" (1978, 56). While "fundamental" points toward what is fixed, foundational, and that which secures thought to regulatory systems, "truth" indicates privilege and power, insinuating a pure form that can (and should) be attained. Through prolix discourse, much of it invested in a yet undetermined truth, Foucault argues that sexuality became epistemological catalyst, inciting the will to know while simultaneously laying claims to authority.

The will to know engages the same muscles as the will to power. Epistemologies of capital operate against *as well as in* queer spaces, but subaltern modes of resistance can be excavated. Foregrounding desire within the episteme, Audre Lorde offered a methodology decades ago. Broadening the scope of knowing to include "deep participation" in a political erotics wherein consciousness is embodied, Lorde's erotics enliven not just the relationship between the queer episteme and desire but she presses the will to know into fissures (1984, 53–9). For Lorde, desire is epistemological, located not only in sexual drive but as a desire of the mind, like a charge, ignited and embodied. Elizabeth Freeman writes, "It is precisely this wide-ranging sense of what Audre Lorde calls the uses of the erotic that allows queer and temporality to touch one another" (2007, 159). By making visible the invisibility of queer desire, and locating it within the temporal, what one reads as "fixed" starts to loosen its hold. Desire, as non-teleological and self-annihilating, motors into a futurity never attained. The horizon glows just out of reach.

And for that reason, queerness is not fully containable or even fully here, in the present. This argument made by José Esteban Muñoz reclaims queerness from regulatory economies and place it on the horizon, to urge subjects toward what is not-yet, beyond the merely human. These queer horizons, a futurity in which "queerness is still forming or in many crucial ways formless," are, he writes, utopic (2009, 29). Whereas epistemologies of capital rely on linear (straight) time to legitimize its insistence on progress and victory, Muñoz's queer time anticipates the ecstatic and echoes Lorde's call for erotic knowing. He positions desire and queerness as not quite here but as an always existing potentiality and as beyond the scope of the human. By focusing on a queer horizon, the pragmatism of the present is destabilized to make possible queerer imaginaries. Muñoz glimpses queer potentiality within the aesthetic, the forward-dawning, and the not-yet-conscious, joined by Halberstam, who leans into the rewards of failure to break open other ways of knowing and being. For Halberstam, failure breaches societally instituted and managed borders, triggering epistemological shifts within the aesthetic and embodied. Attending to fugitive knowledges is also to invest in illegibility. This, Halberstam argues, calls for resistance to mastery and embrace of a "knowledge from below" that is more concerned with unsettling or involving than resolving (2011, 2). Fugitive thought and non-teleological knowledges are often shuttered as state, political, and social power requires category to reinforce itself. Halberstam argues that under such public discourse, the transgender or queer subject specifically is forced to make sense (2005, 54), to placate the needs of those "who want to be fascinated but not challenged, provoked but not transformed" (2005, 58). What is lost are "wild strands of narrative incoherence" that honor the complexities of the subject (Halberstam 2005, 74). Economies of authenticity, he posits, overtake the queer subject, fixing them to category in order to preserve regulatory power (Halberstam 2005, 70). Such function of category is to not only designate value but extract labor, to manage and through regulation reauthorize category. Hetero, racial capitalism requires narratives of becoming to maintain both in/authentic categories. Queer and racialized subjects, then, are coerced into iterations of either assimilation or opposition, even as both serve, fortify, and energize categories of capital. Liberal humanist values further codify the mythos of an authentic self and authorize aspirational models of human expression, expressions that circulate through and strengthen markets made of commodity and positivity. Indeed, one can see also how humanism is swept up into this capitalistic mechanism, reinforcing the human as the maker of meaning, that is, the producer of a valuable product. Muñoz calls for the "radical attempt" to think queerly as a way of "unsettling the settled, sedimented, and often ferocious world of recalcitrant anti-inhumanity" (2015, 209).

Queer epistemological projects have consistently confronted heterocapitalist hegemonies, pointing to ways of knowing unconsumed with dominance and acquisition. But such projects can be pressed even further, to reckon with if not dismantle the figuration of queer wherein merely more knowledge is produced, and to instead elevate the delays and deferrals referenced by the tomboy. This will require an embrace of Muñoz's "radical attempt" of "thinking outside the regime of the human," which he cautions, is a "continuous straining to make sense of something else that is never fully knowable" (2015, 209). In Waite's work, and through the tomboy specifically, queer thriving is not conceived of through assimilation, by making the body more familiar *or* by endorsing deviation for political efficacy, but by estranging ourselves to the horizon. Setting the episteme in its desiring, temporal hum, Waite generously leads readers into ecstatic ways of knowing.

"DEAR GENDER" AND THE TOMBOY'S ECHOING TEMPORALITIES

Two serial pieces, together comprising more than a dozen poems, serve as formal motors in *Butch Geography.* Resisting closure, these poems magnify the formal effects of reiteration and reverberation. They enact echo, that temporal phenomenon that gestures both outward and inward by way of collision. Waite's "Dear Gender" series, for example, consists of six poems, each a letter to gender, each letter responding to the other outside of straight time.[3] Waite's formal movements in "Dear Gender" show how these poems obscure destinations and bungle linear translation, how readers never arrive at gender's defined ends. These poems often feature tomboy figuration, a young butch and their fevering relationship to their gender. But, much like the rest of *Butch Geography*, the voice in these poems belongs both to the child and the adult. Waite collapses time into reiterating temporality, reducing the reliance on chronological logics and dissolving the child/adulthood dichotomy. By so doing, Waite also rejects the aspirational model, a model that translates trans and queer embodiment as advancing toward gendered consummation. They also undermine the dominant logic that children's knowledge of themselves only clarifies in adulthood, and that, queer or not, the child cannot access such "mature" knowing. This structure at once privileges the adult and dismisses the child, reinforcing the dichotomy and concealing the coercive process through which hetero-capitalist epistemology is naturalized.

Framed as letters and inflected with intimacy and estrangement, this series is organized as epistolary missives from a body to their gender(s), which inhibits the conflation of the two. Yet, they also allow the physical body and gendered feeling to blur. The two slip into and away from one another in negotiation, at turns dependent then guarded, suspicious then sentimental: "And when I say, 'Gender, you're going to be all right,' / what I mean is the heart is the most overworked muscle / in the body, that you won't drown out there. Forgive / yourself" (2013, 43). Readers' eyes are in a constant state of focus, but this unease is left unattended. Throughout the series, the speaker fidgets in and against gender taxonomy, aching in the liminalities between rule and deviation. For example, in "Dear Gender 3"[4] the speaker promises to make gender a god; and in "Dear Gender 4" gender is abandoned altogether. To deify is to incarnate, to embed eternality into a finite body, which is (of course) a failing project that in its failure abandons containment. But even the abandonment is temporary as gender finds its way back to the body, reiterating and reintroducing itself in manifold spaces. "Gender, I want you to turn me to chain. I want to bleed you out without dying" (2013, 62). To fully expose the complexities and rewards of this interstitial tension, Waite refuses certainties, leaning fully into a lyrical form that underscores materiality, and the materiality of queer knowing. As Lorde reminds readers, knowing is felt, like desire. "You swing your legs over my hip bones," Waite writes to gender, "you make me your saddle, cold leather // clinging to the back of this animal" (2013, 62).

Indeed, the body is everywhere in the "Dear Gender" series, colliding with, passing through, and veering away from gender. Waite insists on the attention to the material: "It was like this when I saw / the owl lift from the throat / of a tree, the leaves scraping / the thin spine of branches" (2013, 62). Hands also dip into thighs, sleeves are pushed up arms, hands cover eyes, and skin flinches in fear. Waite's metonymic enactments position the uncoded body in its instincts, relegating gender to its (enforced) constructions. By steeping these poems in the material, Waite holds readers fast to iterating, echoing temporalities. And because Waite abstracts gender through the epistolary frame, they interrupt gender as a code of legibility. Readers therefore come to know the body in its liminal aches and joys, within pressed moments, not as a fully conceived thing. "You couldn't see and almost / lost your ground when you tried to stand. / So weak you have always been" (2013, 29). Though tragedy is often located between the queer body and the encountered world, Waite undermines this trope and refuses the teleologies of tragedy. Sara Ahmed explains: "The strangeness that seems to reside somewhere between the body and its objects is also what brings these objects to life and makes them dance" (2006, 163). One could call this ecstatic, an affect particularly attached to ephemerality, to what slips. Ahmed concedes that slipped objects signal distance but also ignite desire. Therefore, ecstaticism contains both ache and longing, blurring their distinctions into unified sensation. In "Dear Gender 2," readers see how the speaker's relationship to gender produces such slippage and disorientation, without collapsing into tragedy: "The truth is I've loved you always / Despite your refusal to play with me," but also, "there were nights, however brief, when you fell to pieces in my lap" (2013, 29). Because queer or trans subjects are often required to have a misaligned relationship to gender, their narratives are often coerced into trajectories of capital with aspirational intonations. That is, it is insisted that the subject fix the misalignment. Waite, however, complicates the relationship, reveals love alongside reservation, estrangement braided with intimacy. Waite shifts the gaze. One is not on their way to an authentic self; they are authentically on their way to themselves, always. Waite makes room for more complex understandings and expressions of gender, affecting the ecstatic—desire imbued in ache—described by Muñoz as a claim, a grunt or yawp even, beyond queer certitude (2009, 32). It extends "a glance toward that which is forward-dawning, anticipatory illuminations of the not-yet-conscious." Cradled by memory, Waite ends the poem tenderly, "Remember? You couldn't see and almost / lost your ground," describing gender as weak, as in vulnerable, but also "so simple and strange" (2013, 29).

The tomboy of the "Dear Gender" series is, of course, never explicitly named, yet can be heard humming in these lines. Gender has been loved, despite its refusals, despite "your stage-fright, stubbornness / and cruel pranks, you have always been / up in tree branches with me like a sibling" (2013, 29). Nearly every poem in the epistolary "Dear Gender" series is organized either into two stanzas or into couplets (perhaps a nod to the binary). Waite rarely breaks with this formal pattern, except in one poem, wherein they rupture the order with two single, floating lines. In "Dear Gender 4," the poem opens with a river holding its breath followed by the punched monostich: "There are rooms I've loved you in" (2013, 48). What rooms, within what containment, does one love or desire gender? The line floats unattended and singular, the emphasis urging readers to consider the complicated relationship between the body and gender taxonomy, a relationship like a river holding its breath, before the watershed. Halberstam might designate Waite's form as "scavenger," in that it resists "compulsion toward disciplinary coherence" (1998, 13). An apt image, the scavenger navigates landscapes both dense and desolate, searching among detritus for survival but also another way. The second monostich both echoes and complicates the first. "I've left you this poem at the door" (2013, 48). At the end of "Dear Gender 4," shouldering a backpack and pocketing some maps and bread, the speaker abandons gender, abandons contained rooms, leaving only a poem (this poem) nailed to the door. Though tempting to translate these lines as definitive with their short and punctuated cadence, or as a linear step across a threshold, readers instead see them as hung in space and hung on the page. Readers know, as made visible throughout *Butch Geography*, that bodies and genders collude again and again, that an echo requires collision. Muñoz argues that queerness is still forming and formless (2009, 29). Taken in this context, one can imagine Waite's speaker—having posted the poem and cinched their pack—headed toward an unattainable horizon like some queer cowboy glowing in dusk's shifting light.

SCREW BALLS: WHEN GENDERING IS MISGENDERING

The second major series in *Butch Geography*, "On the Occasion of Being Mistaken For," consists of seven poems, each featuring a speaker misgendered in an array of spaces, from home plate to the airport, the breakfast diner to the public bus. These packed narrative poems distill a fumbled moment down to its fraught compressions—the body misnamed, mistaken. But these poems also follow more than the panic of public misgendering; without foreclosing the severity often present in such moments, Waite also affects a kind of brevity, in which their speakers are agents of interruption (as opposed to agents of meaning making), illuminating the potentialities within scavenged expression. For instance, Waite's use of repetition signals boundlessness within the parameters of the page. Stimulating an echo, or a ripple of implication, this device rejects declaratives. Rather, it reiterates. Take, for example, the first poem in the series, "On the Occasion of Being Mistaken for a Boy by the Umpire in the Little League Conference Championship." In the poem, the speaker—a tomboy crouched at home plate during a championship game—punches their glove, spits, and waits for the pitch. When the ump calls them "son" and asks if they're wearing their cup, the moment ruptures. With flattened confidence and heightened consciousness, the speaker admits, "I forget the signs for curve balls, fast balls / and screw balls, and all I can think about is no balls, // no little ten-year-old balls to match my spit" (2013, 3). Teammates "correct" the umpire, parents look at their shoes, and Waite's speaker collapses inward. "I think everyone is looking at my no balls. / They're all watching the girl with no balls. / I'm watching her too" (2013, 3). By distancing the speaker again from gender—"I'm watching her too"—Waite interrupts the fallback on binary. The catcher is misgendered by being gendered. Waite's repetition of "balls" no doubt highlights the materiality of the moment, but it also gives their lines a staggered, mutating affect, evoking urgency and attention while delaying ease.

The "Mistaken" series is intoned with irony, encountered as early as the poems' titles. "Occasion" and "mistaken" inform not just how these poems are read but how one feels reading them. While Waite's tone signals informality, playfulness even, they inhibit impassivity on behalf of the reader. Readers always know the stakes. For example, in "On the Occasion of Being Mistaken for a Man by Security Personnel at Newark International Airport," the speaker attempts to pass through airport security only to be stopped and frisked by a male TSA agent. During his search of the speaker's body, moving his hands along their arms and chest, he realizes his "error" and responds with a volatile mix of confusion, anger, and anxiety, forcing (and enforcing) his expectations to adhere to the speaker's body. "He's angry, his blue uniform makes him angry, / so that when he is patting her down now, he does it with force. / He wants her to feel he is stronger than she is" (2013, 39). The rupture of expectation again spotlights the queer body, though with more gravity than it does on the baseball diamond. For in this instance, the expectations of the TSA agent—an agent of the state whose explicit responsibility includes border enforcement—reinforces and reinscribes the demand for coherence. This poem also reveals the precarity of the aging tomboy. What is awkward on the baseball field is nearly violent in the security line. "Occasion," then, nods toward more than some temporal hiccup, and "mistake" is more than just blunder. "What is not yet culturally legible," Freeman writes, "is often encountered in embodied, nonrational forms" (2007, 159). The dissonance between tone (detached) and action (visceral) does more than just reflect the queer experience of incoherence; it simulates it affectively in the reader. That is, the reader *feels* the dissonance because the poem refuses to settle and the specter of violence haunts each line: "He wants me / to keep him secret, to pretend neither of us had ever been born" (2013, 40).

"On the Occasion of Being Mistaken for a Woman by a Therapist," the final poem in the series (when reading linearly), insists the "mistakes" marking these poems are not about being wrongly gendered but about *being* gendered, about the demand for constant coherence. Equally, this demand, by extension, requires Waite's speaker to confess a misalignment that may or may not exist. In this poem, the speaker is asked by their therapist to explain what it feels like "to be" a woman, to disclose the queer body clearly and cogently, not unlike those demands made by the TSA agent. "She thinks, of course / that I must know what it is like, that / somewhere deep inside me lives the life / of a woman, if I would only let her speak" (2013, 82). Though the contexts vary, the stakes remain. And significantly, the stakes expose the ways queer bodies suffer in a world that first demands obedience to category and then demands those subjects adopt aspiration as a way of undoing or mediating perceived misalignment. All of which further reinforces bodies as having authentic forms, that one is either born into authenticity or not, and if not then to cohere is to find and fill the authentic body. Within the therapist's questions, readers see traces of Halberstam's tomboy, the buried girl forced to comply, which is why this series is so interesting. Within the poems that comprise "On the Occasion of Being Mistaken For," the tomboys age out of "appropriate" range. Precarious as the tomboy is, their figuration organizes meaning only temporarily, and is otherwise disruption to and disorientation of straight logics. Paradoxically, as the tomboy figure thins into adulthood, the more they enhance the potentialities of queer epistemologies. The tomboy epistemological project, then, is galvanized as the figuration dissolves.

The "Mistaken" series also reveals how efforts toward legibility, coerced or volunteered, must invest in defined categories, the management of those categories, and applications of force against those who transgress such categories (Halberstam 2011, 9). Dean Spade criticizes the authorization and management of gender under the aegis of medical-therapeutic institutions. In order to receive the medical care one needs, Spade argues, one must concede to the binary, forced to replenish such false concepts as "real" and "legitimate." Spade dismantles the prerogatives of "successful" transition and asks what it may mean to allow people enhancement of gender identity outside the scope of public recognition (2006, 316–29). By pressing gender through the film of the medical institution, gender comes to be viewed as either disorder or disability in need of a coherent fix, convincing alteration, and permanence. The therapist in Waite's poem attends to gender stasis through the interrogative "to be"; but by holding readers in liminality, wherein meaning is deferred and time is dissolved from its linear trajectories and fixed teleologies, Waite resists fixed ends, instead veering from such "failing" trails: "I am the kind of man who rescues, / who thinks to leaving a failing trail in the forest" (2013, 81).

As serial poems, both "Dear Gender" and "On the Occasion of Being Mistaken For" disrupt coercive (i.e., traditional) epistemologies through which political and social reimagining can occur. The drive toward teleological containment, for an epistemology that is productive in its knowing, exposes an unease with uncertainties and illegibility. One longs for an end as a way to make sense of or infuse meaning into process, the mess and meaninglessness of now. And yet, Waite—with poems that fold into, speak across, and unsettle one another—ushers readers directly into that mess.

THE LIMITS OF LANGUAGE: MUÑOZ'S NOT-VANISHING POINT

One is not yet queer yet still stumbles toward a bowed line that is both infinite in its distance and finite in its intimations. The horizon evinces what cannot be handled but longed and ached for. If one heeds Lorde, then this pain of consciousness ignites desire, desire that eludes and leads deeper into ignition, never consummation. One is always in their horizonal stumble. "Queerness is an ideality," writes Muñoz. "Put another way, we are not yet queer. We may never touch queerness, but we can feel it as the warm illumination of a horizon imbued with potentiality" (2009, 1). Who knows *and* feels this more than the tomboy? Muñoz calls this "the not-vanishing point." That which evades but remains (not vanishing) is both queer and aesthetic, the queer not-yet, the fuse of art and making: "At the moment of its creation it is gone . . . No other art is so hard to catch, so impossible" (Muñoz 2009, 81). Impossible and slippery and always (just) beyond grasp, the aesthetic project is not dire. The horizon casts its glow, reinventing the landscape in each moment. Maggie Nelson finds the not-vanishing point synonymous with renewal and marked by constant kinetic energy. She also, like Muñoz, calls it perpetual, "a nominative like *Argo*, willing to designate molten or shifting parts, a means of asserting while also giving the slip. That is what reclaimed terms do—they retain, they insist on retaining, a sense of the fugitive" (2015, 29). For example, Waite's poem "Changing the Names," (which falls outside the scope of the two series) points readers toward an auxiliary aesthetics inflected with its own failures and ephemeralities:

> In the eighth grade, I told a girl
> my name was Ben. I kissed her with my
> mouth in that eighth-grader-in-love
> sort of way. It wasn't the name she loved.
> In Pittsburgh, the rivers want to freeze over,
> but can't stay still long enough. So, for a while,
> I call them ice to honor their wanting,
> their leaving and returning, always the
> slow shift of hands and water. (2013, 67)

What creates also strips away, slow shift of hands and water. But such aesthetic vertigo offers surprising, queer ways of knowing. "Meaning is delayed, deferred," writes Kathryn Bond Stockton, "exactly because we read in sequence, go forward in a sentence, not yet knowing what words are ahead of us, while we must take the words we have passed *with* us as we go, making meaning wide and hung in suspense" (2009, 4). Waite calls this "queer imagination," a way of thinking that breaks with binaried hermeneutics to "imagine the possibilities of queerer worlds" (2015, 113). In this way, suspended punctuation and hung poetics emulate the evasive horizon and evince aching liminalities.

The rewards of Waite's poetry contain epistemological implications that point toward queer thriving. One often thinks of the queer in precarity, as the tomboy running from danger, which locates them in constant reiteration of survival. And while this may be, what about a queer who not only survives, but thrives? Waite's serial poems, though also all of *Butch Geography*, persuade readers into the not-vanishing point. Burying the directions and directives, Waite's poems prize the lost state. "The goal is to lose one's way, and indeed to be prepared to lose more than one's way," writes Halberstam (2011, 6). These poems teach the mind to adjust to and take pleasure in disorientation while resisting destination, to collude in fugitivity, what slips. Their poems ask readers to loosen demands for contained knowledge and to instead enjoy the ecstatic elasticity of not knowing—to get lost in the brambles. And with Waite, readers should not plan on finding their way. Instead, Waite queers the reader's imagination, calls for the retreat from category and teleological ends back into the not-vanishing. In the exigency to name the not-yet, the unknown, Waite stalls the will to know, and in that way sustains desire through the material imagining of the tomboy. This fumbled excursion through knowing, this commitment to desire even as it evades, involves the risks and rewards of failure. The tomboy imaginaries opened by Waite ground readers in the present while pivoting attentions toward the forward-dawning. Halberstam analogizes Judie Bamber's landscape paintings to clarify the temporal and material importance of queer knowing: "Bamber's depiction of the horizon as limit speaks to a queer temporality and a queer spatiality that resists a notion of art as capable of seeing beyond and in fact makes art about limitation, about the narrowness of the future, the weightiness of the past, and the urgency of the present (2011, 106). A queer epistemology is committed to process, to the liminal and interstitial. And in these commitments, queer thriving finds traction in its temporal attentions. Waite offers not a call for greater legibility or assimilative coherence, but a call to queer the world and broaden its possibilities. "If we can teach our students queer imagination, if we can encourage them to cultivate queerer interpretations, if we can help them imagine other, queerer worlds, then perhaps more queer people will survive" (2015, 114). In this move, Waite pivots the gaze away from the subject and toward world-making. Lorde writes, "The quality of light by which we scrutinize our lives has direct bearing upon the product which we live, and upon the changes which we hope to bring about" (1984, 36). She goes on to call this "poetry as illumination" while Muñoz designates it as an "astonishment" that urges one beyond "the limitations of an alienating presentness" and allows one "to see a different place and time" (2009, 5). By deflecting attention away from the subject, the tomboy, as embodied knowledge production (the site of productive information), Waite protects them—at home plate, on the banks of a frozen river, and beyond the page.

Poetry is particularly deft in transgressing literary linearity; but serial poems especially, such as Waite's, reject teleology and incite reverberating echoes. They fold back on themselves, reinstituting the bounds of temporal containment while also implying boundlessness (the poems keep iterating). Which is not to say the series' order is insignificant but that it is both crucial *and* malleable. The poems can be shuffled, re-sorted, and read through one another. Such form expands not just hermeneutical opportunities, but privileges affect over revelation, revealing the "stakes in repeating, looping, summarizing, forgetting, and knowing again" (Halberstam 2011, 59). For Waite, the misgendered child must be in conversation with the misgendered adult; and so these poems not only reveal the lasting presence of the child but, through the fold of the series' form, bungle time. If the queer child, the tomboy, is always present, then queerness gestures toward time's nonlinear distillations. The queer episteme absorbs the temporal struggle but does not designate it as tragic. The possibilities, bound to the page or the present, also signal beyond the page and toward ecstatic horizons. Waite's tomboys teach readers to take on multiple complexities of human feeling—desire that aches, exposure that does not clarify, ecstaticism in the face of totalizing taxonomic force, and meaning beyond or in spite of the human frame.

A SUMMATION, OR SURVIVAL AS THE "ANTHEM OF THOSE PLACES WE'VE ALWAYS BEEN"

Waite tags their title poem, "Butch Geography," with a telling epigraph from Robin Becker: "The desert is butch" (2013, 25). In this poem, Waite distills their two serial pieces into forty-three lines of material-epistemological collision and collusion. They lead readers through all that is butch—cathedrals and suspension bridges, but also wildfires and river rapids. "Butch" translates to "quicksand of subversion" and wild incoherence, "wherever there is / cavernous depth" (2013, 25). An array of wild things inhabit this butch desert—heat, sinewy cats and quick lizards, silence. Waite does not offer mirage; readers stand on sand throughout the poem, within the heat and struggle. The desert, as described by Luciano and Chen, "belongs to a region overlaid with histories of occupation, of settlement, displacement, colonization, and genocide, as well as . . . political and cultural reimagination" (2015, 183). "Overlaid" offers important imagery here. "Overlaid" recognizes enmeshment, that meaning is multiple and layered and cannot be contained within binaries.

Collapsing the past into the present, Waite explains the desert is "survival, the anthem / of those places we've always been" (2013, 26). Whether in the skin of one's own body or within a desert's interior, the horizon glows just out of reach. In the restless desire to know, Waite inspires readers in the interminable horizonal stumble through the butch desert, making the queer world thinkable and imbuing it with potentiality even as, especially as, the sand burns one's feet.[5]

NOTES

1. I use they/them pronouns for Waite and all of the speakers in Waite's poetry.
2. Kara Keeling's definition of queer is helpful here: "'Queer' is not an ontological category—it is not what one is; rather, it is an epistemological category—one that involves life and death questions of apprehension and value production" (2019, 17).
3. Elizabeth Freeman's work on the embodiness of queer temporality in addition to Kathryn Bond Stockton's child growing sideways, show us how time is bungled for the queer. From them we can extrapolate the capitalist mechanism that depends on linearity to function and to make sense of itself.
4. Literature is linear with its pagination, its beginnings and ends. Though I elevate nonlinearity, for logistical reasons and ease of reading, I refer sequentially to the poems in Waite's "Dear Gender" series (e.g., "Dear Gender 1").
5. I want to extend my hearty gratitude to Dr. Jules Gill-Peterson and Dr. Julie Beaulieu for the guidance, insight, and care they offered while this chapter was in progress.

BIBLIOGRAPHY

Ahmed, Sara. 2006. *Queer Phenomenology*. Durham: Duke University Press.

Foucault, Michel. 1978. *The History of Sexuality: An Introduction, Volume 1*. (Trans. Robert Hurley). New York: Vintage Books.

Freeman, Elizabeth. 2007. "Introduction." *Gay and Lesbian Quarterly* 13 (2–3): 159–76.

Halberstam, Jack. 1998. *Female Masculinity*. Durham: Duke University Press.

———. 2011. *The Queer Art of Failure*. Durham: Duke University Press.

———. 2005. *In a Queer Time and Place: Transgender Bodies, Subcultural Lives*. New York: New York University Press.

Heaney, Emma. 2017. *The New Woman: Literary Modernism, Queer Theory, and the Trans Feminine Allegory*. Evanston: Northwestern University Press.

Keeling, Kara. 2019. *Queer Times, Black Futures*. New York: New York University Press.

Lorde, Audre. 1984. *Sister Outsider*. New York: Ten Speed Press.

Luciano, Dana, and Mel Y. Chen. 2015. "Has the Queer Ever Been Human?" *Gay and Lesbian Quarterly* 21 (2/3): 182–208.
Nelson, Maggie. 2015. *The Argonauts*. Minneapolis: Graywolf Press.
Muñoz, José Esteban. 2009. *Cruising Utopia: The Then and There of Queer Futurity*. New York: New York University Press.
———. 2015. "The Sense of Brownness," *Gay and Lesbian Quarterly* 21 (2/3): 209–49.
Spade, Dean. 2006. "Mutilating Gender." *The Transgender Studies Reader: Volume 1*, edited by Susan Stryker and Stephen White, 315–32. New York: Routledge.
Stockton, Kathryn Bond. 2009. *The Queer Child: Or Growing Sideways in the Twentieth Century*. Durham: Duke University Press.
Waite, Stacey. 2013. *Butch Geography*. North Adams: Tupelo Press.
———. 2015. "Queer Literacies Survival Guide." *College Composition and Communication* 67 (1): 111–4.

Chapter 4

Reclaiming Female Power in Postcolonial Africa

The Tomboy in Tsitsi Dangarembga's Nervous Conditions

Tatiana Prorokova-Konrad

Female authors from postcolonial nations and territories often address the degrading and destructive influences of the colonizer on formerly occupied areas. In doing so, they frequently foreground gender, revealing female oppression to be one of the most complex issues in postcolonial spaces. The images of women that these writers construct are those of smart girls/teenagers, caring mothers, hard-working wives, and devoted lovers; yet these very women are also silenced, abused, forgotten, underappreciated, and unjustly deprived of what they deserve. Through such portrayals, these fictional stories emphasize the real problem of subjugated women: the patriarchal belief that being a woman means being inferior to a man. Tsitsi Dangarembga's *Nervous Conditions* is one such narrative. It illustrates how women are trapped in colonialist and patriarchal systems that preclude them from assuming any role except for the ones that have been predetermined for them by men: obedient daughter, dutiful wife, caring mother, and meticulous housekeeper. A woman is thus largely characterized by her femininity which patriarchy interprets as deficient compared to masculinity. And while many women remain trapped within these outlined boarders, there are also those who, as *Nervous Conditions* illustrates, transgress in the name of justice.

Published in the UK in 1988, *Nervous Conditions* is set in the 1960s and narrates the story of Tambu, a young woman from postcolonial Rhodesia (modern Zimbabwe). Exploring the intersections of colonialism, race, and gender, the novel's primary concern is Rhodesia's pervasive gender inequality. This inequality, as the novel demonstrates, is only intensified through colonialist practices and ideologies, including racism, which restricts the role of women to obedient housewives who can exist only within a domestic space. As *Nervous Conditions* engages with the problem of gender inequality, it explicitly targets issues of gender, sexuality, and race through rebellious female characters, who appear as tomboys. There are two such women in the novel: Tambu and her cousin Nyasha. Tambu's main desire is to attend school; yet because they are poor, her family only can afford tuition for her brother. However, after the unexpected death of this child, Tambu is allowed to take his place and starts attending a missionary school. Through the complex relationship between Tambu and her brother, and the Tambu's reimagining of her place in postcolonial Rhodesia as a young woman, the novel comments on the transformation that Tambu must undergo to fight for her place in a patriarchal society. When Tambu moves to her uncle Babamukuru's home, she becomes close friends with her cousin Nyasha who has recently returned from England. While Tambu must be obedient and thankful for the opportunity to go to school (which girls/young women in Rhodesia normally do not do), Nyasha is not as subservient. As a result, she is constantly abused by her father for not being a good-enough "girl." Through both Tambu and Nyasha, the novel illustrates the oppressive nature of colonialism and patriarchy that turns women into objects. These two female characters' choice to rebel and break the rules—make decisions, get an education, control of their own bodies, and discover their sexuality—make them appear different from the vast majority of female characters who can never break the shackles of this oppression. Tomboyism, thus, largely reinforces the characters' ability to fight and potentially win the war against oppression. It validates their womanhood and state of being a woman as not only legitimate qualities but also as powerful enough to withstand oppressive and discriminating maleness and masculinity, as portrayed in the novel. This essay, therefore, not only demonstrates how being a tomboy can be a powerful narrative technique for postcolonial women writers, but also revisits tomboyism from a postcolonial feminist perspective and, thus, reconsiders the term. It is through tomboyism that the novel explores and redefines female identity in postcolonial Rhodesia.

TOMBOYISM AS A POSTCOLONIAL FEMALE IDENTITY: TAMBU

Tomboyism is a unique gender identity category. In the West, and specifically in North America, the word "tomboy" is used to describe "girls who assume the dress, manner, and activities of boys" (Rice 2014, 91). The term itself, however, dates back to the mid-sixteenth century, and was used to describe "rude and boisterous" boys (King 2017). The first tomboys appeared in fiction in the nineteenth century; nonetheless, since that time, the term "tomboy" has acquired different meanings, interpretations, and characteristics, becoming a rather fluid concept, largely due to differing gender norms depending on time and place (Rice 2014, 91). The general understanding of tomboys as "girls" who resist certain gender norms imposed on them can be seen as both positive and negative. To borrow from social psychologists, "tomboys are a significant subgroup of girls during middle childhood, with potentially beneficial and harmful features" (Ahlqvist et al. 2013, 563). Michelle Ann Abate claims that "tomboys are commonly seen as figures who critique women's gender roles" (2008, xxiv). This can be viewed as a positive outcome of tomboyism that directly challenges the patriarchal definition of being a woman as a/an domesticized, hyper-feminized, silent, and ultimately oppressed object. In that regard, scholars acknowledge that being a tomboy may not necessarily be perceived as threatening by society—despite the potential challenge that tomboyism can pose to various patriarchal gender norms—simply because girls acting like boys are generally more easily understood than boys acting like girls, or, to borrow from Linda Brannon, "being a 'tomboy' is more acceptable than being a 'sissy'" (2011, 133). At the same time, Jack Halberstam pinpoints the way in which tomboyism may be dangerous, claiming that "excessively feminine little girls are . . . harmed by the generalization of the tomboy label because when tomboy becomes a normative standard, they look pathologically bound by their femininity to weakness and passivity" (1999, 160).Thus, while tomboyism complicates the patriarchal vision of women's roles and behaviors, it might also reinforce female inferiority as the defining characteristic of femininity, distorting its meaning.

Acknowledging the empowering and harmful aspects of tomboyism, this essay demonstrates how tomboyism can be a manifestation of women's fight against patriarchal norms. It claims that in the writing of postcolonial women, and specifically in Dangarembga's *Nervous Conditions*, being/becoming a tomboy might be the only effective way to fight for gender equality. In the novel, tomboyism is thus portrayed as a necessary gender/identity characteristic that a girl/woman needs to possess to be heard, seen, and recognized.

Nervous Conditions focuses on and is narrated by Tambu, a fourteen-year-old young woman from postcolonial Rhodesia who wants access to the same education available to young men, like her brother Nhamo. Access to (good) education is not available to the economically disadvantaged and girls/young women. Being essentially both, Tambu is not considered a potential candidate. Thus, while Nhamo is recognized as "a promising scholar," his sister is not even given a chance (Dangarembga 2004, 46). Nhamo plainly explains: "Did you ever hear of a girl being taken away to school? You are lucky you even managed to go back to Rutivi. With me it's different. I was meant to be educated" (49). Education becomes a tool through which to reinforce gender oppression and secure female domesticity. Tambu's reaction is, however, not that of a passive observer, for she demonstrates her readiness to fight this injustice. To do that, she has to reject the qualities that are traditionally associated with the young women of Rhodesia (passivity and obedience) and acquire the characteristics that are typical of a young man (defiance and rebellion). After a failed attempt to hit her brother with a rock, Tambu shares with the reader:

> I considered running after him to give him the thrashing he deserved, but judging his head-start, saw that I would not catch him. Besides, we were so evenly matched these days that he might have won a fight or I might have, but I had not fought for a long time and I was out of practice. Today it was better not to fight than not to win. I let him go, still very cross with him for saying such silly things. (49)

Here, Tambu acknowledges herself as physically equal to Nhamo; earlier, she also takes initiative when she asks her father to give her seeds to grow corn and thus pay for her own education from the money that she earns selling the crop. Hence, Tambu is not waiting for any form of patronizing (what essentially happens to Nhamo as he is constantly supported by his parents and then his uncle Babamukuru), but tries to prove herself as equal to her male sibling by demonstrating what she can do and thus breaking the traditional association of women with domesticity.

Tambu overtly "assume[s] . . . the manner, and activities of boys"—the characteristics that make her appear as a tomboy. But her relationship with her mother also indicates her tomboy nature (Rice 2014, 91). Dianne Elise claims that "disidentification of the girl from the mother" is what enables tomboyism (1999, 140). In the novel, there is no conflict between the young woman and her mother; on the contrary, the two constantly support and help each other. Yet it is first through her mother that Tambu learns the truth about gender oppression. Tambu shares with the reader: "The thought of my mother working so hard, so alone, always distressed me, but in the end I decided to prepare the evening meal so that she would be able to rest when she returned. For I knew that if there was still work to be done when she finished her watering, she would tire herself further to do it" (Dangarembga 2004, 10). This is, as Tambu soon realizes, the kind of *choice* that a woman is expected to make. Her mother teaches her daughter how a woman's life is arranged:

> When there are sacrifices to be made, you are the one who has to make them. And these things are not easy; you have to start learning them early, from a very

> early age. The earlier the better so that it is easy later on. Easy! As if it is ever easy. And these days it is worse, with the poverty of blackness on one side and the weight of womanhood on the other. Aiwa! What will help you, my child, is to learn to carry your burdens with strength. (16)

Being a woman in postcolonial Rhodesia thus, according to Tambu's mother, is to *sacrifice* oneself and be able to *accept* this. Yet Tambu starts questioning her mother's words early on and sets different goals for herself: "I decided it was better to be like Maiguru [the wife of her uncle Babamukuru], who was not poor and had not been crushed by the weight of womanhood" (16). This is the crucial moment in the novel when the young woman "disidentifi[es]" from her mother—the process described by Elise that was referred to earlier—and becomes a tomboy.

Gender studies scholars connect tomboyism to female masculinity. From the application of Freud's theories on tomboyism where "the concepts of penis envy and the masculinity complex" are viewed as primary to the interpretations of tomboyism as "an extended childhood period of female masculinity," tomboyism seems to stand for some form of a masculine identity (Elise 1999, 141; Halberstam 1999, 155). In *Nervous Conditions*, this identity is largely manifested through Tambu's behavior and choices. Tomboyism thus becomes Tambu's way of fighting for gender equality, and thus acquires a rather traditional meaning:

> Tomboyism tends to be associated with a 'natural' desire for the greater freedoms and mobilities enjoyed by boys. Very often it is read as a sign of independence and self-motivation. It may even be encouraged to the extent that it remains comfortably linked to a stable sense of a girl identity. (Halberstam 1999, 155)

Yet in the novel, Tambu's tomboyism is unwelcome, and she essentially appears as a deviant young woman in the eyes of men. Clearly referring to western contexts, Halberstam laments: "Despite the rise of feminism and the recognition of the dangers posed by conventional femininity . . . we still hesitate to cultivate female masculinity in young girls" (1999, 154). It is evident that in postcolonial patriarchal contexts, cultivations of female masculinity and tomboyism are considered a threat to the existing patriarchal norms.

Amanda Waugh calls Tambu "a Nietzschean heroine—a woman who embodies the Übermensch by resisting binaries, overcoming good and evil, emphasizing becoming over being, and demonstrating creativity in language and values" (2011, 81). Her story of *becoming*, from a rural young woman trapped within patriarchal limits to a student in a prestigious school, is essentially a story of her identity formation, in which tomboyism plays a crucial role. Noteworthy, Tambu is not a voiceless character who slowly acquires a certain form of equality, but, on the contrary, is a powerful young woman from the onset of the story: this is a direct result of her tomboyism. Scholar Pauline Ada Uwakweh observes that Tambu "achieves voice through narration, an act that gives her liberation from her patriarchal-imposed silence and offers hope in the resilience and success of female challenge" (1995, 77). Dangarembga's choice to narrate the story from the perspective of Tambu, rather than simply *about* her, gives this character the power that the other female characters in the novel lack. Yet as Tambu speaks she, arguably, speaks not only for herself but generally for the women in postcolonial Rhodesia (Zimbabwe). This makes her story not only personal and "autobiographical" but also "communal, a narrative of the entire community: her family, her society, and by extension the story of the nation of Zimbabwe" (Mule 2006, 106). Through her fight for gender equality, Tambu articulates the necessity of such a fight as a national and global movement.

With determination, Tambu uncovers, meditates upon, and deals with the various types of inequality that she faces, gradually learning that those inequalities are the result of the steady dehumanization of her nation during colonial times as well as of patriarchal oppression during and beyond the colonial era. And she manages to fully understand the nature of these various types of inequality and overcomes some of them, "recognizing the limiting function of every value system she experiences—Christianity, colonialism, Shona culture, patriarchy—and transcending them" (Waugh 2011, 93). While colonialism and patriarchy are the major threats she must deal with, Tambu quickly learns that while the effects of colonialism are experienced by everyone in the country, women are doubly oppressed, on the basis of sex, constituting a group that Gayatri Spivak designates as "the subaltern." Tambu unmistakably realizes that *being* a girl/woman (read, being perceived in a certain way in a patriarchal society) is a major obstacle to her progress. Distancing herself from the female sex is thus an option that she believes might help her succeed. Pivotally, she does not consider herself a young man; but she starts acting and behaving differently from what is traditionally expected from her. Though realizing the limits of her gender identity in a postcolonial patriarchal society, she never views femininity and women as inferior. Her aim is thus not to question her gender and sexual identity but rather to make gender inequality visible; to make everyone aware of how perverse, biased, and degrading gender inequality is.

Tambu recognizes domesticity as the space to which women are bound and in which they are further humiliated. For example, she tells the reader about a rather peculiar sleeping arrangement between her father and mother:

> The bed and its mattress belonged to my father. My mother was supposed to sleep on the reed mat on the floor with her babies before they were old enough to join me in the kitchen, although she hardly ever did. Usually she fell asleep in the kitchen and could not be bothered to rouse herself to go up to the house. All the women in the family—Mother, Netsai and myself—preferred it this way, and though my father did not, there was not much he could do about it without making a scene. This he did not often have the energy to do. (Dangarembga 2004, 62)

In Tambu's family, women are excluded not only from those home spaces that are initially designated for men (like her father's bed), but also from the spaces that are meant for adults. Her mother has to sleep with the babies (note that they are described in the novel as "her" babies rather than a shared responsibility). Tambu's mother thus belongs only to the spaces that are allowed to be occupied by babies and children, as well as to the kitchen where she essentially assumes the roles of a cook and a servant. Cooking as such is viewed as an inherently female duty that is religiously conducted on a daily basis, and that reinforces the division between two sexes, excluding women from the world of grown-up decision-makers: "cooking twice a day, a special pot of refrigerated meat for the patriarchy to eat as they planned and constructed the family's future" (138).

Fighting against this narrow understanding of who a woman is and what she can do, Tambu is surprised to hear that a woman can achieve something outside her domestic space. She discovers this when she converses with Maiguru, the wife of her uncle Babamukuru. Taking care of her children, husband, and household chores, Maiguru performs a traditional role of a wife and a mother. Yet, Maiguru, like her husband, has a bachelor's and a master's degree, which astonishes Tambu. Indeed, everyone who knows them thinks that only Babamukuru is educated and Maiguru was with her husband in England simply "to look after" him (102). Maiguru confirms: "I still studied for that degree and got it in spite of all of them—your uncle, your grandparents and the rest of your family. Can you tell me now that they aren't pleased that I did, even if they don't admit it? No! Your uncle wouldn't be able to do half the things he does if I didn't work as well!" (103). Through Maiguru's experience, Tambu reimagines womanhood as not only equal to manhood, but also, essentially, as much more powerful than it. Maiguru challenges the patriarchal definition of a woman as being inferior, implying it as being superior—and it is because of its potency that such an important detail as Maiguru's education is kept a secret.

To fight gender inequality, Tambu needs to distance herself from that domestic place which her society's traditions force her to be part of. Going to school and communicating with her cousin Nyasha—the daughter of Maiguru and Babamukuru—gives her that essential opportunity of turning away from the traditional understandings of womanhood and becoming someone more powerful—a tomboy. When Tambu is fourteen years old, she finds new ways of becoming and being a woman that differ from the ones imposed on her by society:

> Freed from the constraints of the necessary and the squalid that defined and delimited our activity at home, I invested a lot of robust energy in approximating to my idea of a young woman of the world. I was clean now, not only on special occasions but every day of the week. I was meeting, outside myself, many things that I had thought about ambiguously; things that I had always known existed in other worlds although the knowledge was vague; things that had made my mother wonder whether I was quite myself, or whether I was carrying some other presence in me. (94)

This is essentially how the change in place/space, or, as Lily G. N. Mabura terms it, "landscape," helps fight gender oppression that Tambu faces at home (2010, 105). Crucially, Tambu views gender oppression as a corrupt part of her culture, but does not fight the culture itself. In other words, she recognizes the limits and corruption of certain traditions but she never wants to be someone other than a Rhodesian woman—an issue that is largely foregrounded in the novel through the hybrid characters who prefer the English language and culture over their native tongue and traditions. Tambu understands the devastating (continuing) impact of colonialism on her country and people as well as "the dynamics of modernization"; and that is why her fight is aimed at not eradication of her culture but rather at its improvement. Indeed, "her ties to Shona culture . . . allow her to survive and not be overwhelmed" as well as give her strength to fight for Rhodesian women and culture (Schulze-Engler 2007, 29; Sizemore 1997, 71).

While Tambu's tomboyism is apparent in her attitudes, intentions, and actions that are meant to underscore and destroy restrictive patriarchal shackles, it also ambiguously emerges on the level of her sexuality. Her close relationship with Nyasha, which receives greater attention in the next section, prompts one to speculate that the cousins might be lovers. While there is little evidence to suggest that Tambu and Nyasha are lesbians, both characters *do* challenge heterosexual norms, outlining these norms as limiting and thus endangering to gender equality: as noted by Vicki Briault Manus, "Gender and sexual identity are deeply interwoven with modes of domination/subjugation in the colonial sphere" (2003, 24). Tomboyism, in particular, is viewed as harmless as long as it allows space for "femininity, appropriate female aspiration, and as long as . . . [it] promise[s] to result in marriage and motherhood" (Halberstam 1999, 156). After all, as Halberstam notes, "there is always the dread possibility . . . that the tomboy will not grow out of her butch stage and will never become a member of the wedding" (1998, 193). Curiously, there is a wedding described in the novel, and Tambu's attitude to it is rather unusual, as perceived by the other characters. It is Tambu's parents' Christian wedding; and while it is not the personal wedding of the tomboy Tambu, it comments on Tambu's gender identity. Babamukuru, clearly being influenced by the English traditions, suggests that Tambu's parents have a church wedding. This custom is foreign to the Shona people and the very idea provokes anger in Tambu, who believes that such a wedding will only humiliate her parents. In the end, Tambu does not attend the Christian wedding of her parents. Having seen the photos, she regrets that she did not go, but, at the same time, she is also happy because, as Tambu concludes, "the decision at least was mine" (Dangarembga 2004, 171). For her disobedience, she is eventually beaten by Babamukuru. The wedding emphasizes the intersection of colonialism and gender oppression in postcolonial Rhodesia. But it also adds a new dimension to Tambu's tomboy identity. Certainly, her refusal to attend the wedding does not comment on her own sexuality. Yet her refusal to go to the wedding that is traditional to the patriarchal British Empire is a protest against not only the colonial influences but also the colonial ideology in general, where heterosexuality and female oppression play significant roles. Her choice to oppose the opinion of the patriarch Babamukuru is a way to fight oppression on both national and postcolonial levels. The wedding that she does not attend reinforces her tomboyism, without compromising her own sexuality.

REDEFINING THE FEMALE BODY IN NERVOUS CONDITIONS: NYASHA

The tomboy identity is further examined in the novel through Tambu's cousin Nyasha, as well as the relationship between the two young women. Tambu and Nyasha are both the victims of patriarchal norms that they try to overcome, and the way they are punished for their disobedience is essentially the same. Yet it is through the character of Nyasha that *Nervous Conditions* uncovers the most brutal and horrifying aspects of female oppression. Through the treatment of Nyasha's body and its radical transformation, the novel comments on her tomboyism that operates as both a defense mechanism and a tool to fight patriarchy.

Nyasha is the daughter of Babamukuru and Maiguru. Having spent a considerable time in England, she largely differs from her peers in Rhodesia. Because of her parents' higher status, she is better dressed, knows English manners, and at first appears to be more "progressed" than her peers from

Rhodesia. Yet, gradually, the reader discovers that Nyasha is not treated any differently from the other young women—back in Rhodesia she is viewed as a subject inferior to men. Her rebellious behavior largely complicates her life, and she is constantly reminded, in a violent form, who she is, that is, a young woman who must obey her parents and follow the traditions of the society that she is part of. Certainly, her hybrid nature that manifests itself through her behavior, her speech, her choice of language, and so on, makes it harder for her to accept female oppression as a societal norm rather than a form of crime.

The primary conflict in the story is that between Nyasha and her father Babamukuru. The patriarch starts teaching her what being a "true woman" means, first paying attention to her manners and activities. Thus, Babmakuru is upset with Nyasha's choice of literature, pointing out that *Lady Chatterley's Lover* is an inappropriate selection: "No daughter of mine is going to read such books" (Dangarembga 2004, 82). Depriving Nyasha of D. H. Lawrence's erotic novel, her father not only restricts the young woman's access to education but also openly suggests that he is the one to shape his daughter's sexual conduct, clearly finding the title of the book disgraceful. Babamukuru teaches Nyasha to respect him according to society's traditions. At the table, Maiguru behaves as a decent wife should and thus tries to set an example for Nyasha:

> Maiguru said that Babamukuru's old meal was no longer fresh. She said she would eat it herself, that Babamukuru should serve himself another portion of food. Babamukuru thought his wife was, making fuss about nothing, but she insisted, so the ritual dishing out of my uncle's food was performed again. This time Nyasha did not wait for her father to finish. By the time he was on to the third dish, she was helping herself to rice. (82)

Nyasha tries to behave as a woman (in her father's understanding) should, yet she quickly gives up, clearly finding certain aspects preposterous. Without even turning his face to her, Babamukuru expresses his indignation as Nyasha begins to eat, not following her mother's pattern of behavior—waiting until the man finishes his food. To this, Nyasha simply responds: "I don't like cold food" (83). Nyasha recognizes that she is treated differently on the basis of sex, yet in moments like this, she learns that she is deprived not only of larger possibilities (e.g., getting the education of her choice) but also of things that she considers basic, unrecognizable, yet essential for every human being (e.g., being able to eat her food warm).

The conflict between father and daughter becomes more pronounced when Babamukuru explicitly says to Nyasha: "*I* expect you to do as *I* say" (85). For Nyasha, however, such an order is unacceptable because she strongly believes that every human being has the right to decide how to live his/her life, regardless of gender. She is the only character who tells her mother to "stop cooking" so much since a surplus food is not needed and she simply wastes her time, as well as to "learn how to drive" in order not to be late (104). Nyasha's interactions with Tambu also accentuate the young woman's progressive thinking. Here, the term "progressive" is used not to accentuate the revolutionary nature of Nyasha's ideas but rather to emphasize that she is the only character who openly attempts to make her beliefs work in real life. The cousins soon become very close, and it is through their relationship and their responses to various challenges that *Nervous Conditions* explores the problem of female oppression. Tambu confesses to the reader: "There was a certain glamour to the idea of sharing a room with my Anglicised cousin. Nyasha herself was glamorous in an irreverent way that made me feel, if not exactly inadequate at least uneducated in some vital aspect of teenage womanliness" (76). Tambu's reaction to becoming closer with Nyasha prompts further speculation regarding the cousins' relationship. Later, when Nyasha comments on Tambu's appearance, this ambiguity is reinforced: "'Not bad,' she agreed, standing beside me to observe my reflection. 'Not bad at all. You've got a waist. One of these days you'll have a bust. Pity about the backside,' she continued, slapping it playfully as she turned away. 'It's rather large. Still, if you can look good in that old gym-dress, you'll look good in anything'" (92). Some suggest these moments indicate a covert lesbian identity. However, scholar Stephanie M. Selvick does not view the young women as lesbian but instead argues that "Tambu's and Nyasha's intimate relationship is constructed beyond the binary of 'homosexual' and 'heterosexual,' and outside the temporal markers of 'colonial' and 'postcolonial'" (2013, 279). According to Selvick, "Dangarembga utilizes sexual tension and sexual desire to show the queer implications inherent in friendship itself. In doing so, she can celebrate and give credence to an intimacy which, as Tambu points out, words could not otherwise describe" (281). Similarly, Elleke Boehmer notes that "their relationship extends beyond girlhood friendship," suggesting that the close and constant interaction contributes to the young women's mutual transformation, for they learn through each other's experiences and essentially evolve as new selves (2003, 144). This process is enabled "through the body, through their bodily proximity, and mutual bodily awareness, as well as through the striving, once again, for a not-yet-defined beyond" (145). With each other, Tambu and Nyasha can behave not as oppressed women and find ways to empowerment. This is most vividly illustrated through the scenes where "Dangarembga grants Tambu the power to look, whilst still inscribing in Nyasha the power to look back" (Selvick 2013, 283).

The body in *Nervous Conditions* is an instrument through which the horror of female oppression is denuded. The female body is abused on multiple levels, yet it is through physical abuse that female oppression becomes particularly well-pronounced. The conflict between Nyasha and Babamukuru intensifies when she is accused by her father for behaving in a way that he finds inappropriate for a young woman. Yet Nyasha does not passively accept his false accusation but rather chooses to defend herself. Babamukuru loses his temper and, unable to control himself, beats his teenage daughter: "'Today I am going to teach you a lesson,' he told her. 'How can you go about disgracing me? Me! Like that! No, you cannot do it. I am respected at this mission. I cannot have a daughter who behaves like a whore'" (Dangarembga 2004, 116). Nyasha, together with her brother and mother, begs him not to beat her, and after another blow, firmly responds: "'I told you not to hit me,' said Nyasha, punching him in the eye" (117). This makes her father even angrier:

> Babamukuru bellowed and snorted that if Nyasha was going to behave *like a man* [emphasis added], then by his mother who was at rest in her grave he would fight her like one. They went down on to the floor, Babamukuru alternately punching Nyasha's head and banging it against the floor, screaming or trying to scream but only squeaking, because his throat had seized up with fury, that he would kill her with his bare hands; Nyasha, screaming and wriggling and doing what damage she could. (117)

It is Nyasha's (inevitable) choice to act in a way that her father defines as accessible only to men—that is, hitting him and thus encouraging a fight rather than passively accepting beating—that is verbally interpreted as transgression. Nyasha's choice to be equal to men is punished. She is beaten by her father who reminds her that she is weaker and essentially powerless—exactly what he, and patriarchy in general, interprets as *being a woman*. Nyasha's behavior in this scene reinforces her tomboy identity, suggesting that she not only thinks progressively but is ready to literally fight for her views.

Halberstam argues: "Tomboyism is punished . . . where and when it appears to be the sign of extreme male identification . . . and where and when it threatens to extend beyond childhood and into adolescence" (1999, 155). And Nyasha is brutally punished by her father. Babamukuru is shocked by his daughter's behavior: "'She has dared . . . to raise her fist against me. She has dared to challenge me. Me! Her father. I am telling you,' and he began to struggle again, 'today she will not live. We cannot have *two men* [emphasis added] in this house. Not even Chido, you hear that Nyasha? Not even your brother there dares to challenge my authority'" (Dangarembga 2004, 117). Nyasha does not simply "challenge" her father's authority; she undermines it. The father promises to kill his daughter because he becomes *afraid* of her. He is afraid of a woman who can no longer be tamed by patriarchy, who refuses to be oppressed, and who fights for her freedom. Babamukuru calls Nyasha "a man" because the way she behaves does not correspond to his definition of a woman. Yet Nyasha is evidently *a young woman*. Tomboyism becomes a tool for her to fight patriarchy as well as demonstrate a new dimension of a woman that Babamukuru has obviously never witnessed. Tambu wittingly concludes that at the core of the conflict is the belief in "femaleness as opposed and inferior to maleness" (118). And while everyone else slowly forgets Babamukuru's barbaric actions toward his daughter, Nyasha's transformation continues.

Nyasha refuses to eat and gradually becomes anorexic. Her psychological condition also worsens and she is later diagnosed as mentally ill. Through this radical transformation of her body, Nyasha's tomboy identity becomes visible to everyone and has to be finally accepted. Waugh calls Nyasha's illness—anorexia—"a strikingly life-denying act" (2011, 81). Yet this interpretation is rather superficial, for Nyasha does not deny life, but she denies living as an oppressed woman. Hence, Nyasha's deliberate destruction of her health is not a form of suicide but a rebellious act to free herself from imposed norms and standards. In doing so, she changes who she is through the radical transformation of her body. Disabling her body, she frees herself from the stereotypical roles that she is expected to fulfill: care for a husband, have sex with him, give birth, nurse her children, as well as stay at home and tend to the house. Nyasha's anorexic body largely complicates the notion of a female body in a patriarchal society: from an object of reproduction, a female body turns into a de-feminized (in a patriarchal sense) subject, ultimately reclaiming power that girls and women are deprived of. In *Nervous Conditions* thus "the starving African figure"—interpreted in a variety of ways—stands for patriarchal oppression and its murderous nature (Rahman 2014, 275). Or, in words of Muzna Rahman, "Nyasha's starving body is read as a concentrated symbol for colonialism, patriarchy and oppression" (277). But this body is also a sign of rebellion and freedom.

In the novel, Nyasha's anorexic body by no means stands for "the 'disabled' postcolonial nation" (Gorman and Udegbe 2010, 309). It is not a symbol of Rhodesia being, in any way, an inferior nation. It is rather an image of oppression that the people in general and women in particular experience both during and after colonialism. It is thus plausible to argue that "the tragedy of Nyasha's illness serves as a catharsis for purging the knowledge of colonial violence" (313). But her disabled female body, tells the reader more of the type of oppression that she experiences being a woman and the painful ways in which she can fight that oppression. Rachel Gorman and Onyinyechukwu Udegbe claim: "Insofar as anorexia is read as a refusal of female reproductive labor, Nyasha's symbolic refusal causes a resonance between her cultural hybridity and ideas of biological mixity" (316–7). Transforming her body, Nyasha by no means rejects her femaleness; but she attempts to get rid of those visible feminine aspects that, in the eyes of men, make her an inferior object. She foregrounds her tomboy identity through making herself into a woman who is not viewed as such by patriarchy. Lee Zevy notes that tomboys are frequently perceived as "an asexual entity" (1999, 186). And while Nyasha does not become asexual, her detachment from that patriarchal image of a woman makes her appear as such in the eyes of men.

Food plays a crucial role in the novel. Essentially, both Nyasha and Tambu try to fight gender inequality through food. Tambu does so when she grows corn that brings her money she can invest in her education, thus being able to "break free from a life devoted to its [food] cultivation" (Wright 1995, 9). Nyasha fights oppression through her rejection of food. Derek Wright contends: "Dangarembga's novel devises an intricate network of connections between education and consumption, skillfully using eating as the governing metaphor for Africa's consumption—nutritional, cultural, educational—of second-hand, imitative Western values" (1995, 8). But the novel is also a critique of not only certain norms from the West but also of the local political, social, and cultural problems, including gender inequality. Deepika Bahri's interpretation of Nyasha's illness is particularly helpful here: "But it would be entirely too simple to attribute her disease to the ills of colonization alone: Nyasha responds not only as native and Other, she responds as *woman* to the ratification of socially en-*gendered* native categories which conspire with colonial narratives to ensure her subjectivity" (1994, n.p.). It is thus the complex web of colonial, postcolonial, western, and local traditions that Nyasha is trapped within being a woman.

At the same time, "Nyasha's madness can be read as a catharsis of radical political consciousness" (Gorman and Udegbe 2010, 321). Yet her disability largely problematizes her choice to rebel through the body. Gorman and Udegbe raise a crucial issue, discussing the intersection of disability and feminism in the novel:

> If a central function of disability representations in *Nervous Conditions* is to advance the idea that 'patriarchy is disabling,' then the feminist moral implies that 'disability is resistance.' This collapsing of women's consciousness into our bodies (and the inaugural separation between mind and body that this move implies) poses a major problem for disability theorists. Who, then, is the non-disabled woman? If disability is a metaphor for women, then the representation of disability erases disabled women. (2010, 321)

This is an important point to make as the novel indeed foregrounds the disabling influence of patriarchy on women, and in so doing undermines the notions of disabled and non-disabled women. Nevertheless, as Bahri claims, "Nyasha's war with patriarchal and colonial systems is fought on the turf of her own body, both because it is the scene of enactment of these systems and because it is the only site of resistance available" (1994, n.p.). Disability in *Nervous Conditions* is thus both the result of patriarchal oppression but also a way to free oneself from the dominant gender norms.

CONCLUSION

Nervous Conditions is "a novel of development and a novel of social protest, it is also . . . a novel of rebirth and transformation in the Western feminist tradition" (Gray 1997, 116). Feminism in the novel, manifests itself through the behavior of female characters, and especially of Tambu and Nyasha. Breaking the stereotype of the tame, obedient, and powerless woman, both young women cultivate a tomboy identity that helps them fight for gender equality. In doing so, the novel reveals "what it means to become a woman" in a postcolonial environment (Shaw 2007, 8). Scholars are, however, skeptical to claim that *Nervous Conditions* gives hope for any positive transformation for women. Some "point out [the author's] lack of optimism about the possibilities of feminism promoting lasting social changes" (Shaw 2007, 9). Others criticize the ending of the novel since it fails to reveal what will actually happen to Tambu but only comments on the young woman's ability to understand the cultural, political, and social intricacies of postcolonialism and argue that "what emerges at the end of the novel is a female subject who is beginning to be aware of the realities of colonial modernity, and thus she begins to reject the notion that feminist identity can be attained at the price of collusion with imperialism" (Mule 2006, 106). These standpoints are valid; but in addition to them, it seems the ultimate futility of the characters' actions only reinforces the complexity of the violent ideologies that oppress women in postcolonial Rhodesia. One can certainly argue that Tambu's and Nyasha's actions were not entirely for nothing. The young women continue to face violence, racism, the "peripherality" issue that makes them appear inferior compared to the former colonizers, rejection, gender exclusion, and many other problems (Lazzari 2018, 108). But they also learn more about their own womanhood and what it means to be a woman in Rhodesian society. Not providing a satisfying end, the novel successfully reflects the real-life situation that millions of women continue to struggle in even today. It is essentially the concept of "girlpower" that *Nervous Conditions* actively promotes, and it does so successfully through tomboyism (Smith 2000, 250). Here, tomboyism is not only an identity but also a form of feminism that teaches the young women who they are as well as empowers them in their fight for equality.

BIBLIOGRAPHY

Abate, Michelle Ann. 2008. *Tomboys: A Literary and Cultural History*. Philadelphia: Temple University Press.

Ahlqvist, Sheana, May Ling Halim, Faith K. Greulich, Leah E. Lurye, and Diane Ruble. 2013. "The Potential Benefits and Risks of Identifying as a Tomboy: A Social Identity Perspective." *Self and Identity* 12 (5): 563–81.

Bahri, Deepika. 1994. "Disembodying the Corpus: Postcolonial Pathology in Tsitsi Dangarembga's *Nervous Conditions*." *Postmodern Culture* 5 (1): n.p.

Boehmer, Elleke. 2003. "Tropes of Yearning and Dissent: The Troping of Desire in Yvonne Vera and Tsitsi Dangarembga." *Journal of Commonwealth Literature* (38) 1: 135–48.

Brannon, Linda. 2011. *Gender: Psychological Perspectives* (6th ed.). New York: Routledge.

Dangarembga, Tsitsi. 2004. *Nervous Conditions* (2nd ed.). Oxfordshire: Ayebia Clarke Publishing.

Elise, Dianne. 1999. "Tomboys and Cowgirls: The Girl's Disidentification from the Mother." In *Sissies and Tomboys: Gender Nonconformity and Homosexual Childhood*, edited by Matthew Rottnek, 140–52. New York: New York University Press.

Gorman, Rachel, and Onyinyechukwu Udegbe. 2010. "Disabled Woman/Nation: Re-narrating the Erasure of (Neo)colonial Violence in Ondjaki's *Good Morning Comrades* and Tsitsi Dangarembga's *Nervous Conditions*." *Journal of Literary & Cultural Disability Studies* 4 (3): 309–25.

Gray, Rosemary. 1997. "'Unnatural Daughters': Postmodernism and Tsitsi Dangarembga's *Nervous Conditions*." *The European Legacy: Toward New Paradigms* 2 (1): 115–20.

Halberstam, Jack. 1998. *Female Masculinity*. Durham: Duke University Press.

———. 1999. "Oh Bondage, Up Yours!: Female Masculinity and the Tomboy." In *Sissies and Tomboys: Gender Nonconformity and Homosexual Childhood*, edited by Matthew Rottnek. 152–79. New York: New York University Press.

King, Elizabeth. 2017. "A Short History of the Tomboy." *The Atlantic*, January 5, 2017.

https://www.theatlantic.com/health/archive/2017/01/tomboy/512258/.

Lazzari, Gabriele. 2018. "Peripheral Realism and the Bildungsroman in Tsitsi Dangaremga's *Nervous Conditions*." *Research in African Literatures* 49 (2): 107–24.

Mabura, Lily G. N. 2010. "Black Women Walking Zimbabwe: Refuge and Prospect in the Landscapes of Yvonne Vera's *The Stone Virgins* and Tsitsi Dangarembga's *Nervous Conditions* and Its Sequel, *The Book of Not*." *Research in African Literatures* 41 (3): 88–111.

Manus, Vicki Briault. 2003. "The Interaction of 'Race' and Gender as Cultural Constructs in Tsitsi Dangarembga's *Nervous Conditions*." *Commonwealth: Essays and Studies* 26 (1): 23–32.

Mule, Katwiwa. 2006. "Blurred Genres, Blended Memories: Engendering Dissidence in Nawal el Saadawi's *Memoirs of a Woman Doctor* and Tsitsi Dangarembga's *Nervous Conditions*." *Meridians: Feminism, Race, Transnationalism* 6 (2): 93–116.

Rahman, Muzna. 2014. "Bodily Secrets: The History of the Starving Body in Tsitsi Dangarembga's *Nervous Conditions*." *Forum for Modern Language Studies* 50 (3): 275–88.

Rice, Carla. 2014. *Becoming Women: The Embodied Self in Image Culture*. Toronto: University of Toronto Press.

Schulze-Engler, Frank. 2007. "African Literature and the Micropolitics of Modernity: Explorations of Post-Traditional Society in Wole Soyinka's *Season of Anomy*, Nuruddin Farah's *Sardines* and Tsitsi Dangarembga's *Nervous Conditions*." In *Texts, Tasks, and Theories: Versions and Subversions in African Literatures 3*, edited by Tobias Robert Klein, Ulrike Auga, and Viola Prüschenk, 21–35. Amsterdam: Rodopi.

Selvick, Stephanie M. 2013. "Beyond the Binary: Same-Sex Desire and Gender Defiance in Tsitsi Dangarembga's *Nervous Conditions*." *Journal of Postcolonial Writing* 49 (3): 278–90.

Shaw, Carolyn Martin. 2007. "'You had a daughter, but I am becoming a woman': Sexuality, Feminism and Postcoloniality in Tsitsi Dangarembga's *Nervous Conditions* and *She No Longer Weeps*." *Research in African Literatures* 38 (4): 7–27.

Sizemore, Christine W. 1997. "Negotiating Between Ideologies: The Search for Identity in Tsitsi Dangarembga's *Nervous Conditions* and Margaret Atwood's *Cat's Eye*." *Women's Studies Quarterly* 25 (3/4): 68–82.

Smith, Ann. 2000. "Girl Power in *Nervous Conditions*: Fictional Practice as a Research Site." *McGill Journal of Education* 35 (3): 245–60.

Uwakweh, Pauline Ada. 1995. "Debunking Patriarchy: The Liberational Quality of Voicing in Tsitsi Dangarembga's *Nervous Conditions*." *Research in African Literatures* 26 (1): 75–84.

Waugh, Amanda. 2011. "'Willing Liberates': Nietzschean Heroism in Tsitsi Dangarembga's *Nervous Conditions*." *Pacific Coast Philology* 46: 80–96.

Wright, Derek. 1995. "'More than Just a Plateful of Food': Regurgitating Colonialism in Tsitsi Dangarembga's *Nervous Conditions*." *Commonwealth: Essays and Studies* 17 (2): 8–18.

Zevy, Lee. 1999. "Sexing the Tomboy." In *Sissies and Tomboys: Gender Nonconformity and Homosexual Childhood*, edited by Matthew Rottnek, 180–95. New York: New York University Press.

Chapter 5

Tomboy Ethos in Children's Non-Fiction

Jennifer Harrison

In light of the increasing critical preoccupation with materialism, embodiment, and subjectivity, the "tomboy" question has been handled in critical discourse in two distinct and wholly disparate ways. In the humanities, scholars of queer and gender studies in history, popular culture, and literature have begun to unpick the entanglement of the tomboy character with issues of constructed identity and social justice, pointing to its transformative and revolutionary potential as well as its iconoclastic status. The tomboy has become a cultural icon, constructed and shaped by centuries of gender conservatism in the West. Moreover, the evolution of the tomboy in American history points strongly to commercial, consumerist roots: as well as its establishment through iconic characters from literature such as Scout and Jo March, tomboy identity was established through motion-pictures, comics and popular magazines, sodas, Cracker Jack box prizes, and—today—through fashion and media products targeting the LGBTQ+ market (Abate 2008, x–xi). According to Michelle Ann Abate, whose *Tomboys: A Literary and Cultural History* is one of the few full-length cultural studies of the tomboy currently available, in the United States "[c]hanges in the nation's social, political and even economic climate . . . facilitated the expansion of this [tomboy] figure" (2008, x). While Abate is concerned primarily with the emergence of the tomboy figure as a literary and cultural phenomenon, her observation nevertheless reveals the extent to which the fictionalized figure of the tomboy is rooted in concrete constructions of gender performance within specific social contexts. In fact, in an exhaustive discussion of "tomboy taming" in American children's and YA texts, Shawna McDermott argues that "taming"—understood as the depiction of tomboys who are taught to be "proper" girls and women—"has become widespread in media targeted to adolescents in the late twentieth and twenty-first centuries" (2019, 134). The tomboy figure, then, has not always been revolutionary in nature.

In contrast to this constructivist approach in the humanities, attention in the science and medical fields has focused increasingly on tomboyism as a disease: a problem to be solved or an indicator of problems to come. Such studies not only attempt to define tomboyism as a biological characteristic, but also work backwards from observations of very real social disadvantages suffered by children who identify as or are identified as tomboys: "Tomboys may be stressed by paradoxical gender expectations, involving nicknames, criticisms, gender-conformism about body types and movements, teasing, and ostracism" (Hall 2008, 561). While the first approach has tended to focus primarily on depictions of tomboys in fiction—literature, film, and television—the latter has relied on fieldwork conducted with groups of children, parents, educators, and so on. Surprisingly, however, virtually no work has been conducted on the intersection between these two approaches: namely, the nonfiction texts and cultural productions from which young people of all genders learn the behaviors, values, and practices associated with scientific inquiry.

This chapter will explore how the fictionalized figure of the tomboy has come to merge with the reality of gendered performance through depictions of female subjects in nonfiction children's texts in the fields of nature and science. In particular, it will describe how in non-fiction targeted toward young readers, the question of whether science is gendered—of whether girls who "do science" are tomboys—is handled in three distinct ways: 1. Feminine characteristics are emphasized; 2. Boys and girls are shown as equal in both appearance and behavior; or 3. Characters are androgenized and gender is erased.

TOMBOY CHARACTERISTICS

What, then, is a tomboy? Here, at least, there is some accord between the scientific and humanities communities—at least on the surface. According to the *Oxford English Dictionary* (OED), since its first recorded use in 1592, the term has historically "been connected with connotations of rudeness and impropriety" ("Tomboy" 1989, 211). Abate states that "[t]he traits most Americans are likely to name as constitutive of this code of conduct include a proclivity for outdoor play (especially athletics), a feisty independent spirit, and a tendency to don masculine clothing and adopt a boyish nickname" (Abate 2008, xvi). Hall states simply that "[s]ome girl children act like boys" (2008, 555), while the researchers on The Tomboy Project define tomboys as girls who "behave like boys in some respects," including interest in sports, a proclivity for "boy's toys," and an "aversion to dresses" (Bailey et al. 2002, 333–4). However, such definitions raise a number of questions. For example, what makes "outdoor play" a "boyish" activity? What exactly is a "boy's" toy, and who gets to decide which gender category a particular toy falls into? While such issues may have been clear-cut five-hundred years ago, they are far from so today. As Abate points out, "[Y]oung women now commonly participate in many of the same activities as young men" (Abate 2008, xi), and "it is now routine for girls to wear pants, play sports and have short hair" making it possible that "nearly all contemporary young women could be placed on the spectrum of tomboyishness" (Abate 2008, xxiii).

It is distressing that, in order to try and pin down the concept of "tomboy" as anything beyond a literary phenomenon—as in Abate's work—theorists are forced to turn to a scientific/medical establishment which seems determined to remain firmly rooted in conservatism and gender binaries. The researchers on The Tomboy Project, for example, describe it as "a longitudinal study of girls identified by their parents as tomboys" (Bailey et al. 2002, 333). They ask, in the introductory literature review of their published study, the following questions:

> For example, do tomboys behave like boys in all respects or only in some? Tomboys may be male-typical in their interest in sports and their aversion to dresses, but are they also more physically aggressive than other girls? Increasingly, psychologists have conceptualized sex-typed behaviors as a multidimensional space (Ruble & Martin, 1998), meaning that individuals can be male-typical in some respects and female-typical in others. In which behaviors do tomboys differ from other girls? (Bailey et al. 2002, 333)

This article maintains a strictly objective tone and a veneer of scientific language and convention, simply glossing over the complexity of terms such as "girl," "boy," "male-typical," "masculine," "sex-typical behaviors" and so on, and treating them as concrete, measurable, scientific realities rather than as malleable and fluid social and cultural constructs. Even more worrying is the fact that the girls themselves have not self-identified in this study, raising the question of whether they themselves understand certain behaviors and characteristics as gendered. Another study conducted in 2002 found "[m]asculine characteristics such as independence, aggression, competitiveness, leadership ability, ability to defend, stand by beliefs" positively correlated to both "self-perceptions" of being a tomboy and to "confidence" (Hilgenkamp and Livingston 2002, 743). The study made use of the BEM Sex Role Inventory (744), which asks participants to self-identify with different characteristics which are categorized by the test as either masculine, feminine, or neutral. Problematically—and similar to the researchers on The Tomboy Project—this study makes no attempt to understand why particular traits should be considered "masculine," nor—most importantly—whether the subjects under observation considered these traits to be gendered. In other words, studies such as these are not observing individuals who *self*-identify with the tomboy as a cultural phenomenon; instead, such studies are themselves *labeling* girls and women with particular characteristics and behaviors as "tomboy." Furthermore, as Paechter and Clark point out, many scientific studies of tomboyism focus on "gender identity, particularly child gender identity disorder and adult transsexuality, and its relation to tomboy roles, and the relationship between tomboy behavior in childhood and a variety of features of adulthood, such as adult lesbianism" (2007, 343). According to these studies, nonconformity to social stereotypes of gendered behavior can be quantified, diagnosed, and identified as a root cause of lived experiences of injustice. Such an approach troublingly indicates the fine line between recognition of and enforcement of gender stereotypes.

TOMBOYS AND SCIENCE

When considering the disparity between these two views of tomboyism, it is worth remembering that science and nature studies are fields which have been historically gendered (Kourany 2010, 5; Tuana 1989, vii): feminists have identified, e.g., the stereotypes of both the male scientist (Dean-Ruzicka; Bodzin and Gehringer) and the earth-mother figure (Leach; Gibson). At the same time, the dearth of girls and women willing to enter STEM fields, along with the rigidly gendered and sexist conditions women who do enter those fields encounter, has been a growing cause of concern for academia and industry alike (Dean-Ruzicka). Writing about the representation of queer identities in STEM education (a field related to if not actually parallel with this current exploration), Letts and Fifield describe STEM as an "[i] nsitutionalized regulatory process of naming, categorizing, normalizing, and explaining" processes which necessarily "induce transgressions via infidelities, slippages, resistances, improvisations, and perverse repurposings that both define and undermine what's normal and natural, and what's not" (2019, 3–4). They describe STEM education as susceptible to "the normalizing pull . . . of indelible, knowable, institutionalized identities" (13). The place of the tomboy within science, therefore, is especially difficult.

In the article "Tomboys, Dykes, and Girly-Girls," Adams, Schmitke, and Franklin discuss the more visible arena of sports and athletics, and point out that for second-wave feminists in the 1960s and 1970s, "[s]ports was seen as a critical arena for women to contest stereotypical images of the docile, passive, inert, incapable female body, thus challenging the patriarchal control and regulation of the female body" (2005, 18). That these feminists focused on sports rather than science—the body rather than the mind—is, perhaps, telling: the cultural stereotype of the scientist/scholar often compares unfavorably to that of the athlete in terms of "acceptable" masculinity as well, but the woman, who supposedly lacks both reason and physical capacity, ranks lower still.

As already described, moreover, tomboys have become the target of a gendered scientific agenda in the modern Western world. It is interesting that, as Michelle Ann Abate describes in the epilogue to *Tomboys*, anxieties about gender and tomboyism in the late twentieth and early twenty-first centuries have been absorbed into scientific discourse; Abate describes, for example, a "scientific blurring between childhood tomboyism, Gender Identity Disorder, and adult lesbianism" (2008, 231–2), with non-conformity to cultural gender norms becoming a subject for scientific study and medical diagnosis. Science is, furthermore, one arena in which patriarchal control and regulation of the female body continues strong: in the current political climate within the United States, medical interventions in birth, birth-control, and gender conformity disease, have become matters of national debate. For the tomboy in science, then, gender identity must be defended on two fronts: that of the mind and that of the body.

In a study concerning gender and sexuality representations in a range of UK science textbooks, Michael Reiss found that they tended to favor a policy of silence and "omission" (1998, 147) when approaching these culturally sensitive topics, as if they might be an unfit subject for a supposedly factual and objective medium. Jay Lemke, conducting a similar analysis on biology textbooks, notes that "the nuance and complexity of how people become sexed and gendered is not represented" in such works (Milne 2011, 308). Where, then, can one look for a positive depiction of the tomboy in science?

In the introduction to *Women in STEM on Television,* Ashley Lynn Carlson makes the grim observation that the largely absent or negative stereotypes of women in STEM in popular culture both dissuade girls and young women from excelling at STEM in school and pursuing STEM degrees, and create hostile and unappealing work environments for those women who do enter into STEM careers (2018, 1–3). Rachel Dean-Ruzicka, writing about the representation of "girl" and female scientists in young adult dystopian fiction makes a similar observation that young women lack positive role models in the field of science. She writes that as well as real-life role models, young women also "look to popular culture for fictional role models" but discover that "one rarely finds female characters worth looking up to in popular culture texts dealing with science and technology" (2016, 51). She describes tropes in popular culture such as the "babe scientist, the mad scientist's beautiful daughter, the gadgeteer genius, the motherly scientist, or the wrench wench" and argues that such tropes are "pervasive in popular culture and often define how the categories of 'girl' and 'scientist' overlap in ways that rely on emphasizing feminine characteristics in order to balance out the supposed masculine ability to work in STEM fields" (52). A study conducted by Cheryan et al. in 2011 found that "women who interacted with nonstereotypical role models believed they would be more successful in computer science than those who interacted with stereotypical role models. Differences in women's success beliefs were mediated by their perceived dissimilarity from stereotypical role models" (2011, 656). The need for positive gendered depictions of women within STEM is clear: women need to be able to identify other women in STEM and see them succeeding.

Michelle L. Knaier, however, in an exploration of the representation of sex and gender in STEM classrooms, discusses the problem of language and imagery targeted toward inclusiveness, and especially targeted to toward including "girls" in STEM education; as she points out, more specialized language and strategies in fact reinforce the idea of sex and gender binaries and ignore the real-life complexity of these categories. She argues that "perhaps the solution to the problem of a restrictive two-category system (i.e., boy/girl, masculine/feminine) is not simply adding more categories. Perhaps categories themselves are the problem. What if we move beyond gender identities?" (2019, 216). Her recommendation is simple: avoid depicting normatively gendered and sexed behaviors (216). She explains, "normative gender-binary assumptions (like masculine/feminine) hurt those who do not conform—especially when they are applied to children. These assumptions may also narrow the minds of those who do conform—especially when they try to understand nonconforming children" (209) such as tomboys.

This range of observations addresses itself to two polar extremes: fictional depictions of science in popular culture compared to straightforwardly nonfictional depictions of science in classrooms and textbooks. However, what of those works that fall in between: the narrative nonfiction picture books and magazines aimed at young readers? These works depend heavily on imagery to convey both information and narrative, and as Perry Nodelman explains in *Words About Pictures,* these images make explicit and deliberate use of the cultural assumptions of the implied reader in order to convey meaning; images in picture books are often simplified, generalized, and deliberately stereotypical as a means of facilitating easy interpretation, and children viewing generalized images in picture books learn to decode those images as representative of a cultural norm (1988, 27–30). Avoiding the depiction of "normatively gendered and sexed behaviors," therefore, while simultaneously supporting the inclusion of more women in STEM, may well be a near impossible task.

Recent best-seller lists have seen an explosion of titles aimed at encouraging girls into STEM fields. Author and illustrator team Andrea Beaty and David Roberts, for example, published *Rosie Revere, Engineer* in 2013, and further titles featuring characters such as Ada Twist (*Scientist*) and Sophia Valdez (*Future Prez*) have followed, emphasizing the spheres of science and politics as appropriate for and open to girls. However, depictions of tomboy characters nevertheless remain scarce. Avid young readers of nonfiction might, in fact, be justified in questioning whether an interest in science can coincide with tomboy identity.

The following sections will examine three different ways in which the question of whether science is gendered—of whether girls who "do science" are tomboys—has been handled by recent children's nonfiction publications: 1. Feminine characteristics are emphasized; 2. Boys and girls are shown as equal in both appearance and behavior; or 3. Characters are androgenized and gender is erased.

FLOWERY GALOSHES: THE FEMINIZED "GIRL" SCIENTIST

Nonfiction picture books in which gender is deliberately emphasized are pervasively present on current best-seller lists, but two stand out in particular as typical of current trends in gender depiction: Joanna Gains's *We Are the Gardeners* and Andrea Beaty's *Rosie Revere, Engineer.*

Written by popular HGTV star Joanna Gains, *We Are the Gardeners* exemplifies many of the qualities extolled in her TV series, *Fixer Upper.* The book, which claims on the front cover to be "written by Joanna Gains and Kids," details the family's discovery of the joys of homestead gardening, and serves as an adjunct to the depictions in the series of keeping chickens and goats, growing vegetables and herbs for the table, and exploring the natural world through DIY work, gardens, and landscaping. Family life, as shown in the TV series, is a predominant theme in the book.

Long-running *The New York Times* best-seller *Rosie Revere, Engineer* was first published in 2013 and has been followed by a long string of spin-off titles; the most recent, *Rosie Revere and the Raucous Riveters* (2018) and *Sofia Valdez, Future Prez* (2019), hold a steady place on the Amazon and *The New York Times* best-sellers lists and have garnered similar critical and popular acclaim. The book tells the story of Rosie, a young girl with a flair for engineering ingenuity, as she learns that perseverance is the key to success in science. These two titles, both widely read and critically acclaimed, take different approaches to the question of gender and science. However, in both texts gender is emphatically stable and, moreover, stable gender identity is celebrated.

The front cover of *We Are the Gardeners* sets the tone for the rest of the book: the happy family is pictured busy amidst the riotous growth of the garden, with Joanna's two daughters and the baby pictured on the right, and the two boys pictured on the left. The characters are clearly gendered: the two girls have long hair, and one wears a dress while the other wears a pink, dress-like tunic. The boys are attired identically in blue jeans, and each has short hair and broad shoulders. While the two boys are engaged in physical endeavors—one holds a trowel and the other a large watering can—the girls and the baby are more passive—two are chasing butterflies and the other holds a large flower. The physical attributes are clearly intended to mimic the identities already familiar to readers from the HGTV show, but the behaviors and choice of dress also clearly point to demarcated gender characteristics. This theme continues throughout the book. The seventh double-page spread, for example, depicts the family seated around the table, planning their garden. The text reads: "We all gathered around the kitchen table and got to work dreaming, planning and drawing things out" (Gains 2019, n.p.). While the text is gender-neutral, the imagery is not. The girls, once again, are depicted in dresses, and their long hair is loose and flowing. Chip (the father) is prominent as the largest figure at the table, writing on a large notepad. The two other boys are equally actively engaged: one writes on a smaller notepad while the other clutches an open seed-packet, from which seeds are tumbling. Neither Joanna nor the two girls is shown as actively participating; the spaces in front of them are empty, and they are neither writing nor engaging with the other materials (seed packets, crayons, garden plans, trowels) spread out across the table. One of the girls clutches her father's arm, while the other has her hand politely raised. It seems clear that for the young women, their role falls more on the side of dreaming than planning. Much of the text deals with learning: learning about soil and water, layout, garden pests, and companion planting. However, only one image in the book depicts active scientific investigation (although all four children engage in the more passive activity of reading up on gardening on the fourth double-page spread), and this is the image of one of the boys peering intently through a magnifying glass on the twelfth double-page spread. A total of eight different images (not counting the front cover) show one of the girls either holding flowers or chasing a butterfly, and a further four images depict the girls holding—but not using—a gardening implement. Of the remaining images, twelve depict the female characters doing nothing whatsoever, while only six images show the characters actively engaged in gardening. In comparison, the male characters are shown actively engaged in the physical labor of tending or planning the garden—writing, watering plants, toting a wheelbarrow, tying up plants, and so on—in fifteen different images throughout the book. Although this is a depiction of a real family (whose members are presumably more fluid in real life), the representation of gender (in both the book and the well-known *Fixer Upper* series) is carefully orchestrated to tell a conservative gender narrative.

We Are the Gardeners leaves no space for the tomboy. In this text, the context of the traditional nuclear family leaves the female characters enmeshed in rigid gender roles and stereotypes. The girls behave and dress in a manner instantly recognizable as traditionally feminine, and no room has been left for ambiguity, slippage, or experimentation. The narrative fits within the wider historical context of American pioneer-ism, depicting the act of understanding and tending a garden as a merging of scientific curiosity and socio-familial bonding. Moreover, the depiction of nature as firmly demarcated as well—there are wheelbarrows and shovels for the men, and flowers and butterflies for the women—juxtaposed with the gendered depictions of the characters implies that gender conformity is something "natural." There is no room in this depiction for the disturbance that might be created by a fracturing of familiar gender identities.

Where *We Are the Gardeners* is conservatively traditional in its approach to femininity, *Rosie Revere* is just the opposite: this text openly declares its defiance of traditional gender roles and advocates the colonization of traditionally masculine fields by women. Throughout the text, Rosie is depicted actively engaged in scientific pursuit: she draws, builds, tests, and scavenges for materials. She is frequently depicted working alone, and where other characters are mentioned or depicted, they are downplayed by the text itself, which keeps the focus firmly on Rosie herself. Unlike the girls in *We Are the Gardeners,* Rosie has actively taken on the masculine characteristics—physical activity, a liking for "boys" pursuits, and so on—that should mark her as a tomboy. Nevertheless, all hints of tomboyism have been carefully excluded from the text. In the first place, Rosie is—in name and appearance—decidedly feminine. Throughout the text, she is depicted invariably in dresses (when she is not in her pajamas), and emphasis is placed on her long, styled hair, which is described as "swooping over one eye" (Beaty and Roberts). Rosie is also depicted as "girlish" in her behavior: she is shy and her posture in many images is timid and closed. In one memorable scene, in which she scavenges in a park trash-can for materials, she is shown on tip-toe, barely able to reach into the can, her hair falling stylishly over one eye, and pink blush-marks coloring her cheeks. Even when she is depicted inventing, she sits hunched in on herself, dwarfed by the science that surrounds her, her tiny feet just poking out from her pajamas and her long eyelashes accentuating her wide eyes. The story also emphasizes characteristics traditionally associated with femininity: Rosie is shy, afraid, self-doubting, and lacking in confidence, and her story is less about her progress in her chosen field as it is about her ability to overcome these emotional drawbacks.

Rosie Revere, it seems, leaves as little space for the tomboy as *We Are the Gardeners* does. Rosie is not a tomboy; she engages in traditionally feminine behaviors and displays traditionally feminine physical and emotional characteristics as a balance to her "masculine" interest in engineering. The text seems to be openly declaring that this is a GIRL as well as a great engineer—a GIRL about whose GIRLISHNESS there can be no mistake. The field of engineering is saved from gender exclusivity by this text, but girls themselves are not.

For a tomboy to "do science" would be to insist that there is no need for girls and women to display clear femininity to counter their involvement in traditionally masculine pursuits. This is the message that texts such as *Rosie Revere* and *We Are the Gardeners* seem to work actively against.

OBJECTIVE AND NEUTRAL: DEPICTIONS OF GENDER EQUALITY

Where narrative tales such as *We Are the Gardeners* and *Rosie Revere* foreground the need to adhere to gender stereotypes, nonfiction that eschews a narrative stance often strives to downplay the importance of gender. These texts tend to opt either for depictions of boys and girls (or men and women) as equal, or to avoid the depiction of human characters at all. Choosing texts for this analysis was challenging, because non-narrative texts are rarely foregrounded in the media and by award-presenting bodies in the same way that narrative texts are. The texts chosen for analysis in this section—*The Everything Kids' Science Experiments Book* by Tom Robinson and the *Human Body Activity Book for Kids* by Katie Stokes—rank on Amazon's best-selling kids science books list for 2019 and are fairly typical of the "hands on" science genre they fall into. While their appearance on this list is by no means a commentary on their quality, it nevertheless implies that these books are at least being widely purchased—and therefore, presumably, widely circulated.

Published in 2001 by Everything Kids, *The Everything Kids' Science Experiments Book* introduces readers to scientific principles and the scientific method by means of experiments conducted within the home and making use of common household materials. The author, Tom Robinson, is a high school science teacher, and the book is—according to its Amazon listing—targeted at children ages 7–12 (grades 3–6). The front cover is fairly typical of the illustration contained within this type of volume: alongside bold lettering in bright primary colors, two cartoon characters are depicted—one in each of the bottom corners—engaged in different experiments. On the left, a boy with dark curly hair and dark skin examines something being weighed on a scale. On the right, a girl with bobbed hair pulled back by a headband examines differently colored liquids in beakers. There is an obvious attempt in this depiction to foreground equality: the characters depicted are of equal size and their positioning on the page is balanced. The colors chosen for the characters' clothing is also gender-neutral: the boy wears a red pull-over and the girl wears a yellow under-garment with a blue over-garment. The activities in which they are engaged are also gender-neutral: there is no indication of either experiment being more difficult, complex, or challenging than another. The utilization of two different skin-colors as well as both male and female characteristics in the depictions sends a clear message that science is race-and gender-neutral. Despite this emphasis on equality, however, gender (and race, although that is a discussion for another time) is clearly indicated through a number of visual cues. Foremost, the girl is distinguished by her hair, which is longer, styled in a feminine cut and held back by a headband—an accessory most often associated with girls. The girl is also dressed in clothing which suggests—without explicitly depicting—a dress: the garment is long, flares slightly toward the girl's waist (the picture is truncated below this point), and in two pieces. Together, these visual cues clearly indicate not only the female gender, but characteristics culturally coded as feminine. These visual cues are not accidental: with so much current emphasis being placed on the encouragement of girls and women in STEM education and careers, books such as *The Everything Kids' Science Experiments Book* strive to send a clear message that girls can and do participate equally in STEM. In the attempt to normalize depictions of women and girls in STEM, these volumes use such visual coding precisely to draw attention to gender equality. As argued by Michelle. L. Knaier, however, this deliberate inclusion of distinctly male and female characters is in itself problematic, as it both excludes non-binary readers and normalizes the idea of binary gender (2019).

Inside *The Everything Kids' Science Experiments Book*, the depiction of human figures is limited: an approach which is also common in this type of book. The deliberate erasure of gender from science books intended for children, while it may seem the complete opposite of the deliberately gendered approach described so far, actually serves a similar purpose: to suggest that gender is not a limiting factor in the pursuit of STEM knowledge. In *The Everything Kids' Science Experiments Book,* only two human characters appear inside the book: a caricature of a scientist which accompanies a series of text-boxes called "Cool Quotes," and a bored-looking child accompanying the activities labeled "Kid's Lab Lessons." Both are androgynous: the scientist wears a too-big lab coat and glasses, and has shoulder length hair. However, there are no visual cues that might allow a reader to determine whether this character is intended to be male or female, masculine or feminine. The child attached to the "lab lessons" wears a T-shirt and has shorter hair parted in the middle. Again, no visual cues indicate an assigned gender for this figure. If tomboys were to find themselves at all in STEM books for children, it would be in this type of depiction. It would be, however, difficult for a self-identifying tomboy to identify with these characters fully: in the absence of any gender coding at all, it is as easy to imagine these characters as boys/men as it is to imagine them as non-conforming girls/women. These images do not support gender fluidity; instead they suggest the absence of gender. Even more troubling is the depiction of the human body found in the *Human Body Activity Book for Kids.* Page nine, entitled "All About Your Body," achieves the somewhat astonishing feat of erasing sex and gender from the human body itself. A full-page spread depicts a human body illustration with a visible interior: shown as though the pinkish skin were transparent, bones, muscles, veins and arteries, and interior organs are depicted and labeled. One side of this figure's face has been left intact, to allow surface details—eye, nose, ear—to be identified and labeled as well. The figure is childish in build, with rounded limbs, a large head, and short stature. The figure has short, brown hair styled in what might be a gender-neutral manner; with no clothing or other visual gender markers, this figure could be female. Further than this cannot be determine, however, because the image includes no sex organs. The bladder is depicted, but neither scrotum/testicles nor a womb are included in the image. As a depiction of a typical human body, therefore, this image is severely lacking. This full-page androgynous figure appears several more times throughout the volume, and in each instance the biological markers of sex have been omitted. Not only does this imagery fail to support the possibility of gender fluidity, but it also fails to support the idea of gender equality or even neutrality. Instead, this biology-based instructional image attempts to pretend that gender and sex do not exist.

The practice of erasing gender and even sex from STEM works for children is most likely an attempt to avoid depicting one body-type, gender, or sex as normative. Choosing to do so by depicting *no* sex or gender, however, runs the risk of leaving important questions unanswered for child readers. After all, even very young children—and certainly those of the age delineated by the product listing—understand that the bladder is for excreting liquid waste and that that waste exits the body from somewhere. Choosing not to depict that somewhere calls into question the accuracy and completeness of the whole image, as well as raising more questions than it avoids. If gender and sex are insignificant in STEM, why would it be necessary to deliberately introduce such issues to a text? As discussed with reference to *Rosie Revere* and *We Are the Gardeners,* for a tomboy to "do science" would be to insist that there is no need for girls and women to display clear femininity to counter their involvement in traditionally masculine pursuits. Books such as *The Everything Kids' Science Experiments Book* and the *Human Body Activity Book for Kids*, by refusing to depict any gender or sex coding at all, fail even more explicitly to deliver this seemingly obvious truth. Rather than run the risk of depicting a non-feminine female character engaged in the STEM pursuits, these volumes attempt to deny that the categories of female and feminine exist at all: a fallacy so obvious that even children must surely notice it.

As this brief exploration has indicated, the position of the tomboy in STEM texts for children is far from secure and stable. Whether these texts seek to encourage gender equality in STEM or not, many of them fail to leave the requisite room for gender fluidity that would enable self-identifying tomboys to see themselves reflected in STEM pursuits. In fact, many of these texts seem to demand either gender conformity or gender denial as prerequisites for STEM participation.

How these issues might be positively approached is a difficult question. However, it seems fair to say that STEM-focused non-fiction could stand to learn from the tomboy characters of popular and classical fiction. As discussed by Shawna McDermott, the most problematic aspect of most fictional portrayals of tomboys is not the depiction itself, but tendency to use plot detail—and specifically endings—to "tame" the tomboy figure; lacking any narrative drive toward a socially acceptable ending, this is an error nonfiction STEM texts are in a unique position to be able to avoid. Rather than showing readers engineers with long, feminine eyelashes and anatomy illustrations with suspiciously absent genitals, these texts could show scientists whose sex is evident, but whose gender is absent: characters engaged in scientific inquiry without the need to prove their femininity through the wearing of a dress or an interest in butterflies; characters who can have both breasts and practical jeans, and who can measure accurately or lift heavy objects despite a proclivity for long hair. Is this really so hard to imagine?

BIBLIOGRAPHY

Abate, Michelle Ann. 2008. *Tomboys: A Literary and Cultural History*. Philadelphia: Temple University Press.

Adams, Natalie, Alison Schmitke, and Amy Franklin. 2005. "Tomboys, Dykes, and Girly Girls: Interrogating the Subjectivities of Adolescent Female Athletes." *Women's Studies Quarterly* 33 (1/2): 17–34.

Bailey, J. Michael, Kathleen T. Bechtold, and Sheri A. Berenbaum. 2002. "Who are Tomboys and Why Should We Study Them?" *Archives of Sexual Behavior* 31 (4): 333–41.

Beaty, Andrea, and David Roberts. 2013. *Rosie Revere, Engineer*. New York: Abrams Books.

Bodzin, Alec, and Mike Gehringer. 2001. "Breaking Science Stereotypes." *Science and Children* 38 (4): 36–41.

Carlson, Ashley Lynn. 2018. "Introduction." In *Women in STEM on Television: Critical Essays*, edited by Ashley Lynn Carlson, 1–6. Jefferson: McFarland.

Cheryan, Sapna et al. 2011. "Do Female and Male Role Models Who Embody STEM Stereotypes Hinder Women's Anticipated Success in STEM?" *Social Psychological and Personality Science* 2 (6): 656–64.

Dean-Ruzicka, Rachel. 2016. "Of Scrivens and Sparks: Girl Geniuses in Young Adult Dystopian Fiction." In *Female Rebellion in Young Adult Dystopian Fiction*, edited by Sara K. Day, Miranda A. Green-Barteet, and Amy L. Montz, 51–74. Oxon: Routledge.

Gains, Joanna. 2019. *We Are the Gardeners.* Nashville: HarperCollins Christian Publishing Inc.

Gibson, Lois Rauch. 1988. "Beyond the Apron: Archetypes, Stereotypes, and Alternative Portrayals of Mothers in Children's Literature." *Children's Literature Association Quarterly* 13 (4): 177–81.

Hall, Joanne M. 2008. "Tomboys: Meanings, Marginalization, and Misunderstandings." *Issues in Mental Health Nursing* 29 (6): 555–65.

Hilgenkamp, Kathryn D., and Mary Margaret Livingston. 2002. "Tomboys, Masculine Characteristics, and Self-Ratings of Confidence in Career Success." *Psychological Reports* 90 (3): 743–9.

Knaier, Michelle L. 2019. "What Makes Girls and Boys So Desirable?: STEM Education Beyond Gender Binaries." In *STEM of Desire*: *Queer Theories and Science Education*, edited by Will Letts and Steve Fifield, 209–21. Leiden: Brill Sense.

Kourany, Janet A. 2010. *Philosophy of Science After Feminism*. Oxford: Oxford University Press.

Leach, Melissa. 2007. "Earth Mother Myths and Other Ecofeminist Fables: How A Strategic Notion Rose and Fell." *Development and Change* 38 (1): 67–85.

Letts, Will, and Steve Fifield. 2019. "Prolegomenon: Queer Theories and STEM Education." In *STEM of Desire*: *Queer Theories and Science Education*, edited by Will Letts and Steve Fifield, 3–40. Leiden: Brill Sense.

McDermott, Shawna. 2019. "The Tomboy Tradition: Taming Adolescent Ambition from 1869 to 2018." *Children's Literature Association Quarterly* 44 (2) (Summer): 134–55.

Milne, Catherine. 2011. "A convenient dichotomy: critical eyes on the limits to biological knowledge." *Cultural Studies of Science Education* 6: 305–10.

Nodelman, Perry. 1988. *Word About Pictures: The Narrative Art of Children's Picture Books.* Athens: University of Georgia Press.

Paechter, Carrie, and Sheryl Clark. 2007. "Who Are Tomboys and How Do We Recognise Them?" *Women's Studies International Forum* 30 (4): 342–54.

Reiss, Michael. 1998. "The Representation of Human Sexuality in Some Science Textbooks for 14–16 Year Olds." *Research in Science and Technological Education* 16: 137–49.

Robinson, Tom. 2001. *The Everything Kids' Science Experiments Book: Boil Ice, Float Water, Measure Gravity-Challenge the World Around You!* Avon: Everything Kids.

Stokes, Katie. 2019. *The Human Body Activity Book for Kids: Hands-On Learning for Grades 4–7.* Emeryville: Rockridge Press.

"Tomboy." 1989. *The Oxford English Dictionary* (2nd ed.).

Tuana, Nancy, ed. 1989. *Feminism and Science*. Bloomington: Indiana University Press.

PART III

THE SMALL SCREEN: THE TOMBOY ON TELEVISION

Chapter 6

"Whoever I Want to Be"

Tomboy and/as Femme Fatale in Marvel's Agent Carter

Cara McClintock-Walsh

The image of the tomboy does not immediately leap to mind when considering the female figures who occupy the Marvel Cinematic Universe (MCU). With the exception of Captain Marvel, who does move within the typical contours of the tomboy, most of the female characters and superheroes of the MCU skew more closely to the archetype of the femme fatale, a position that seems diametrically opposed to the qualities, strategies, and values of the tomboy. However, several films and television series that comprise the MCU upset this dichotomy, and instead illustrate the ways in which we could understand the figure of the femme fatale as an extension of the gendered ethos represented by the tomboy. I will focus my attention on the figure of Peggy Carter, who appears as a pivotal character in the Captain America movies and who is the titular character of the series *Agent Carter*. Both the Captain America films and *Agent Carter* deploy storylines and characters that challenge and undo the gender expectations underlying figures who, at first glance, appear to be hypermasculine and hyperfeminine (Captain America, for instance, despite his spectacular physique and desirability, is revealed to be sexually inexperienced, if not a virgin; he also begins his career not on the battlefield but as the lone man on a stage full of showgirls). Agent Peggy Carter, in her various roles as codebreaker, agent of the Strategic Scientific Reserve, and co-founder of S.H.I.E.L.D. (Strategic Homeland Intervention, Enforcement, and Logistics Division), is one such figure in the ways that she charts women's historical efforts to enter the workforce during and after wartime, but she also, by embodying and slipping between various female identities and roles (tomboy, femme fatale, working woman), encourages the audience to see them not as separate identities but instead as part of the same sexual strategy. During the second season of *Agent Carter*, the episode titled "Smoke and Mirrors" explores Peggy's backstory but also the origin story of her nemesis, Whitney Frost. Compellingly, this episode reveals that both women, hero and villain, began their lives as tomboys: Peggy in England, dressed as a knight rescuing her doll from a tree, and Whitney as a young boyish girl in the American South who finds within the identity of the tomboy the freedom to experiment with scientific ambitions and the ability to avoid her mother's fate as a woman ruled and degraded by men's sexual demands. In *Agent Carter*, the symbol of the tomboy has the power to collapse dichotomies: between masculine and feminine but also between hero (Peggy) and villain (Whitney). It is the sexual ethos of the tomboy, uncovered in the linked origin stories of the female hero and female villain, that remains with both figures and ultimately manifests in their subversive attempts at self-invention. Indeed, both Peggy and Whitney's initial identification as tomboys allows each woman to become, throughout her life, "whoever [she] want[s] to be," as Whitney memorably says at the close of the episode. In this chapter, I will first explore the ways in which the MCU in general and the Captain America storylines in particular destabilize gender roles; then, I will show how *Agent Carter* deploys the archetype of the tomboy both as a general symbol of sexual subversion but also as a gendered ethos and energy that later manifests itself, surprisingly, in the figures of the double agent and the femme fatale.

CIVIL WAR: MARVEL, MASCULINITY, AND THE QUESTION OF GENDER

Though Marvel films were initially invested—literally and figurately, economically and thematically—in an exploration of masculinity and masculine crisis, they have developed an increasing commitment to a diverse and varied representation of women's roles both within their films and within the Marvel studio system. A franchise grounded in the story arcs of two (apparently) hypermasculine, white, male characters—Iron Man and Captain America—over time expanded its universe to include one of the first superhero films both named for a female character and directed by a woman (*Captain Marvel*). In 2018, Kevin Feige, president of Marvel Entertainment, articulated a vision for the future of the franchise that grounds itself in a commitment to women and people of color. He assured audiences and the press, in advance of the release of *Captain Marvel*, the twentieth film in the franchise and the first directed by a woman, that "I cannot promise that all 20 Marvel movies will have female directors but a heck of a lot of them will" and that "diversity is something that's necessary to be able to continue to tell stories."[1] *Black Widow* (2021) will follow the example of *Captain Marvel,* as a film both named for a female superhero and helmed by a female director, and two upcoming series/films will transfer male superhero story arcs to female leads (the upcoming *Thor: Love and Thunder* will feature Dr. Jane Foster as the possessor of Thor's hammer and power, and Peggy Carter, in an upcoming *What If. . .?* series, will become Captain Britain in the place of Steve Rogers's Captain America). A study of the progression of Marvel films reveals not only more female characters, but more complex roles for women within the films. Whereas the first establishing films of the series (*Iron Man, Captain America: The First Avenger, Thor*) feature few female roles, by the end of the franchise's third phase, the Marvel Universe is populated by female characters who speak more, act more, and occupy more pivotal, complex roles. A brief rollcall makes this point clear: Dr. Jane Foster, Agent Peggy Carter, Okoye, Shuri, Black Widow, Scarlet Witch, Gamora, Nebula, Valkyrie, Pepper Potts/Rescue, Wasp, Dr. Van Dyne, and Captain Marvel are only a partial list of rounded, active female characters in the Marvel Cinematic Universe.

The increased visibility and variety of female roles in Marvel films mirrors a similar pattern in Marvel comic books. In her exhaustive study entitled, "Analyzing Female Gender Roles in Marvel Comics from the Silver Age (1960) to the Present," Katherine J. Murphy uses statistical analysis to reveal patterns of gender representation. Her study, which encompassed "68 Marvel titles for a total of 788 Marvel comic books broken down by decade from 1960 to 2014," revealed clearly that representations of women in Marvel Comics became both "less stereotypical and more equitable" during that time period, along all seven lines of quantifiable measurement, which include "comic book cover art, the Bechdel Test, storyline, occupation, balance of power, female sexualization, and violence against women" (2016, 1). Gender representation became more varied, active, and complex across all categories of measurement during this time, culminating in the storylines of the 2010s.[2] While I will not spend time discussing the Marvel comics, this shows an ideological shift that spans the Marvel Universe in terms of print, film, and as a corporation. If, according to Bradford Wright, "Just as each generation writes its own history, each reads its own comic books," we might also say that each generation gets its own Marvel films—and the current generation of Marvel films represents a commitment to a representation of women and female power that can only be called disruptive (2001, xiii).

FROM IRONMAN TO FAMILY MAN: CHALLENGING THE HYPERMASCULINITY OF SUPERHEROES

To credit the Marvel franchise with a progressive, complex portrayal of gender and gender roles might seem surprising at first, especially considering where the franchise begins. *Iron Man*, released in 2008, follows the story of Tony Stark, a once-wunderkind now greying at the temples and a self-proclaimed, "Billionaire, Playboy, Philanthropist." The opening of *Iron Man*, and by extension the entire MCU, showcases Tony in all of his exaggerated masculine dimensions: when we first see him, he rides in an armored vehicle, neat scotch in hand, as he tosses banter back and forth with the soldiers who will deploy the armaments he and his family are responsible for designing, creating, and selling; Stark's bonhomie and casual sexual predation demonstrate that he is unmolested by the role he and his family play in the military industrial complex. Stark is, at this point, not a character but a stereotype: a predictable playboy whose cavalier attitude toward his own charm and toward women as a whole threatens to reduce the film and the franchise to a dull and indulgent cinematic recycling of gender stereotypes. Stark's hypermasculinity is on display in the opening moments of *Iron Man*: Tony compulsively flirts with any woman who crosses his path, even if she is a soldier covered head to toe in a military field uniform and tactical armor. Immediately after he praises the female soldier's cheekbones, he brags about his recent sexual conquest of twin sisters . . . and at this moment his hypermasculinity is violently disrupted and permanently altered when the vehicle he is traveling in is hit by an IED and he is subsequently wounded by a weapon of his own making (literally, since it bears the imprimatur of Stark Industries).

Although *Iron Man* briefly flashes back to this hyper-sexed, caricatured version of Tony,[3] the film—and indeed the rest of the film franchise as a whole—makes patently clear that from the moment Tony Stark is injured by his family's own weapons of war, his job is to denounce the destructive and lethal legacy passed on by his father and instead turn toward peacebuilding. The rest of the *Iron Man* films show Tony Stark gradually (and, at times, reluctantly) shedding the "playboy" part of his title and becoming instead a philanthropist who eschews war and builds peace ("Peace would bankrupt me," he glibly says in the first *Iron Man* film, yet by *The Avengers* [2012] he is turning his attention toward questions of ecological sustainability). His gestures and creations become protective rather than destructive, more maternal than paternal.[4] If Tony laments that he "never got to say goodbye to [his] father" in this film, the subsequent *Iron Man* films (through *Endgame*) find him confronting, forgiving, and eventually releasing the man whose legacy of violence he must reject. Tony's trajectory is one in which he recognizes and abandons his hypermasculinity as destructive; for Tony Stark, fathers and father-figures (like Obadiah Slane, his paternal stand-in and eventual enemy in this film) are figures to be overcome, not emulated. Ashley Sufflé Robinson argues in her essay "We Are Iron Man: Tony Stark, Iron Man, and American Identity in the Marvel Cinematic Universe's Phase One Films," that Tony Stark "is a superhero that embodied Americans' frustration with their country" (in his original comic book incarnation, a figure who "helped readers wrestle with American identity during the politically contentious Vietnam era") (2018, 824). If this is the case, the final iteration of Stark in *Endgame* helps Americans express a frustration with a country that repeatedly, destructively, and exclusively concentrates power in the hands of men.

Indeed, the latest film in the franchise (as of this publication) and the last in which Stark appears, *Endgame*, suggests that Stark's legacy will be carried on not by sons, but in large part by his wife and daughter. It is Stark's daughter Morgan who finds (and dons the helmet of) the mech suit he is in the process of constructing for his wife Pepper Potts, and Pepper, at a key moment in the battle against Thanos, dons and wields the suit that will transform her from quiet-wife-reading-a-book-on-composting to a superhero in her own right (called "Rescue"). Indeed, Pepper Potts's trajectory alone illustrates nicely the *Iron Man* films' renunciation of hypermasculinity and the embrace of increasing female power: Pepper begins the films as Tony's helpmate (*Iron Man*), becomes CEO of his multinational conglomerate (*Iron Man 2*), rescues Tony from destruction by harnessing the power of one of Tony's own suits (*Iron Man 3*), and finally becomes a superhero (*Endgame*).Tony's story—and the movement of the entire MCU—reverses the male-gendered appropriation of power and, instead, releases power and legacies of power into the hands of women. It is not surprising, then, to find that the other superhero who grounds the MCU, Captain America, is influenced and shaped by the series' first tomboy: Agent Peggy Carter.

PERFORMANCE PROBLEMS: CAPTAIN AMERICA, LEARNED MASCULINITY, AND THE TOMBOY TRADITION

Judith Butler famously claimed, in *Gender Trouble*, that gender is both performative and constitutive; that an "essence of gender is manufactured through a sustained set of acts, posited through the gendered stylization of the body" (1990, xv). Tony Stark of the first *Iron Man* movie embodies Butler's sense of performative masculinity; indeed, he is the consummate performer, one who enacts his hypermasculinity through his performances on stages, in boardrooms, and in bedrooms, as well as through a set of cultivated and coordinated characteristics. His famous *cri de coeur* that ends the first film—"I am Ironman"—stands as a declaration of a successfully constituted and synthesized masculine identity. Steve Rogers (aka Captain America), on the other hand, is a terrible performer, a man who longs to physically embody and enact his own internal qualities of patriotism and idealism, but who repeatedly and spectacularly fails to do so. To use Butler's language, Rogers cannot "produce through certainly bodily acts" the "internal feature[s]" that he feels constitute him (1990, xvi). Indeed, Rogers cannot enact his masculinity—crucially, he cannot *become* Captain America convincingly—until he meets Agent Peggy Carter, whose tomboy ethos and identity is first hinted at in her tutelage of Steve Rogers. Before Agent Carter's backstory as a tomboy has been revealed, by way of the television series *Agent Carter* (2015–2016), Peggy Carter performs two of the tomboy's lesser-known characteristic functions in *Captain America: The First Avenger* (2011): she first gains access to spheres of masculine power and privilege; and she then finds her counterpart in an effeminate man, and through her ability to navigate male spaces teaches *him* how to perform his own masculinity successfully. In this case, the feminized man Agent Carter finds and tutors is none other than Steve Rogers, who requires her guiding influence in order to become Captain America.

Peggy Carter acts as an instrumental character in Captain America's development throughout the MCU: she is his officer, his love interest, his lost possibility, and, through a trick of time travel in *Avengers: Endgame*, his final, long-awaited choice (a close-up of Steve Rogers and Peggy Carter kissing is the shot that ends the entire arc of the first twenty-three MCU films). Peggy Carter also emerges as notable among the pantheon of female characters in the MCU because of the extensive development of her character. Although Carter's appearances in MCU films after *Captain America: The First Avenger* are brief, ultimately, she emerges as perhaps the most well-developed female character within the MCU owing to the television series *Agent Carter*, which ran for two seasons. Although it might seem more obvious to discuss Captain Marvel or Black Widow when examining the figures of the tomboy and the femme fatale, respectively, neither of those characters enjoys the depth of development that Peggy Carter does (this is likely to change with the release of a Black Widow film in 2021, and with any future Captain Marvel films). Carter is not, at first, obviously a tomboy figure: although in a uniform for most of *Captain America: The First Avenger*, she cuts a distinctly feminine form, evoking an Alberto Vargas pin-up girl more readily than a stereotypical tomboy. Although audiences will not learn of Carter's backstory as a tomboy until many years later, in the spinoff TV series *Agent Carter*, Peggy Carter performs and embodies two compelling aspects of tomboyism during her inaugural appearance in the MCU.

In the introduction to her engaging and comprehensive study *Tomboys: A Literary and Cultural History*, Michelle Ann Abate enumerates the qualities of tomboyism that tend to remain stable throughout her otherwise various and shifting cultural iterations. They include "a proclivity for outdoor play (especially athletic), a feisty independent spirit, and a tendency to don masculine clothing" (2008, xvi). Other qualities of the tomboy, according to Abate, include "physical strength, emotional fortitude and intellectual cunning. . . [and] frequent harangues against sentimentality and submissiveness" (2008, 11). Scholars Samantha Holland and Julie Harpin, in their essay "Who is the 'girly'-girl? Tomboys, hyperfemininity, and gender," add to this list the observation "that the tomboy encompasses a sense of freedom, mobility and physicality" (2015, 296). While all of these traits are routinely attached to the figure of the tomboy, Abate expands upon this "Tomboy Index" and includes two slightly lesser known identifying characteristics of the tomboy: the power to (often temporarily but occasionally permanently) enter and occupy otherwise exclusively male spaces; and "the tendency for tomboys to form close relationships with effeminate male characters" and to educate them on how to *become* men (2008, xvi). It is these less common tomboy traits that first suggest that Peggy Carter's outwardly glamorous, sexualized appearance belies the tomboy ethos that informs and directs her character.

Carter makes her debut in *Captain America: The First Avenger* as an officer with the Strategic Scientific Reserve (SSR), notable as the only female officer in its hypermasculine, military ranks (other women appear in the military, but all in the role of secretaries or office workers). As Traci Craig and Jessica LaCroix note in their essay "Tomboy as Protective Identity," "tomboy identity can gain women limited privilege to spaces for which masculinity is an unspoken requirement" and that the tomboy should be understood as "an agentic identity that allows girls and women . . . protected access to male privileged spaces, activities, and conversations" (2011, 450). Carter certainly enjoys this freedom of movement and identification offered by the tomboy ethos—but her character takes this a step further. Specifically, Carter's position as an *officer* in the SSR reveals the ways in which she is doubly iconoclastic: she has gained access to the military, itself a notoriously male-dominated and homosocial field, but she has also risen through the ranks of an inner sanctum of the military (the SSR, which is, as one of the commanding officers elaborates, "an Allied effort made up of the best minds in the free world" whose goal is "to create the best Army in history" headed by "a new breed of Super Soldiers"). When eulogized by her great niece in *Captain America: Civil War* (2016), we learn that Peggy Carter sustained a career as a master of "diplomacy and espionage at a time when no one wanted to see a woman succeed in either." Carter's career trajectory finds further definition in *Endgame* (2019), the final of the twenty-three films that currently constitute the MCU, when, during a time travel sequence, we learn that Carter moved on from the SSR to eventually co-found S.H.I.E.L.D. The length of her military service and the consistent upward trajectory of her career in espionage also mark her as unique: as Craig, LaCroix, and other scholars of tomboyism point out, even tomboys often enjoy only limited access to realms of masculine power and privilege. Craig and LaCroix aver that "the temporary nature of the protections provided to tomboys undermines the ability of tomboys to truly transcend the binary gender system" (2011, 450). Carter, then, acts as an example of a tomboy whose access to privileged male spaces persists,[5] but only because of her own deft maneuverings within a resolutely and abidingly sexist workplace, a point I will return to later. Carter is an example of a tomboy untamed, a figure who does not outgrow this identity but who finds her entire life directed and fueled by the ethos found in tomboyhood.

While Carter's presence in these otherwise exclusively masculine spaces acts as the first clue to her underlying identity as a tomboy, over the course of the film, Carter enacts another narrative of tomboyhood: she finds and befriends a weak male outsider and tutors him on how to become a man. Carter and Rogers are linked because neither of them fits into the military they are trying to serve, and both because of gender: she as a woman, and he as a man who is physically weak to the point of disability (not even his helmet fits him; it slides around on his head as it would on a child's). Their shared outsidership finds voice as they ride together in the back of a cab through New York City. Rogers narrates his landscape of persistent physical humiliation, pointing out every alleyway in which he was beaten up. Carter, as the only woman in every workspace she has occupied, relates to Rogers: "I know a little of what that's like. To have every door shut in your face." Rogers then confesses to his own virginity (using the metaphor of never having danced before because he is "waiting for the right partner"), a virginity that likely remains intact throughout the entire franchise (even after his transformation, other Avengers chide Rogers for being sexually inexperienced, even to the point of being a bad kisser).[6] Their conversation reveals the ways in which Agent Carter and Steve Rogers are both excluded from realms of power because they are *not men* (Carter) or not "real men" (Rogers).

As his officer in the SSR, Peggy Carter trains Steve Rogers during boot camp when he is physically weak but morally exemplary, and again after his transformation into Captain America. While Carter's role as his boot camp officer is important, her tutelage takes on subtler and more profound dimensions after Rogers undergoes his dramatic physical transformation from eager weakling into Captain America, paragon of patriotic masculinity. Indeed, the sense of Rogers not being a "real man" persists even after his startling physical transformation from "90-pound asthmatic" Steve Rogers to the embodiment of physical perfection and desirability that is Captain America. Rogers expects that once he receives the Super Serum he will be instantly deployed to the battlefield, where he can demonstrate his newly acquired physical prowess and finally enact his patriotic ideals in a meaningful manner. But instead, Captain America begins his life not on the battlefield directing troops but as a character on the stage, backed by a patriotic kick-line of showgirls. He is appropriated as a symbol that can be deployed "on the most important battlefield of the war": the marketplace of ideas and public opinion. At first, this newly minted, abundantly muscled "Captain" America is Captain in name alone: he is a character, not an officer, existing somewhere between the realms of sex symbol and symbol of patriotism, and launched as a marketing ploy to sell war bonds. Here Captain America's kinship with Peggy Carter becomes even clearer in that they emerge as gendered inverses of one another: she is the only woman in a hypermasculine workplace (the military), while he is the only man on stage with a bevy of showgirls.

Despite his new very masculine contours, Captain America remains feminized and recognized as essentially feminine by other men. Audiences on the home front pack theatres to watch Captain America, the stage character, punch out a wily Adolph Hitler, yet when Captain America takes the stage and performs the same act in front of deployed troops during a USO tour, he is repeatedly hooted down by soldiers and derisively referred to as "sweetheart" and "Tinker Bell." Enlisted men treat Rogers not as a man but as a shirker, and a poor substitute for the dancing girls that support his act. If gender is performative, Captain America, despite his physical transformation, is, at this point, still understood not as a man but as a "chorus girl" (a title his commanding officer gives him repeatedly). When Rogers laments his situation to Peggy Carter, he confesses, "You know for the longest time I dreamed about coming overseas, and being on the front lines, serving my country. I finally got everything I wanted . . . and I'm wearing tights." His masculinity is only partial, or incompletely performed; if one end of the spectrum is fascist masculinity, a fate to be avoided, Captain America cannot author a correlative vision of masculinity that is convincing to the audience he most desires to convince. It is at this point in the narrative that Agent Carter intervenes and redirects Rogers's defeatism into a clear and direct plan of action.

When "Captain" Rogers, laid low by the demeaning catcalls lobbed at him by the troops at the USO show, sits morosely in the rain in his Captain America costume, sketching a representation of himself as nothing more than a trained monkey, Agent Carter, in her military uniform, refuses to let him wallow in self-pity and, instead, shows him the way to become Captain America, the war hero, instead of "Captain" America, the stage star. Whereas

Rogers laments that he has only been given two options to serve his country, as a "lab rat" or as a glorified pitch man, Peggy Carter not only reminds him that "You were meant for more than this," but also provides him with the necessary intel for the mission that will take him from the stage and onto the battlefield, hence initiating the second part of his transformation into the heroic Captain America. Once Agent Carter tells Rogers about a troop of soldiers trapped behind enemy lines, he resolves to rescue the survivors (including, he hopes, his childhood companion Bucky Barnes). Their shared outsider status simultaneously causes the commanding officer to reject their plan and ultimately allows Peggy and Steve to conduct this rescue mission on their own. The colonel silences Peggy when she is about to offer her plan for this rescue mission and dismisses Steve entirely because he is not a soldier but a "chorus girl" or, alternately, "the star spangled man with the plan." Because they are dismissed as incompetent, feminized others, they are able to operate outside of the colonel's gaze and devise their own successful plan to rescue the remaining members of the 107th. As Michelle Abate notes in her study, "tomboys often help masculinize effeminate boys: they teach their weak counterparts to be adventurous, assert themselves and even fight. By the close of [these narratives], the previously sissy boy has been transformed by his tomboy friend into a strong and even powerful man" (2008, xvii). In this instance, Peggy provides Steve with both the mission (she is the one who informs him of the stranded troops) and the means by which he can accomplish it: she enlists the help of Howard Stark, who flies them over enemy lines and drops Steve at his mission point. She directs, arms, and equips him for his mission, and later in the film, even helps him choose (and test: she takes aim and shoots at him when she catches another woman kissing him as a way to express the gratitude of the nation) his iconic shield.

We know this is a transitional moment in Steve's development from "showgirl" to superhero by his very dress: still in his fairly outlandish Captain America costume (complete with winged hood, red Peter Pan boots, and tights), he pulls the slacks of a military uniform over his costume, and tops this off with the only helmet he can find: not a military-issued one but one that belongs to a chorus girl. In other words, as Captain America arms himself for battle, his shield, shirt, and helmet are still part of costume, not a uniform. He, himself, while on his rescue mission, slips between roles; when the soldiers of the 107th see this hybridized hero who still resembles a character more than a soldier, they ask, baffled, "What are you supposed to be?" At this moment, Captain America is stranded between performative identities: he is not yet convincing as a man in the military, yet he feels painfully out of place on the stage among women, where he functions as a symbol and not a hero. He reveals his unstable position between gendered identities during the rescue mission itself; when the skeptical soldier ask this curious figure if he knows what he is doing, Rogers naively and earnestly replies, "Yeah. I've knocked out Adolph Hitler over 200 times," an answer in which he conflates the real threat on the battlefield with the scripted threat he faced on stage and screen by an actor playing Hitler. This conflation of real and fantasy, "Captain America" the character with Captain Steve Rogers the soldier, reveals his transitory state between feminized man and masculinized hero. Although he occasionally slips between his performative identity as a "showgirl" and his developing identity as a hero, Rogers is able to demonstrate his tactical and physical prowess in a way that finally gains him legitimacy among military men and become a fully realized version of Captain America, a figure who now successfully performs his masculinity to all audiences. He achieves this unified masculine identity under the guiding influence of Peggy Carter, a woman whose identity as a tomboy has allowed her access to the masculine world Steve cannot access alone. She models for him what it means to operate in a masculine world, and more specifically she demonstrates how to overcome barriers the masculine world erects for outsiders like them. The closing credits of this film project the image of Rosie the Riveter over Hayley Atwell's name, thereby further announcing to audiences that they have met the franchise's first and most well-developed tomboy.

AGENT CARTER: TOMBOY, DOUBLE AGENT, FEMME FATALE

The series *Agent Carter*, set in 1946 after Cap's death and the Allied Victory, dramatizes Peggy Carter's challenges as a postwar career woman whose desire to continue her successful career in the military contravenes the nation's desire to restore gender roles and hence, pre-war order. Much of the first season of *Agent Carter* juxtaposes Peggy's adventures in espionage with her life in the office, in which her male co-workers make every effort to relegate her to the role of coffee fetcher and lunch server. In the show's first episode, the SSR office receives an all-hands-on-deck call, but when Peggy responds to this along with her co-workers, she is told to cover the phones while the male agents strategize. Her relationship with Captain America—a relationship, it should be recalled, in which *she* trained *him*—is reduced to its imagined sexual dimensions; her coworkers refer to her as "Captain America's . . . liaison" and her formerly valued knowledge is reduced to sexual innuendo ("She's used to working under a Captain"). Peggy laments the difference between her life during the war and afterwards when she wistfully recalls that "during the war I had a sense of purpose, responsibility . . ."; although the nature of her work remains the same, her acceptance in the male sphere of work has been revoked. *Agent Carter* shows the ways in which the tomboy represents not only a gendered figure but also a strategy that allows women like Peggy to enter masculine spaces, pursue and exploit ambiguous alliances, and subvert male power. The essentially and thoroughly transgressive power of the tomboy grounds Carter and other women in the series in an ethos that prizes defiance and individuality as its central tenets.

In the second season of *Agent Carter*, the episode "Smoke and Mirrors" reveals the origin story of both Peggy Carter and her nemesis, Whitney Frost. Peggy—British, and the series' hero; Whitney—American, and the series' villain, both begin life as tomboys. Separated geographically and culturally, their shared identity as tomboys suggests a common ability to challenge and disrupt gendered societal boundaries. The episode opens with an adolescent Peggy Carter dressed as a knight and riding a hobbyhorse in a moment of play with her brother. She gallops around her backyard, sword drawn, and announces her mission to "Slay [the] dragon and save the princess." When her brother interferes with her fantasy world, she tackles him to the ground and straddles him in an effort to retrieve her weapon. At this moment, she is admonished by her mother, who tells her that "one of these days you're going to have to start behaving like a lady." This scene cuts to modern day Peggy, in a laboratory, heartily and sloppily eating a sandwich while she talks to an African American colleague. The sly and playful juxtaposition of these scenes show that Peggy remains, underneath her red lipstick and pin-up girl looks, a tomboy who has not learned her gendered place in the world, who recognizes and feeds her own hungers—be it for food, sex, adventure, success, recognition—both as a youth and as a woman. For Peggy, her identity as a tomboy, both in her adolescent form and as a grown woman, allows her access to male spheres of work, culture, and power. Although Peggy's nemesis, Whitney Frost, also adopts the strategies of her childhood tomboyism throughout her life, she will follow a different trajectory altogether.

The episode shifts in time to Broxton, Oklahoma in 1920, where Whitney Frost (born Agnes Cully, later dismissively dubbed by one of Peggy's colleagues as "an Okie . . . kind of like the heartland's Marie Curie") reaches pre-adolescence in her mother's house, a household precariously balanced on the ragged edge of poverty and propriety. In this scene, young Whitney (then Agnes) deconstructs and reconstructs a radio at the family's kitchen table. In a household without a father, Whitney/Agnes takes it upon herself to fix the radio in order to please her mother; this is also an outlet for her budding scientific and mechanical prowess. Whitney/Agnes's mother, rather than evincing pleasure in her daughter's obvious gifts, is instead displeased by her daughter's tomboyishness, and admonishes her to "clean up" and "be sweet" for "Uncle" Bud, a man who preys on Whitney's mother's financial desperation by offering her money for sex. Witness to her mother's sexual degradation at the hands of this man, Whitney refuses to "be sweet" to Uncle

Series heroine Peggy Carter (figure 6.1, top, played here by Gabriella Graves) and series villain Whitney Frost (figure 6.2, bottom, played here by Ivy George) share a twinned point of tomboy origin, which reframes much of what we know about these characters.

Bud when he tries to cajole a smile out of her. She instead rejects the call to please the man who demands sexual favors for money and tells him she will not smile "because I'm thinking." Whitney/Agnes refuses to don the mask of acceptable femininity. She demands that Uncle Bud return her pencil so she can work out her formulas, and, for her efforts, earns the title "strange" from both Uncle Bud and her own mother. (We might substitute *queer*, with its lexical challenge to compulsory heterosexuality, for *strange* in this instance.) The radio that Whitney/Agnes repaired with her skills and knowledge ultimately is not used to please her mother; instead, young Whitney/Agnes turns up the volume to drown out the sounds of her mother prostituting herself to the man who demands feminine acquiescence.

As with Peggy's mother, Whitney's mother objects to her daughter's identity as tomboy; in this case, Whitney does not need to learn to act "like a lady," as Peggy does, but instead must learn to make herself sexually desirable and sexually available to men in order to secure an existence, however unstable. Whitney's mother does not encourage her daughter to use her intellectual gifts to escape this situation; she instead insists that Whitney learn her ways in order to attract and hold male attention because her livelihood depends on it. Whereas Peggy's role as a tomboy taught her how to access realms of male influence, Whitney turns to tomboyhood in search of what Traci Craig and Jessica LaCroix call a "protective identity" (2011). Tomboyhood forestalls the commitment to heterosexuality; as Holland and Harpin note in their sociological study of tomboys and their mothers, "tomboy identities . . . kept them [girls] 'safe' from, and unaware of, the (hetero)sexualized attention that hyper-femininity could attract" (2015, 305). In the words of one mother involved with their study, tomboyhood "kept her a girl for longer" (2015, 305). Whitney craves this protection from the predatory sexuality that her mother attracts and is exploited by. Left without a parent to protect her from the unwelcome attentions of men, she constructs her own role as a tomboy as a shell, a shield against the attentions and sexual expectations of men.

As with Peggy's origin story, Whitney's then jumps to her present day, in which Agnes Cully has been transformed into Whitney Frost, movie star and covert mad scientist. In this scene, juxtaposed with the first part of her origin story, Whitney's current situation reveals how she has learned to camouflage her knowledge and skill underneath her cultivated female beauty. Present-day Whitney, like her young tomboy iteration, engages in scientific experiments (she is the unacknowledged and invisible brains behind Isodyne Industries, an atomic energy company, and successfully contributed inventions to the Allies during World War II), but she does so in her dressing room surrounded by the extravagant gowns and feminine accoutrements of a movie star (it bears mentioning that the radio from her childhood rests on her vanity). Whitney, like Peggy, remains grounded in her tomboy identity beneath her glamorous exterior; she has learned to disguise her talents and ambitions, deemed masculine, under a carefully constructed feminine exterior. Although neither Peggy nor Whitney maintains the look of a tomboy into adulthood, their career trajectories, personal ambitions, and sexual strategies belie the persistence of a type of tomboy ethos; indeed, their personalities cohere around the trope of the tomboy. Peggy's and Whitney's shared origin as tomboys is richly evocative, and indeed reframes much of what we know about these characters. The ability to traverse gendered identities, learned in her childhood as a tomboy, now informs the way Carter can, does, and must operate in a male workspace; indeed, for Peggy Carter, the tomboy is the ideal proving ground for her future as both a woman in the sexist workplace and a double agent. For Whitney Frost, her youthful origin as a tomboy translates into a lifelong desire for power, individuality, and a life free from predation; her glamorous visage as a screen star masks her tomboy origin while simultaneously transforming it into a similarly disruptive figure of female power: the femme fatale.

If one of the tomboy's key tenets is her mutability, it follows that the ethos embodied in this figure would find expression in other gendered embodiments of female defiance. Rebecca Jennings, in her study *Tomboys and Bachelor Girls: A Lesbian History of Post-War Britain 1945–1971*, argues that gendered identities such as the tomboy, bachelor girl, and career woman "were situational and contingent, enabling individual women to alternate between a number of sexual identity models in distinct locations and different times" (2007, 2). Michelle Ann Abate agrees, noting that the figure of the tomboy is not "singular [or] static. . . [but instead] unstable and dynamic . . . changing with the political, social and economic events of its historical era" (2008, xii). Indeed, much of Abate's study shows how the iconoclastic energies attributed to tomboyism find themselves reborn in other disruptive female figures such as the New Woman (2008, 57) and the flapper (2008, 120); tomboyism then becomes both a precursor to these figures as well as a "code of conduct" transmitted through these iterations of female individuality and power. The second season of *Agent Carter* dramatizes this transformation of tomboy into femme fatale, and then shows the way in which this transformation of the tomboy actually answers one of the key critiques of this figure: that of tomboy taming. The characters in this season of *Agent Carter* suggest that perhaps the tomboy is not tamed after all: instead, this ethos reemerges and reasserts itself as a controlling code of conduct in other embodiments of defiant femininity, such as the double agent and femme fatale. What I suggest here is that the femme fatale should be understood as a strategy of female rebellion and independence related to and rooted in the figure of the tomboy.

Many scholars who study the figure of the tomboy point out the tomboy's temporary nature. Holland and Harpin, in "Who is the 'girly' girl? Tomboys, hyper-femininity and gender," note that "tomboy behavior is portrayed as a common aspect of pre-pubescent childhood . . . but beyond puberty tomboy behavior often becomes seen as rebellious or even pathological" (2015, 297). Shawna McDermott, in "The Tomboy Tradition: Taming Adolescent

Ambition from 1869 to 2018," sees the tomboy as a figure that ultimately fails women and girls because her power to defy gender norms is always temporary; eventually, McDermott asserts, society tames even the boldest tomboy until she conforms to compulsory heterosexuality and traditional gender roles: McDermott writes that across time and genre, "disparate . . . texts . . . consistently result in the abandonment of adolescent ambition and the capitulation to gendered normativity" (2019, 137). She calls this tendency "tomboy taming" and argues that this act of taming is so common as to be an essential part of the tomboy trope. McDermott shows, through an analysis of figures as diverse as Katniss Everdeen in *The Hunger Games* and Regina George in *Mean Girls*, that although the tomboy enables stories of "desperately earnest girls who queerly desire futures beyond what their culture prescribes for them," the end of the tomboy story "inevitably show[s] them tamed into a conventional version of femininity" (2019, 138). Even Jo March, the ur-tomboy, finds herself yoked to the uninspiring Frederick Bhaer and running a school for boys at the close of *Little Women*. How radical is the tomboy, then, if her rebellion is fleeting? McDermott calls the tomboy's promise both "powerful and deceptive . . . This genre has long been invested in showing girls what they could have and then convincing them that heteronormativity is better" (2019, 148). McDermott chillingly suggests that society itself, in its acceptance and promulgation of tomboy stories, does not celebrate female rebellion but instead codifies female rebellion as harmless play. She presents the possibility that the tomboy, with all of her rebellious potential, is not a figure of rebellion at all.

Agent Carter (and, to some degree, the Marvel franchise as a whole) restores the tomboy's defiant possibilities by suggesting a different narrative. The rest of "Smoke and Mirrors" reveals that, in the case of Peggy Carter and Whitney Frost, the tomboy does not go gentle into that good heterosexual future; she does not age out of or abandon the identity that allowed for her youthful defiance and self-expression. After we are introduced to Peggy Carter's and Whitney Frost's twinned point of tomboy origin, the episode extends the tomboy's narrative to several key developmental moments when Peggy and Whitney face challenges to their tomboy ethos and ultimately have to choose whether to preserve or abandon it. Not surprisingly, these moments involve the competing pressures to marry or to pursue careers. In Peggy's case, her story moves from the tomboyhood she enjoyed in adolescence to a scene set at Bletchley Park in 1940, where Peggy worked as a codebreaker. As the scene opens, Peggy receives two proposals simultaneously: a ring from her fiancé, and a letter from her supervisor inviting her to become a member of the Special Operations Executive (SOE). Should she choose to marry, she would fulfill the gendered expectations of a woman's narrative and leave her tomboy ethos behind as a youthful indulgence or a phase to be outgrown. Should she choose to join and train under the SOE, a "new war division spearheaded by Winston Churchill himself," she would move from the role of codebreaker in an office to an agent in the field, to be trained in "irregular warfare. Espionage, sabotage, guerilla tactics." This option would allow her to extend her story as a tomboy, from adolescent knight to World War II codebreaker to active agent, a role in which her invisibility as a woman would work in her favor. Mr. Edwards, her supervisor, explains that her sex actually works in her favor for this job because "resistance networks all over Europe need people who won't draw attention walking down the street. They need women."

Although Peggy initially hesitates, deferring the decision to the authority of her fiancé, she ultimately chooses the path that honors her origin as a tomboy, and she does so precisely *because* she is reminded of this origin. Peggy's story continues at her engagement party in Hampstead in 1940, where she sits uneasily between the influence of her brother (a soldier on the front lines of World War II and the person who nominated her for the SOE position) and her fiancé (an officer operating out of the safety of the home office who glibly declares that "a boring life is a privilege"). Peggy's brother Michael acknowledges and celebrates her origin as a tomboy by nominating her for the SOE, a point he elaborates on when he tells Peggy that "This [marriage] isn't what you want . . . [You want] the same thing you've wanted since you were a little girl. A life of adventure." When Peggy objects and declares that "I've grown up. My dreams changed," Michael quickly replies, "No, you've just let everyone else drum them out of you . . . Don't worry what other people think . . . Stop pretending to be someone that you're not." Despite the wave in her hair, her deep red lipstick, and her form-fitting dress, Peggy's identity as a tomboy is recognized by her brother Michael as constant and ascendant; Michael sees Peggy's childhood self not as a phase to be outgrown but instead as an expression of her abiding selfhood. Later in this episode, Peggy learns of her brother Michael's death in battle as she is trying on her wedding dress, seemingly having chosen the path the world expects of her. But this news does not cause her to run into the safety marriage would offer her; Peggy instead honors her brother's memory by taking off her engagement ring and picking up the invitation to join the SOE. When Michael nominates Peggy for the SOE position, he acknowledges her tomboyishness as essential to her being and simultaneously attempts to save her from heterosexual conformity; his nomination helps clear the path that will allow Peggy to remain an untamed tomboy until the very end of her story.

Whitney's story also situates her at a developmental crossroads, but whereas Peggy receives two proposals as a young woman, Whitney receives no such invitations. Whitney's story picks up in 1928, as she overhears her mother and "Uncle" Bud fighting over his infidelity with a woman only a year older than Whitney. When Whitney's mother loses the attention of Uncle Bud she loses not only his affections but also the precarious financial footing he provided as part of their transactional sexual relationship. When Whitney's mother cites her daughter's failure to please Uncle Bud as the reason for their breakup, Whitney defends her right to refuse male attention, no matter how it might benefit her or her mother financially. At the same moment that Whitney attempts to hold on to her tomboy ethos, one that allows her to reject male attention and approval in favor of her own singular ambitions, Whitney's mother forces her to confront her limited options, options limited explicitly by gender: she thrusts a rejection letter from the University of Oklahoma into Whitney's face and says, "You really think that that fancy science program is gonna take a girl? It don't matter how smart you are. You're stuck here, same as me." When Whitney again declaims her desire to use her mind as her escape from her mother's fate, her mother drags her in front of a mirror, forces her to look at herself and offers her daughter this lesson: "No one cares what's in your head. If you were half as smart as you think you are you'd fix on this [grabs Whitney's face]. This is the only thing that's gonna get you anywhere in this world." The setting then jumps forward to present-day Whitney being badgered over the phone by her husband, who wants her to participate in a photo shoot so that he can further his own political ambitions. When he insists that she attend because "It's your face they [*Life* magazine] want," she refuses his demands with a smile as the camera pans around her to reveal the growing black crack running down her cheek caused by her contact with a substance called Zero Matter. This shot reveals the ways in which Whitney maintains her right to refuse male attention and approbation in favor of her own quest for knowledge and power. Although to the outside world it appears that Whitney has abandoned her tomboy identity and been "tamed" by societal expectations, this moment illustrates that Whitney's tomboy ethos has not been abandoned but instead sublimated and transformed. The ethos that drove her in childhood remains a central part of her character; what she has learned to do is adopt a mask of conformity while carrying out her true transgressive desires in private.

This evocative episode ends with the tomboy rallying cry repeated: once uttered by a man against Whitney, and once uttered by Whitney as a full-throated pronouncement of her own power. The scene shifts to 1934, when a young Agnes Cully arrives in Hollywood, poor but ambitious. Unable to afford the price of a matinee, she is accosted outside of the movie theater by a talent agent who, like Uncle Bud before him, approaches her with the words, "I bet you're real pretty when you smile." Whitney's disgust remains constant but, without the options Peggy Carter enjoyed, she grudgingly acquiesces to his interest. Whereas Peggy is offered the option to become a secret agent, Whitney is approached by a talent agent who rechristens her "Whitney

Frost" on the spot because "That's the beauty of Hollywood. You can be whatever you want." This phrase, previously associated with the freedom the tomboy offers, becomes instead an assertion of male power over Whitney's identity. Abate notes that the phrase "'I can do anything' . . . could serve as the motto for tomboys in U.S. literature and culture. From their inception, tomboyish characters and their accompanying behaviors have been linked with such elements as social surprise, gender duplicity and unlimited possibility" (2008, xiii). At the end of this episode, set in the show's present, Whitney uses, for the first time, her full power to destroy and absorb the strength of a human being (a man, notably, who stands in the way of her pursuit of Zero Matter). When her husband, a witness to her new monstrous power, asks in horror, "What are you?" she replies, "Whatever I want [to be]." Whitney deploys the language used against her by the agent and reclaims it as tomboy rallying cry, claiming for herself her original transgressive identity and the possibilities it should have allowed her. Hers is a quest toward self-authorship, toward a desire to slip the bonds of gendered expectations and emerge into herself. Whitney is no more tamed than Peggy is, but whereas Peggy's opportunities to live a life of action allow her to enact her tomboy identity through a life of individual achievement and adventure as an agent and career woman, Whitney's lack of opportunities at a crucial moment in her life take her tomboy identity and transform it, ultimately, into a monstrous display of female power. As Craig and LaCroix note in "Tomboy as Protective Identity,"

> Women who have the privilege of choosing rather than being strongly pressured to conform to gender norms have a different view of gender. Rather than feeling a need to defend one's tomboy[ishness] . . . or resign oneself to feminine display, it becomes a tool that can be used to navigate interactions with others. (2011, 460)

By extending the tomboy's narrative beyond adolescence, this episode of *Agent Carter* shows two examples wherein the tomboy is not tamed but instead goes underground and reemerges as either the double agent (Carter) or the femme fatale (Whitney).

Whereas Peggy's tomboyishness prepares her to become a double agent and finds expression through this role, Whitney's transformed tomboy energies find expression in the figure of the femme fatale. Certainly, the setting of Season 2 of *Agent Carter* prepares us for this figure: while the first season was set in New York City, Season 2 takes place in the blasted desert landscapes and movie lots of the California of the forties, iconic settings of both classic and modern film noir. As a femme fatale, Whitney takes the energies and ideals of her tomboy nature and marries them to the physical beauty and sexuality she has spent so long trying to diminish or avoid. What at first appear to be two distinct, near-opposite figures of femininity—the tomboy's typically asexual, adolescent independence seems a far cry from the femme fatale's hypersexual, ultra-feminized appearance—find common ground in their ethos and their ability to defy and subvert gendered ideals and spaces. Whereas the tomboy frequently expresses her masculine identification through her appearance or self-naming (Josephine becoming Jo, for instance), the femme fatale expresses her masculine identification through her desire for power and use of her own physical and sexual power. Susana Nicolás identifies the femme fatale's predecessor as a Renaissance figure known as the *femme forte*, "a distinctive social and literary figure, a renovated strong woman possessing masculine qualities such as fortitude or bravery" (2017, 96). This figure of the *femme forte* accrues darker dimensions both sexual and destructive during and immediately after times of global conflagration, such as World War I and World War II, and is largely understood to be emblematic of male paranoia about female access to hitherto exclusively male realms of power.[7] The femme fatale takes the tomboy's desire for independence, power, and freedom and makes it lethal; she illustrates what happens to the tomboy should these desires forever be denied her. The femme fatale, in some ways, is a version of the tomboy all grown-up.

In his study of this figure, Scott Yarbrough elaborates upon the "paradigm-establishing femme fatale":

> She is beautiful, intelligent, and corrupt. She uses her sexuality as a weapon that can turn men against themselves, and she is ultimately self-serving and ambitious. She is an ambiguous character: powerful and strong while evil . . . [S]he is then able to learn how to apply the masquerade to herself, such that she is always hiding behind a mask, creating distance between her body—which has so betrayed her—and her true self . . . [The femme fatale] turns to the innate weapon of her body, the sexuality she has divorced from her true self by use of the masquerade . . . Strength is one of the core characteristics of the femme fatale, of course. (1999, 52, 56, 57, 60)

While Peggy is capable of temporarily adopting the role of femme fatale when the mission calls for it—she uses her body as a weapon quite literally at times, weaponizing a tube of lipstick, for example, so that whoever she kisses becomes poisoned, or seducing men into giving up their secrets—Whitney's story arc conforms to that of femme fatale at every turn. Whitney Frost learns the lesson her mother taught her—that the world will only allow female ambition to go so far, and will insist on beauty as a woman's most valuable asset—and prepares a beautiful mask that allows her to hide her true ambitious nature and to seduce men who can bring her closer to the power and freedom she desires. The protective nature of tomboy identity cited earlier fails her: harassed by men her entire life, demonized by her mother for failing to conform to gender standards, rejected by college on the basis of her sex alone, she ultimately pursues power as a femme fatale because she is kept from power as a girl and a woman.[8] In other words, Whitney takes the sexuality that has been thrust upon her and embraces it as the very instrument of her revenge. The tomboy is the identification that she is wrested from by society, and so she adopts the role of femme fatale as a way to bring down the patriarchal forces that have disrupted and continue to disrupt her natural state.

To Whitney, power would lend her both independence from the men she loathes relying on and revenge against them as well as the exclusive enclaves of privilege they populate and patrol. In the episode titled "Monster," Whitney endeavors to absorb as much Zero Matter as she can, now heedless of the effect it has on her mask of beauty. When Whitney absorbs the Zero Matter and, symbolically, male power, her mask cracks, at first to her alarm but then to her delight. Indeed, Whitney longs to destroy the beauty that has come between her and her nature as a tomboy because "it has taken too much from me, my childhood, my innocence." Whitney frames her quest for power as a corrective meant to wrest power from men and patriarchal systems and claim power for the otherwise disempowered, a point dramatically illustrated by Whitney's choice of targets. Zero Matter makes Whitney's body lethal: when she touches foes, she is able to absorb their power and destroy them. Once endowed with this power, Whitney takes revenge not simply on individuals but on systems of male power and privilege that have actively excluded her or exerted control over her and her identity. The director who simultaneously tells her she has lost her sex appeal and then propositions her for sex is her first victim; the all-white, all-male board of the company that controls Zero Matter is her next target; following that, she destroys and absorbs the power of her husband. In short, Whitney absorbs the power of men *in* power, and of men who have unjustly exerted power over her and other women. As with her tomboy identity, Whitney's femme fatale longs to strike out at the forces that refuse to leave her alone, the forces that dictate what she must do, be, think, and how she must appear. What makes Whitney monstrous, ultimately, is the enforced separation, over the course of a lifetime, of her and women like her from power, dramatized by the very way her appearance begins to crack. She is not a tomboy tamed but a tomboy transformed, and a testament to what the world does to a woman who refuses to leave that ethos behind.

As scholars of tomboyism show, the figure of the tomboy, while stable in some aspects, is a largely dynamic figure, one that evolves with the pressures and opportunities of her time. While many critics rightly highlight the tomboy's oftentimes transitory nature, the narratives uncovered in the Marvel Cinematic Universe restore the tomboy's promise and show the ways in which tomboyism can become what Abate calls "a lifelong identity" (2008,

13). Peggy Carter and Whitney Frost adhere to the tomboy ethos learned in their girlhoods throughout their lives, and this code of conduct orders their ability to infiltrate and overturn systems of male power; in this way, the series *Agent Carter* helps to extend and expand the possibilities embodied in the ever-creative figure of the tomboy. Indeed, we may look back on 2019 as the year the tomboy narrative evolved. Three blockbuster films, two of them ending eras of long and much-loved franchises and one reclaiming a beloved feminist text, revisit the figure of the tomboy and, like *Agent Carter* before them, utterly un-tame her: *Avengers: Endgame* (April 2019), *Star Wars: The Rise of Skywalker* (December 2019), and Greta Gerwig's *Little Women* (December 2019). *Star Wars* delivers the fate of the franchise (and the universe) into the hands of Rey, a traditional tomboy *par excellence*; Greta Gerwig, director of 2019's *Little Women*, through a deft and moving sleight of hand rescues ur-tomboy Jo March from her otherwise bedevilingly unsatisfying and unsettling fate[9]; and *Avengers: Endgame* completes the story arc of Peggy Carter and Steve Rogers, the figures who began this study. In the very closing moments of the final film in this phase of the MCU, Steve Rogers—and, pointedly, *not* Peggy Carter—uses a trick of time travel to refuse his call to become Captain America and instead chooses a life of domestic pleasures with Peggy Carter. Steve Rogers's abdication of his heroic storyline and Peggy Carter's ability to choose and sustain her career as a double agent simultaneously upend a deeply rooted gendered narrative and open up new narrative possibilities for male and female characters alike, narrative possibilities in which tomboys can, indeed, become whoever they want to be.

NOTES

1. See Dave McNary. "Kevin Feige Promises More Female Directors on Marvel Movies." *Variety,* June 2018.

2. For a more detailed discussion of these statistics, see "Analyzing Female Gender Roles in Marvel Comics from the Silver Age (1960) to the Present" by Katherine J. Murphy. The one measurement that did not change significantly over time was the rate of violence against women in the comic books, which Murphy identifies as a disturbing constant across decades. See also "Analyzing the Gender Representation of 34,476 Comic Book Characters" by Amanda Shendruk, which includes an analysis of which powers are most often attributed to male vs. female superheroes, as well as patterns in gendered nomenclature. This is best viewed online for its interactive and entertaining disaggregation of results.

3. Perhaps the most egregious example of this in Iron Man occurs in an early flashback when Tony reduced a well-educated and critical female reporter (who pointedly and accurately accuses him of war profiteering) to a quivering body on a bed, her own reservations about his morals easily overturned by his apparently irresistible charm.

4. Tony's desire to shield and protect rather than ruin and destroy eventually will help create his wife's superhero identity. The Marvel comics reveal that Tony Stark initially builds the Rescue suit for Pepper Potts as a protective device; in the film *Endgame*, Pepper dons the Rescue suit in order to participate in the battle against Thanos, and not merely as a shield that would guarantee her own safety.

5. Carter's storyline also demonstrates the ways in which this access comes with a price. Carter's access to masculine realms of power does not inoculate her against the misogynist attitudes that dominate this sphere; she is, as the only woman who is not a nurse or secretary, subjected to pointed sexual harassment in the workspace, both from her superiors and from the men she is in charge of training. Further, Carter herself, when in the presence of other officers, must act like "one of the boys," a fate shared by many other tomboy figures in literature and film. This helps explain the otherwise baffling moment when Carter, herself a strong and accomplished woman, calls the weakest recruits to the SSR "girls" or likens them her grandmother. As Craig and LaCroix note, tomboys, even when they successfully maneuver themselves into masculine spheres of power, "may be expected to objectify others in order to fit in and 'be one of the guys'" (2011, 456). Furthermore, tomboys, because of their ability to modify or transcend sexual boundaries, are then "presumed to be immune to sexism and therefore subjected to blatant and hostile examples of such sexism . . . tomboy identity is not an all-access pass" (2011, 457). Carter, though, even amid the pervasive and suffocating sexism of the postwar workplace, instead exploits the sexist codes of the office to her advantage. In episode one of *Agent Carter*, for example, Carter insinuates that she has her period and asks for the day off; when her boss complies, disgusted by her femininity, she instead takes the day off to pursue and apprehend the culprit the entire office cannot locate. Carter's identity as the lone woman in the office paradoxically makes her more and less visible simultaneously.

6. Chris Evans, the actor who played Captain America in the MCU, discusses Cap's likely virginity in an interview with *Time* magazine. Though this declaration startled some fans, it does not take a particularly canny viewer to arrive at this same conclusion.

7. See Yarbrough, 51.

8. For more on this, see Yarbrough, 53–54.

9. In the epilogue to her study, Abate includes a brief but insightful analysis of the 1994 iteration of *Little Women*, in which she notes that the film's "version of Alcott's character [Jo March] [is] scarcely tomboy enough to be tamed" and instead stands as a stark example of the coopting and "heterosexualization of tomboyism" (2008, 227).

BIBLIOGRAPHY

Abate, Michelle Ann. 2008. *Tomboys: A Literary and Cultural History*. Philadelphia: Temple University Press.

Allen, Lindsey, writer. *Agent Carter*. Season 2, episode 5, "The Atomic Job." Directed by Craig Zisk, featuring Hayley Atwell, James D'Arcy, and Enver Gjokaj. Aired February 9, 2016. Disney+ 2019.

Butler, Judith. 1990. *Gender Trouble: Feminism and the Subversion of Identity*. New York: Routledge.

Chung, Sue, writer. *Agent Carter*. Season 2, episode 4, "Smoke and Mirrors." Directed by David Platt, featuring Hayley Atwell, James D'Arcy, and Wynn Everett. Aired February 2, 2016. Disney+ 2020.

Craig, Traci and Jessica LaCroix. 2011. "Tomboy as Protective Identity." *Journal of Lesbian Studies* 15 (4): 450–65.

Dingess, Chris, writer. *Agent Carter*. Season 1, episode 1, "SNAFU." Directed by Vincent Misiano, featuring Hayley Atwell, James D'Arcy, and Chad Michael Murray. Aired February 17, 2015. Disney+ 2020.

Easton, Brandon, writer. *Agent Carter*. Season 2, episode 7, "Monsters." Directed by Metin Hüseyin, featuring Hayley Atwell, James D'Arcy, and Enver Gjokaj. Aired February 16, 2016. Disney+ 2019.

Englestein, Brant and Linsey Allen, writers. *Agent Carter*. Season 2, episode 8, "The Edge of Mystery." Directed by Metin Hüseyin, featuring Hayley Atwell, James D'Arcy, and Chad Michael Murray. Aired February 23, 2016. Disney+ 2019.

Fazekas, Michelle and Tara Butter, writers. *Agent Carter*. Season 1, episode 8, "Valediction." Directed by Jennifer Getzinger, featuring Hayley Atwell, James D'Arcy, and Chad Michael Murray. Aired February 24, 2015. Disney+ 2019.

———. *Agent Carter*. Season 2, episode 10, "Hollywood Ending." Directed by Christopher Misiano, featuring Hayley Atwell, James D'Arcy, and Chad Michael Murray. Aired March 1, 2016. Disney+ 2019.

Holland, Samantha and Julie Harpin. 2015. "Who Is the 'Girly' Girl? Tomboys, Hyper-Femininity and Gender." *Journal of Gender Studies* 24 (3): 293-309.

Jennings, Rebecca. 2007. *Tomboys and Bachelor Girls: A Lesbian History of Post–War Britain 1945–71*. Manchester: Manchester University Press.

Johnston, Joe. 2011. *Captain America: The First Avenger*. DVD. Directed by Joe Johnston. Hollywood, CA: Paramount Home Media.

Markus, Christopher and Stephen McFeeley, writers. *Agent Carter*. Season 1, episode 1, "Now is Not the End." Directed by Louis D'Esposito, featuring Hayley Atwell, James D'Arcy, and Chad Michael Murray. Aired January 6, 2015. Disney+ 2019.

McDermott, Shawna. 2019. "The Tomboy Tradition: Taming Adolescent Ambition from 1869 to 2018." *Children's Literature Association Quarterly* 44 (2): 134–55.

Molina, Jose, writer. *Agent Carter*. Season 1, episode 5, "The Iron Ceiling." Directed by Peter Leto, featuring Hayley Atwell, James D'Arcy, and Chad Michael Murray. Aired February 3, 2015. Disney+ 2019.

———, writer. *Agent Carter*. Season 2, episode 3, "Better Angels." Directed by David Platt, featuring Hayley Atwell, James D'Arcy, and Chad Michael Murray. Aired January 26, 2016. Disney+ 2019.

Murphy, Katherine J. 2016. "Analyzing Female Gender Roles in Marvel Comics from the Silver Age (1960) to the Present." *Discussion: The Undergraduate Research Journal of CWRU* 12, no. 2: 1. http://www.inquiriesjournal.com/articles/1449/analyzing-female-gender-roles-in-marvel-comics-from-the-silver-age-1960-to-the-present.

Nicolás, Susana. 2017. "'She Sleeps Inside like a Lion and a Lamb and a Child': Revisiting Shakespeare's Female Evil through Edward Bond's *Lear*." In *Re-visiting Female Evil: Power, Purity, and Desire,* edited by Melissa Dearey, Susana Nicolás and Roger Davis, 95–111. Leiden, The Netherlands: Brill Rodopi.

Pearson, Eric and Lindsey Allen, writers. *Agent Carter*. Season 2, episode 2, "A View in the Dark." Directed by Lawrence Trilling, featuring Hayley Atwell, James D'Arcy, and Enver Gjokaj. Aired January 19, 2016. Disney+ 2019.

Robinson, Ashley Sufflé. 2018. "We Are Iron Man: Tony Stark, Iron Man, and American Identity in the Marvel Cinematic Universe's Phase One Films." *The Journal of Popular Culture* 51 (4): 824–44.

Russo, Anthony and Joe Russo. 2019. *Avengers: Endgame*. DVD. Directed by Anthony Russo and Joe Russo. Burbank, CA: Marvel Studios.

———. 2018. *Avengers: Infinity War*. DVD. Directed by Anthony Russo and Joe Russo. Burbank, CA: Marvel Studios.

———. 2016. *Captain America: Civil War*. DVD. Directed by Anthony Russo and Joe Russo. Burbank, CA: Walt Disney Studios.

———. 2014. *Captain America: The Winter Soldier*. DVD. Directed by Anthony Russo and Joe Russo. Burbank, CA: Walt Disney Studios.

Wright, Bradford W. 2001. *Comic Book Nation: The Transformation of Youth Culture in America*. Baltimore: The Johns Hopkins University Press.

Yarbrough, Scott. 1999. "The Dark Lady: Temple Drake as Femme Fatale." *The Southern Literary Journal* 31 (2): 50–64.

Chapter 7

Tomboys, *Annedroids*, and the New Normal

Rebecca Feasey

A myriad of children's animations include a tomboy in their otherwise predictable character biographies, be it Mulan (*Mulan* 1998), Edith (*Despicable Me* 2010), Merida (*Brave* 2012), or Wyldstyle (*The Lego Movie* 2014) on the big screen; or Buttercup (*The Powerpuff Girls* 1998–2005, 2016–2019), Dora (*Dora the Explorer* 2000–2015) or Rainbow Dash (*My Little Pony: Friendship in Magic* 2010–2020) in contemporary popular programming. However, these girls tend to be singled out for their sartorial efforts, mannerisms, and interests as they negotiate traditional codes of femininity and push the boundaries of acceptable girlhood to include strength and rebellion over and above coquettishness, pastel palettes, and subversive niceness. What these animated girls, be they anthropomorphic or otherwise, have in common, is that they stand out as exceptional . . . they are the tomboy amidst an otherwise predictable backdrop of gendered clothing, traits, and mannerisms.

And although it is routinely animation that can push the boundaries of appropriate sex, gender, family, and social codes, this chapter will suggest that it is children's live-action programming that presents the most progressive take on the contemporary tomboy. Building on its animated predecessors, the live-action Amazon original, *Annedroids* (2014–2017) presents the tomboy as a routine, accepted, and, indeed, ordinary iteration of girlhood. Eleven-year-old Anne/Addison Holley is the central protagonist, and, based on appearance (dungarees and unkempt hair), interests (science, engineering, and making mechanical companions) and bedroom culture (robots alongside florals), she is presented as the show's tomboy lead. Anne is a very smart girl in a junkyard world, taking a seat amidst a growing friendship group

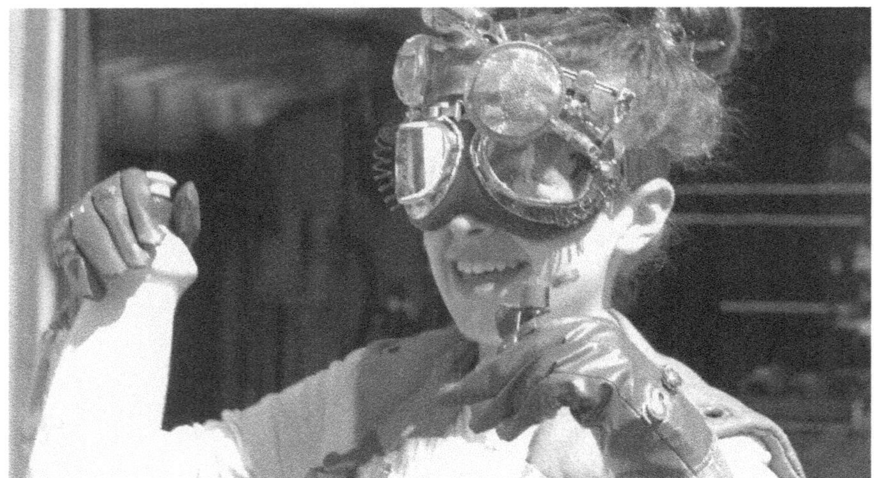

Figure 7.1 ***Annedroids*****. S1:E4 "Helping Hand." Anne played by Addison Holley.**

that carefully introduces the program's young audience to different ways of performing gender, removed from judgment or hierarchy.

Annedroids presents the tomboy, not as the exception that proves the more predictable feminine rule, but as a mainstream depiction of contemporary girlhood. The characters, be they girls, boys, men, women, or robotic creations, play with science, gender, and sartorial choices. *Annedroids* has perhaps unsurprisingly won the "Parents' Choice Gold Award" and received eleven daytime Emmy nominations. After all, the program presents a variety of warm and welcoming family units, gives valuable screen time to a diverse multi-generational cast, and brings STEM subjects into popular children's entertainment. Such diversity provides the backdrop to the show's mainstream tomboy. The *Annedroids* tomboy is rarely singled out or asked to justify her gendered self, and as such, the program can be seen to be presenting its whip-smart and tech-savvy tomboy as just another way of experiencing girlhood: as the new normal.

ANNEDROIDS

Annedroids is a Canadian television series created by J.J. Johnson, released on Amazon Video in both the UK and United States in 2014. The show combines live-action and CGI over four seasons in order to introduce a pre-teen audience to the subjects of science, technology, engineering, and math (STEM). The series, like much pre-teen and teen programming, is told from the point of view of an adolescent[1] peer group, namely Anne Sagan,[2] Nick/Jadiel

Dowlin and Shania/Adrianna Di Liello. Anne,[3] the central protagonist, wears utilitarian fashions while creating engineering adventures, proposing scientific advancements, and indulging in robotic exploits in her own personal junkyard. Although Anne has spent her childhood making, quite literally, her friends in her android engineering bay, the series begins with Anne befriending Nick, the new boy to the neighborhood who lives across the street from the junkyard, and Shania, the local-girl-*cum*-wannabe-princess-gymnast-popstar.

While Anne lives in the junkyard with her robotics-expert dad/Wilbert/James Gangi and three androids (Hands, Eyes, and Pal), Nick lives with his television reporter mom/Maggie/Raven Dauda and Shania lives with her foster "grandma" and siblings. At the outset of the first season, we are told that Anne does not know the whereabouts of her mother who left when she was an infant, Nick has brief contact with his absentee father, while Shania has little knowledge (but several elaborate theories) about her biological parents.

At the same time that the program is introducing its adolescent audience to a diverse cast and a variety of family units, so too, it opens a dialogue about gender that can be seen to challenge stereotypical iterations of boyhood, girl culture, masculinity, and femininity that are more routinely associated with children's television fare. Indeed, *Annedroids* is said to take "what you and your kids have come to expect from gender roles on the screen, yank out the circuitry, and rework it entirely" (Ashby 2022). Although the anthropomorphic Eyes and Hands are both programmed as gendered, popular media commentators have picked up on the fact that Pal, Anne's final and most challenging android, has not been programmed in this way. Throughout the show's history, Pal is never knowingly referred to as male or female, he or she. Rather, we are told that Pal is . . . well . . . Pal is, just Pal. In their work on genderless characters in children's television, Sara Beck, Rebecca Hains, and Colleen Russo state that "[u]pon creation by Anne, PAL has no hair or any attire that would mark PAL as gendered. Furthermore, PAL's childlike voice is digitally processed in such a way that it sounds robotic and of indeterminate gender" (Beck, Hains, and Johnson 2017, 225).[4] However, although there is much scope here to unpack the broader representation and reception of these android creations, this chapter is more interested in the depiction of Pal's creator, the socially awkward STEM genius, Anne. It is worth exploring the ways in which Anne can be understood as masculinized girl, androgynous adolescent, as gender fluid femininity, or as tomboy.

GENDER ROLES, GENDER IDENTITY, AND FEMALE MASCULINITY

Before we look to the media representation of the tomboy, it is important to briefly outline the debates, discussions, and routine disagreements as they speak to the ways in which masculinity and femininity "relate to being male and being female" as it exists in the fields of gender education, sociology, history, psychology, and literary criticism (Paechter 2006, 253).

In 1968, Robert Stoller spoke of individual males and females having variable levels of masculinity or femininity (1968). Since that time, masculinity and femininity have been and routinely continue to be understood in relation to male and female bodies, respectively. That said, in his seminal volume *Female Masculinity* (1998), Jack Halberstam was keen to "denaturalise the discourse of masculinity, demonstrating its performative dimension, and to create a discursive space in which masculinity can be read in relation to the female body" (Robinson and Davies 2010, 26; see also Davies 2008). Likewise, Christine Skelton and Becky Francis have suggested that we are able to name particular behaviors as masculine, irrespective of whether they are being performed by girls or boys (Skelton and Francis in Paechter 2006, 253). However, while many from the field of gender education and beyond agree that the concept of "masculinity must not and cannot and should not reduce down to the male body and its effects," Halberstam's notion is challenged for its reliance on masculinity as fixed and stable (Halberstam 1998, 2). Carrie Paechter makes the point that "[t]his would not be such a problem if we actually had a clear picture of what men and boys *do* do, but we do not, and, indeed, cannot" because "men and boys, and what they do, are many and varied" (Paechter 2006, 254). In short, the problem here stems from the fact that we are unable to "define either masculinity or femininity except in relation to each other and to men and women" (Paechter 2006, 254).

Either way, irrespective of whether theorists "situate tomboyism within the realm of masculinity taken up by girls and women" or note that "tomboyism can exist within the realms of femininity" (Robinson and Davies 2010, 26), the debate about gender identity is "unlikely to be able to move away from having two main genders, in the sense that each one of us knows whether we are male or female, or, less frequently, something different or in between" (Paechter 2006, 261). Moreover, we need to acknowledge that "knowing that someone is male or female says very little about how their masculinity or femininity is constructed" because although most bodies are fixed and stable "how we understand ourselves as masculine and feminine varies according to time, place and circumstances" (Paechter 2006, 261).

This consideration of the terminology surrounding the ways in which masculinity and femininity relate to being male and being female is crucially important. After all, within and beyond extant research from the social sciences, humanities, and education, popular media culture refers to the tomboy as an iteration of female masculinity, as a girl who plays with, borrows, or exploits traditionally masculine interests, behaviors, and sartorial choices.

It is useful to consider the competing ways in which the tomboy has been read and understood in such literature. Lynn Carr provides a useful overview of competing accounts, noting that while some theorists "have asserted that tomboyism is an instance of 'cross-gender' or 'masculine' identification . . . others have maintained that tomboys are better classified as 'androgynous' people who exercise both 'masculinity' and 'femininity'" (Carr 2005, 121). Although early work on the tomboy linked tomboyism with "lesbianism, abnormal gender development, and confused gender identity" (Carr 2005, 121), these findings have been challenged to the extent that tomboyism has more recently been read as a "healthy" iteration of girlhood, to be encouraged rather than rejected (Carr 2005, 121).

MASCULINIZED GIRL, ANDROGYNOUS ADOLESCENT, OR CONTEMPORARY TOMBOY

Irrespective of the longevity and continued popularity of the term "tomboy" within society and media culture, "no satisfactory definition of tomboyism has emerged" within extant literature (Stahl 2016, 52). There is little consensus or agreement on the characterizations of the figure in question. Indeed, a sprawling array of "traits and behaviors prompt attributions of tomboyism, from an affinity for horseback riding . . . to having short hair and spunk" (Stahl 2016, 52). In their work on girly girls, tomboys, hyper-femininity, and gender, Samantha Holland and Julie Harpin present what might be understood as the most useful overview of the figure in question when they note that:

> The tomboy is the active girl or young woman who resists gender norms, especially during childhood; her clothes are not restrictive, and her appearance is mostly low maintenance. She works against the limitations of traditional femininity, without ever really acquiring the currency of masculinity . . . but she refuses to "throw like a girl" and enjoys her physicality. (Holland and Harpin 2015, 305)

To pick up on this last point, the physicality routinely associated with the tomboy was front and center in Carrie Paechter and Sheryl Clark's findings from the Economic and Social Research Council funded Tomboy Identity

Study. The authors investigated both "the enabling and constraining factors for girls in taking up and maintaining tomboy identities, and the relationship between these and the perpetuation of active girlhood during the later primary school years" (Paechter and Clark 2007, 317). The study found that children use playground spaces as a means of constructing gendered identities, with tomboys spending their playtimes "participating in activities that are usually associated with masculinity" such as football and team games rather than the "walk and . . . talk" more routinely associated with girlhood on the playground (Paechter and Clark 2007, 321). Of interest here is the fact that "both masculinity and tomboydom were constructed by the children . . . around physical aggression" (Paechter and Clark 2007, 318).

Although aggression comes with negative connotations, the broader role of physicality and a space demanded for movement can be seen to pick up on Holland and Harpin's work on the tomboy as they refer to the figure as encompassing "a sense of freedom, mobility and physicality" (2015, 296). The authors make it clear that their reading of tomboy freedom is not reduced to a girl who is out "climbing trees all day" but rather, to those girls and boys who feel that they have "more physical agency than a girly-girl" (Holland and Harpin 2015, 296). When appearance is in question, freedom is again key. The tomboy, we are told, is "careful to be 'low maintenance' and not overly feminine, and instead wears trousers, sportswear, and short or no-fuss hair" (Holland and Harpin 2015, 296–7). To embrace freedom means opposing normalized feminine positions and rejecting the "disempowerment" that comes with it (Paechter 2006, 257). Paechter comments on Halberstams's seminal work when she notes that girls should dismiss femininity in favor of what is deemed to be a "healthier" masculinity. In this way, "renouncing femininity . . . becomes an act of renouncing powerlessness, of claiming power for oneself" (Paechter 2006, 257).

GROWING UP OR GROWING OUT OF TOMBOY IDENTITY

Michelle Abate's seminal research charts the tomboy's "long, complex, and largely overlooked" literary and cultural history, from the mid nineteenth century hoyden to the "Girl-Power" post-feminists at the turn of the millennium (Abate 2011, 407). We are informed that the term "tomboy" gained prominence in America during the Civil War as a way to help educate privileged, white women about physical strength and health.[5] In an effort to maintain white power, girls were encouraged to eat well and play actively, outdoors, so that they would be better able to procreate (Abate 2008, 55–8). Although there was agreement about the early use of the term, there is friction around the way in which the tomboy is understood in relation to contemporary debates around sex, gender, and identity.

Although Abate maps over 150 years of tomboyism, it has been suggested that these figures are dated and/or sexist and, therefore, the tomboy could be read as a figure from a pre-feminist era before girls were encouraged to play sports, take part in STEM, and asked to look at and take on the world as equals. That said, recent structured interviews with children from the New York area concluded that the term "tomboy" continues to be used as a "meaningful label to young girls in the present day and age"[6] (Ahlqvist et al. 2013, 577). The operative word here is *girls*. The question then is why we should "call a girl a quasi boy just because she likes to dress comfortably, play sports, climbs trees, go on adventures, or have boys as companions"? (Thorne 1993, 113). After all, those traits, mannerisms, and behaviors that have been used to classify the tomboy such as "rough-and-tumble play or intense energy expenditure; preference for stereotypical boys' toys and male playmates; lack of interest in clothing and adornment; lack of interest in infants, motherhood, and marriage; and an interest in career for later life" are all also found in girlhood (Devor 1989, 14–5).

In Halberstam's work on female masculinity in childhood, we are asked to consider if "masculinity were a kind of default category for children, surely we would have more girls running around and playing sports and experimenting with chemistry sets and building things and fixing things . . . and so on" (Halberstam 1998, 269). Indeed, we are asked to consider the "possibility that tomboys view themselves not as outcasts of their gender, but as girls with options" (Ahlqvist et al. 2013, 576). A number of theorists have suggested that "tomboy traits may have positive outcomes for girls, in that they are often associated with assertiveness and self-reliance" (Holland and Harpin 2015, 297). And yet while tomboy identities "are thought to be a common occurrence in girlhood . . . beyond puberty tomboy behaviour often becomes seen as rebellious or even pathological" (Holland and Harpin 2015, 297). It has been argued that tomboy behavior is tolerated in part because it is seen as a child development phase rather than a longer-term model of womanhood or mature femininity. Lynn Carr informs us that "most girls are believed to renounce their tomboy ways in adolescence" (Carr 1998, 530; see also Halberstam 1998, 6) because, to cite Dawn Currie, "young women are pressured to conform to dominant ideals of femininity" (Currie 1997, 462).[7]

TOMBOY TAMING

Patriarchal society in general, and popular media narratives in particular look to tame tomboys because of a fear that "rebellious females left unrehabilitated into society could overturn the male-dominated social order" (Stahl 2016, 66). Indeed, it is precisely because these girls are regarded as a threat to patriarchal supremacy that society, with its masculinist paranoia and its accompanying stories, "mandates their 'expiration'" (Stahl 2016, 66). So routine is the turn away from tomboy identity post adolescence, that what has been termed "tomboy taming" is spoken of as a common feature of popular art, literature, comics, television, and feature films (Abate 2008, 31; Clayton 2010; Stahl 2016).

As previously noted, tomboys are said to have emerged on the back of the Civil War, becoming a staple of children's literature of the time with titles such as *Gypsy Breynton* (1866), *Little Women* (1868), and *What Katy Did* (1872) (Segel 1989, 67–71). However, the depiction of "self-willed, passionate, often deeply earnest girl characters whose aspirations go beyond the roles prescribed them by their societies' conceptions of gender" is not unique to that period (McDermott 2019, 134). Rather, contemporary theorists are pointing to the representation of tomboys in texts such as *The Little Mermaid* (1989), *Mean Girls* (2004), and *The Hunger Games* trilogy of novels and their filmic adaptations (2008–2010, 2012–2015) (McDermott 2019, 134–55).

Although the earlier texts depict the tomboy as a girl who has "a proclivity for outdoor play . . . a feisty independent spirit, and a tendency to don masculine clothing and adopt a boyish nickname" (McDermott 2019, 135; see also Abate 2011, 407) Shawna McDermott makes the point that:

> These tomboy traits—marked as inappropriate and worrisome in girls in the late nineteenth century—have become standard in girls' lives. In the late twentieth and early twenty-first centuries, it was and is a normal part of American girlhood to play outside, to engage in sports . . . to wear pants and sporty clothing, and to have boyish nicknames. According to the classic definition of tomboyism, then, all girls who today participate in these fully acceptable aspects of American girlhood are tomboys. (McDermott 2019, 135)

Perhaps it is unsurprising then that Anne Balay notes that "it is almost standard now for girls to identify as tomboys" (Balay 2010, 11). While Renée Sentilles picks up on the themes of age and gender ambiguity, stating that "tomboys are intrinsically queer, regardless of how that tomboyism is expressed or repressed" (Sentilles 2018, 16), other theorists have suggested that queerness extends to all children (Stockton 2009, 1). After all, the "theory of queer childhood understands all children as as-yet outside of heteronormative structures of gender and time" (McDermott 2019, 135). So too, Kerry Robinson and Cristyn Davies note that:

> Through their transgressions from gender norms and the taking up of different ways of doing gender, we can understand childhood as a potentially queer time and space—a space in which children can subvert dominant discourses of childhood through taking up alternative ways of performing gender and relating with each other. (Robinson and Davies 2010, 24; see also Robinson and Davies 2007)

Rather than overlook the tomboy as a role or representation from a bygone era, we should re-imagine and reconfigure tomboyism for the contemporary period. Traci Craig and Jessica Lacroix pick up on Joanne Hall's work when they say that "the tomboy identity must be understood as multifaceted and created in a social, cultural, and political environment that shapes the definition and use" of the term (Craig and Lacroix 2011, 451). With this in mind, the focus shifts from clothing and physicality to "queer ambition" (McDermott 2019, 134–55). We are informed that "[a]mbition is the constant trait in tomboy stories in the nineteenth century as well as today. What is different today is the ways in which girls outwardly perform their tomboyism. What the tomboy wears, how she acts, how she then en-acts her desires is flexible and changes according to each girl's era and experience" (McDermott 2019, 136). We are reminded that "[t]hese internal feelings and desires, and especially the ambitions that they generate, are the consistent traits that place these characters within a tradition that spans centuries" (McDermott 2019, 136). When Abate refers to tomboys as being "linked with such elements as social surprise, gender duplicity, and unlimited possibility," it is the notion of unlimited possibility that could be seen to engage with ambition, picking up on the energy, aspiration, and initiatives of the tomboy—removed as they are from hegemonic gender codes and strict societal conventions (Abate 2008, xiii).

However, irrespective of the tomboy traits in question, the conclusion remains the same—these tomboys are routinely tamed and contained in line with more traditional, stereotypical iterations of heteronormative femininity. McDermott makes the point that although earlier efforts to contain and constrain the tomboy "focused on the shedding of tomboyish dress and boyish antics," "it is the taming of queer ambition that represents the true downfall of the tomboy and the possibilities that she represents" (McDermott 2019, 135). McDermott continues:

> Time and time again, authors choose to give their tomboys dreams beyond what their gender will allow, and then they shatter those dreams in order to demonstrate that they were not the correct ambitions and should be replaced with the joys and benefits of traditional womanhood. The ideal of the tomboy who persists untamed is, according to this tradition, impossible, an enigma, an oxymoron, not to be realized. (McDermott 2019, 138)

In this way, McDermott's readings of *The Little Mermaid*, *Mean Girls* and *The Hunger Games* make it clear that "thwarting adolescent ambition ha[s] persisted across time and genre" (McDermott 2019, 135). In short, the "continuation of this plotline beyond the golden age of tomboy fiction represents a systemic taming of aberrant adolescent ambition that is at least a century old and still going strong" (McDermott 2019, 134).

AN(NE)DROIDS AND TOMBOYS

With a consideration of the roles, rules, and repercussions for tomboys in mind, it is important to turn to *Annedroids* in general, and the central female protagonist specifically. The shy yet spirited Anne who lives with her socially awkward and reclusive father in the junkyard does not refer to herself as a tomboy, nor do those around her, and yet, if one considers, as Halberstam does, that tomboyism can be "read as a sign of independence and self-motivation" (Halberstam 1998, 6), linked to "a 'natural' desire for greater freedoms and mobilities," then Anne can be read as such (Halberstam 1998, 6). Both gender and cultural studies theorists (and the actor who plays Anne) have been seen to read and respond to the character with a tomboy figure in mind. In their work on the representations of gender and STEM in children's television, Ashley Lynn Carlson and Hope J. Crowell state that Anne:

> Is not overly feminine or fashion conscious. Instead, Anne is portrayed as a tomboy. For example, in the pilot episode when Nick and Shania first meet Anne, she is wearing a welding helmet and overalls. When she takes off the helmet the other two children are surprised to discover that she is a girl. (Carlson and Crowell 2018, 12)

Holley (who plays Anne) picks up on this same reading when she notes that:

> Anne is definitely a tomboy, and she dresses kind of like a boy. I do relate to Anne in that she is not afraid of trying new things, and she's not afraid of new adventures and exploring. I do really admire Anne because she doesn't mind what other people think of her, and she's not trying to be like other girls. I like that Anne is her own person! ("Meet Addison Holley!" 2019)

The fact that Anne dresses in utilitarian workwear and resourcefully leans on junkyard materials as clothing staples such as belts, braces, and hair ties, positions her some way toward a tomboy identity.[8] The fact that she is interested in science, space, robotics, engineering, and all manner of scientific experiments and advancement puts her even further into tomboy territory. However, as is the case with existing tomboy fictions, it is what these girls are not and what they stand against that cements their tomboy status. In this way, it is not merely Anne's interest in science or her array of denim dungarees that position her as a tomboy, but rather, her opposition to, and bemusement with more predictably feminine interests and activities.

While Shania resides in a pink bedroom, surrounds herself with unicorns, dreams of being a princess-gymnast-popstar, lives to try on clothes and create new hairstyles and gymnastic choreography, Anne flinches at the thought of exploring or exploiting her femininity.[9] Time and again, Shania makes it clear that Anne needs a style and sartorial makeover, but rather than look awkward or embarrassed, these asides do nothing to change Anne or her wardrobe. And although Anne questions Shania's interest in fashion, make-up, and clothing, neither girl changes. Both remain resolutely their own version of femininity, without explanation or apology. While Anne is reluctant to engage with the more predictable world of feminine fashions, she does not speak of it with hostility. In this way, Anne's iteration of tomboy identity can be seen to lean on Pat Plumb and Gloria Cowan's work on the tomboy, wherein they discovered that "tomboys did not necessarily see feminine activities as aversive but rather enjoyed a less restrictive gender-role" (Craig and Lacroix 2011, 451).

Although Carlson and Crowell state that Anne appears "horrified by the amount of pink in Shania's room" and is "repulsed" by the end result of Shania's makeover,[10] my reading is that both Anne and Shania are confused and bemused by the other, rather than anything more divisive here (Carlson and Crowell 2018, 12). Indeed, the girls' day (which transpires as a result of Anne's dad stepping in last minute to support Nick in a father-son mini-vehicle challenge) involves watching a movie, ordering pizza, and hanging out at the request of Nick's mom.[11] When, as already noted, Anne seems taken aback by the sheer volume of pink involved, it is Shania herself who points out that girls' day "doesn't have to be" pink . . . it is simply that she, Shania, rather than all girls, loves the color (S2:E4). Anne is not looking to a tomboy identity as a form of protection "from negative aspects of what it means to be female in society" (Craig and Lacroix 2011, 451) and, as such, when Shania wants to watch television rather than search for a meteorite, they are each demonstrating their own agency and presenting alternative feminine possibilities, without judgment.[12]

Anne's friendship with Shania and Nick is seen as meaningful and supportive: she needs both in her life and finds herself troubled with the news that, in different seasons, they may be moving away from the junkyard. While tomboys routinely play like boys and with boys as a way of negotiating power within and beyond the playground, here, the junkyard is Anne's playground, and as such, she has little need to play such games (Paechter and Clark 2007, 317–31). With the junkyard in mind, one might routinely look to the space as stereotypically masculine because of its associations with heavy duty labor, physicality, and the need for operatives to work with metals and machines; however, this junkyard is routinely referred to as Anne's, and the various androids, robots, experiments, and creations are of her making. If one considers the ways in which spaces for play are crucial to the construction of social identity, then the junkyard could be understood as more relevant to Anne's tomboy identity than the paternal role, lack of maternal role, or peer group. There is never any sense that Anne is masculinized because of her time spent in the junkyard, yet likewise, the junkyard is never feminized because of Anne's time and commitment to it. Neither is fully feminized nor masculinized.

STEM OVER SPORTS

Physicality has long been a mainstay of tomboy culture and identity, and when Craig and Lacroix speak of the tomboy being "used to convey . . . a particular masculinity focused on skills or competencies rather than appearance," one might think of tomboys on the playing field (Craig and Lacroix 2011, 451). However, it is interesting to turn this particular skill set from sports to the junkyard. Anne demonstrates tomboy learning, with STEM interests overtaking sporting prowess as a site of freedom and mobility. The fact that Anne's father is unaccustomed to physical activity and uninterested in the world of sports might be part of the reason why Anne herself has little investment in physicality beyond that needed to make and mend her android creations. And although an interest in sports and outdoor play is routinely seen as informing a tomboy identity, Anne's authority over the outside world exists, but here in relation to STEM over sporting prowess. While tomboys within and beyond the entertainment arena routinely draw on masculine strength, male-defined team games, physicality, and aggression, so too, Anne engages in "activities atypical for [her] gender," albeit removed from the more routine physical prowess of the tomboy (Ahlqvist et al. 2013, 564). McDermott makes the point that tomboys are dynamic, in that gender performance is able to change "according to time, media, genre, and wave of feminism" (McDermott 2019, 134–55). Therefore, in the same way that earlier iterations of the tomboy were seen as active, ambitious, and challenging the status quo by whistling during the Civil War years, cycling during the Progressive Era, and dressing in male attire in the twenty-first century, Anne takes an active, in every sense of the word, interest in STEM (Abate 2008).

Anne is perfectly at home in her junkyard surroundings, with her eccentric yet awkward technology-minded father and robotics laboratories, and yet, beyond the screen space, qualitative data from the Economic and Social Research Council-funded ASPIRES 2 project makes it clear that while there may well be space for the male-leaning tomboy, that space is not available to her other, the hyperfeminine girly girl. Becky Francis et al. have suggested that the limitations of traditional femininity are amplified in relation to science, wherein feminine attributes are mocked and denigrated. We are told that hyperfemininity is viewed as vacuous and risible.[13] It is unsurprising then that our female lead is more tomboy than girly girl (Francis et al. 2017, 1097–110). While Allison Gonsalves discovered that "girly girls" are less likely to continue with physics at A Level (Gonsalves 2014, 503–21), Francis et al. more recently noted that those girls "who did intend to take physics at A level invested in various disassociations from femininity and/or actively performed masculinity" (Francis et al. 2017, 1103). The risk here then is that Anne's tomboy tendencies, as they incorporate an interest in science and technology, add to the weight of a culture that links STEM with masculinity, at the expense of femininity.

CHOOSING MASCULINITY AND/ OR REJECTING FEMININITY

We find that "[t]omboys are nearly always motherless in film" (Stahl 2016, 51) and literature . . . and *Annedroids*, as a small screen addition, is no exception (Abate 2008, xviii).[14] When we meet Anne, there seem to be no parents present, and over subsequent episodes we hear about and then meet her father, then find that her mother is neither in their lives nor whereabouts known.[15] And yet, although a lack of a maternal presence in the home has been said to play a part in tomboys leaning on masculinity, there is also evidence to suggest that having a mother in the home encourages a rejection of femininity (Holland and Harpin 2015, 305). Lynn Carr suggests that it is the maternal role that encourages young girls to reject traditional femininity in favor of the tomboy. Drawing on life histories with women who "identified themselves as tomboys," research finds that mothers were not seen as role-models to admire or emulate, rather, they were seen as boring, weak, emotional, helpless, unintelligent, overworked, underappreciated, and lacking in ambition (Carr 1998, 537–8). The author mentions that "[f]athers and other male role models seemed very important to most tomboys" and were "often discussed at great length" before going on to mention that she had to "pry information about mothers from respondents" (Carr 1998, 541). In the same way that women speaking about their pre-adolescent tomboy selves noted the importance of masculinity and paternity and the limitations of femininity and maternity, so too Anne is pulled toward masculinity at the expense of femininity. However, when the participants speak of the pull toward masculinity and the rejection of femininity, they are speaking of somewhat traditional gender spaces, roles, and identities. Back to *Annedroids*, Anne's dad may well be the breadwinning head of the household, but he is not "a man in power, a man with power [or] a man of power" at the pinnacle of the hegemonic hierarchy (Kimmel 2004, 184). Intelligent, caring, thoughtful, and awkward, yes . . . wealthy, physically assertive, or dominant in the public sphere, no. In this way, Anne may well be leaning toward a masculine caregiver, but this offers little in the way of a traditional hegemonic role model of masculinity.

The "distinction between the 'pull' of 'masculinity' and the 'push' of 'femininity'" that forms Carr's work might also be useful as a way of understanding adolescent identity based on schools, socializing, clubs, and societies (Carr 2005, 121). However, as an only child, self-schooled over the internet with few interests beyond her own back "junk yard" garden,[16] Anne has little gendered frame of reference here. In this instance, one might suggest that her tomboy identity says less about choosing masculinity or rejecting femininity, and more about Anne being herself. Anne is a product of her environment in the same way that Carrie Paechter and Sheryl Clark's primary school participants were products of their playground experiences (Paechter and Clark 2007, 317–31). The difference here is that Anne had, for the first decade of her life, limited social interaction, little interest in media fare, and, therefore, scant reason to see herself as gendered. Without parental, peer, or playground pressure, Anne was free to be herself, without limitations. This notion of freedom links in with earlier iterations of tomboy identity. Anne does not see femininity as a limitation, nor masculinity as a strength, and as such she has not adapted her own behaviors and mannerisms with the more predictable gender stereotypes and constraints in mind. However, when we read Anne, it is clear that based on existing work on femininity, girlhood, masculinity, and opportunity, Anne is a tomboy. Her aspirations and ambitions for herself, her friends, and her future speak of a childhood without limitation or restriction. When we hear Shania announce her plans to be a singer/actor/figure skater, we do not question her. So too, when Anne speaks of wanting to be the "first [person] to make contact with aliens on another planet" (S2:E5) and (not or) win the Nobel Prize (S4:E2), we do not doubt her. Tomboys are routinely seen to act upon the world, rather than being "an object to be viewed and subjected to the world" (Craig and Lacroix 2011, 462).

Lynn Carr's work on the life histories of tomboys draws attention to the ways in which her participants speak of both "choosing masculinity" and "rejecting femininity." She explains that "'boy stuff' seemed 'more fun,' womanhood appeared to hold 'no future,' [and that] to be a girl was to be vulnerable to male violence" (Carr 2005, 121). Carr goes on to note that "boys and men enjoyed more privileges, and fathers and male role models bestowed more attention on boys and 'boyish' behavior" (Carr 2005, 121; see also

Carr 1998). With this in mind, it is interesting to consider the ways in which *Annedroids* can be seen to adhere to or negotiate these life histories. There is no question that, like Carr's participants, Anne chooses masculinity in terms of her attire, activities, and interests while also rejecting the accoutrements of femininity. However, the program gives us the sense that she is choosing masculinity, not because of its supposed privilege,[17] but rather, because it is comfortable and available. Likewise, she is not rejecting femininity because she sees it as trivial or limiting, rather, it simply does not sit or fit comfortably as clothing, costume, or broader traits or mannerisms. In this way, it is as if Anne's formative years in the junkyard have been gender neutral, and that Anne is simply herself. Her activities and aspirations tell us little about gender; they simply help us to understand Anne. In this way, we can talk about the character as tomboy, androgynous, as borrowing from both masculinity and femininity, or as broadening the horizons of twenty-first century girlhood. Anne seems to be echoing Carrie Paechter when the theorist states that "[o]nce we understand that not all masculinities are entirely masculine, or femininities feminine, we may be able to think of ourselves as humans who construct our identities in various ways, some of which are related to ideal typical forms of masculinity and femininity, and some of which are not" (Paechter 2006, 262).The program picks up on this reading when the characters offer Pal the opportunity to select a gendered identity:

> Shania: Boys are smelly, gross and messy, they like fart jokes, not showering, running around and breaking stuff.
>
> Pal: But Nick is not like that and he is a boy.
>
> Shania: Girls like dressing up, doing their hair, doing their make-up, unicorns, the colour pink, dancing, unicorns, gymnastics and dreaming of becoming a princess.
>
> Pal: But Anne is not like that and she is a girl.
>
> Anne: Everyone is different. Not all girls are the same and not all boys are the same. You have to figure out what makes you, you . . . that is what growing up is all about: discovering yourself and who you want to be. (S4:E13)

While tomboy taming routinely sees girls leaving behind their "ambitions in order to embrace traditional female roles," Anne is not without ambition (McDermott 2019, 148). So, while McDermott speaks of the *Hunger Games* series and *Mean Girls* as primers in "feminine disappointment," *Annedroids* is proposing something different (McDermott 2019, 148). Tomboy texts routinely tease audiences with the possibility of queer readings before "showing girls what they could have and then convincing them that heteronormativity is better" (McDermott 2019, 148). In this way, the "tradition does not cover up or elide queer possibilities and identifications, but instead works to convince girls that heteronormativity is superior, easier, or inevitable" (McDermott 2019, 148). From *Little Women* to *The Little Mermaid*, we have been witness to a genre "that purports to recognize wild ambitions, queer identities, and female empowerment only to repudiate them" (McDermott 2019, 149). McDermott puts it eloquently when she states that tomboy texts may well "open doors to queer identities," but that in the final outcome, "what these texts actually offer is not a guide to queerness, but a guide *through* queerness, toward heteronormative femininity" (McDermott 2019, 147, emphasis added). In this way, the final season of *Annedroids* could, according to the tomboy taming trope, have chosen to present Anne as transitioning through her tomboy phase, through her tween and early teenage years, through puberty and out the other side of acceptable femininity.

Anne speaks of a fascinating future, moving through elite science academies to a world-changing career in STEM (particularly, robotics); however, when the opportunity arises and she is offered a scholarship at an elite STEM academy, she turns it down to stay with her friends and father. Although one might look to this narrative as evidence of tomboy taming, with the suggestion that Anne is taking on domestic responsibilities over and above her scientific aspirations or being asked to curtail her dreams in favor of a contained and constrained iteration of normative femininity, it must be noted that Anne's dreams do not change and her desire to learn, understand, and make a difference in the world are not diminished. The conventions of the tomboy taming genre speak of a climactic scene whereby "a sympathetically presented adult, emotionally central to the tomboy's life, persuades her to give up her rambunctious ways in order to be loved. Sometimes this lesson is underscored by events which make unmistakable the change in the tomboy protagonist" but this is not the case here (Segel 1989, 70). There is no parent gently steering her toward heteronormative femininity, and although her friends speak of missing her if she leaves, the peer group is not asking her to quash her ambitions. There are no other adults looking to challenge Anne; rather, her peer group and their parents all make it clear that Anne has the knowledge and capacity to make her own decision.

Although the show looks to have ended, with no plans or rumors of a fifth season in the pipeline, a more grown up Anne is no less ambitious, intelligent, creative, or enterprising than she was at the outset of the first season. Moreover, hair styles and sartorial choices have changed very little over the course of the show's history. As such, *Annedroids* concludes with Anne as tomboy, rather than a more predictable reading of a tomboy tamed. While "social scientists tend to assume that most girls cease tomboyism in adolescence," this popular children's program shows little sign of complying (Carr 2007, 439). Indeed, even though there is evidence that some girls "identify as tomboy and mobilise femininity to their advantage on occasions"[18] (Robinson and Davies 2010, 26), Anne is more consistent in the sense that she mobilizes tomboy-leaning thoughts, interests, and behaviors "in various sets of circumstances" throughout and beyond her formative years (Robinson and Davies 2010, 26).

Extant literature suggests that tomboy behaviors can be seen to end "around the age of 13" (Burn, O'Neil, and Nederend 1996, 424). Anne is around this age as the show concludes, with little sign of growing out of her tomboy identity, interests, or behaviors. Anne's future tomboy self is more than hinted at when, in an action-driven final episode, she rides her largest android as if wearing a power-loader suit to protect her dad from her mentor-*cum*-evil-robotics-nemesis, Ada Turing/Nicola Correia-Damude. Anne snarls, "get away from him you witch" (S4:E13). The *Aliens* (1986) pastiche, harking back to Ripley/Sigourney Weaver's untamed tomboy from the long-standing horror franchise, is a timely reminder about the courage, resourcefulness, and nurturance exemplified by the tomboy, irrespective of age, genre, format, or franchise. The tomboy in general, and Anne in particular, remains "a liminal figure, traversing the spaces between masculine and feminine, active and passive, child and adult" (Skerski 2011, 471). Indeed, Anne's refusal to enact traditional femininities by outgrowing her tomboy identity can be seen as a challenge to existing norms of gender development. After all, a tomboy identity post-puberty could "shatter the mandate for compulsory heterosexuality and female subordination" (Skerski 2011, 467; see also 471).

CONCLUSION

This chapter looks to the ways in which *Annedroids* can be seen to confirm or challenge existing themes and debates as they relate to media representations of the tomboy. I argue that the program presents a contemporary iteration of tomboy identity through the character of Anne. *Annedroids* offers its pre-adolescent audience a smart, capable, thoughtful, and ambitious central protagonist who leans toward a tomboy identity, a tomboy identity for the twenty-first century wherein an active interest and aptitude for STEM overrides an earlier drive for sporting prowess as a challenge to former feminine restrictions. While all of the lead characters, by which I am referring to Anne, Nick, Shania, and Pal, play with gender codes and debunk stereotypical gendered expectations, it is the tomboy Anne who is most significant here. Significant not because she fits into a neat definition of the tomboy, but rather, because her interest and excellence in science, technology, math, and engineering can be seen to update working definitions of both the tomboy and acceptable girlhood. Unlike former iterations of the tomboy, Anne should not be read or received as an "honorary boy," but nor should she be read as a challenge to the parameters of girlhood (Paechter 2006, 257). Anne has not been written as a way of dismissing or deriding traditional femininity, but rather, as a way of expanding our understanding of femininity, which, unlike the tomboy, should not be seen as a passing phase.

NOTES

1. Adolescence is a "transitional phase of growth and development between childhood and adulthood. The World Health Organization (WHO) defines an adolescent as any person between ages 10 and 19. This age range falls within WHO's definition of *young people*, which refers to individuals between ages 10 and 24" (Csikszentmihalyi 2021, emphasis in original).

2. Several characters have been given the surname of well-known scientists, including: (Carl) Sagan, (Alan) Turing, and (Giovanni Domenico) Cassini.

3. The program was originally conceived with a boy as the central protagonist; however, on the back of a report from Prix Jeunesse International relating to the fact that girls are "woefully underrepresented in kids TV shows," the decision was made to switch the central male character to a central female character, interested in STEM in general, and robotics in particular. Johnson states that "[a]t the time, I didn't think it was going to be that big a deal" and goes on to admit that he "couldn't have been more wrong" (Götz, Nastasia, and Johnson 2018, 47).

4. The final episode of the popular program saw Pal decide whether it wanted to be a girl or a boy, the android reflected that "I do not want to be a boy or a girl . . . I just want to be me" (S4:E13). Anne pronounces that "androids are just like people—they should have the choice to be who they are" (S4:E13). With this in mind, the show has been applauded for opening a dialogue about gender and diversity for its audience. Caroline Siede points out that while "op-eds continue to talk about how to make Hollywood less sexist, Amazon just went out and did the damn thing" (Siede 2014). And yet, it is important to note that the show, in general, and the character of Pal, in particular, has made some parents uncomfortable. Under the title of "Suggestive Material" on the Common Sense Media website, one mother penned: "What really alarmed my husband was the fact that in an episode, the discussion of Pal choosing 'its' gender was brought up. This aroused questions from my 10 year old that *we* do not feel that she is old enough to be discussing" (Correia Kenny commenting on Ashby 2022, emphasis added). And with added hostility, another parent writes on the topic of "introducing kids to transgender culture . . . My daughters 9 and really liked this show so it's disappointing they had to add this garbage into it. Trying to brainwash the kids into thinking its ok to pick their gender" (Nglass commenting on Ashby 2022).

5. Although not the focus of this chapter, it is worth noting, as Michelle Abate does in her seminal work on the topic, that tomboys have not always been girls/

women (Abate 2008, xiii). Abate gives a sense of the longevity, complexity and contradictions within tomboyism when she states that "[o]ver the centuries, this code of female conduct has assumed both masculine and feminine forms, been found in both urban and rural locales, been associated with both heterosexual and homosexual sexualities, been attributed to dispositional and circumstantial origins, been viewed as a temporary development phase as well as a lifelong identity, and been present in both Western and non-Western cultures. In this way, while it is commonplace to refer to tomboyism as a singular and static classification, it is actually far more fluid and multivalent" (Abate 2011, 407).

6. Kerry Robinson and Cristyn Davies tell us that although our readings of the tomboy have changed according to generation, it is younger women who view the term most positively. This is, we are told in part, "because of the term being re-signified through gender discourses, and also through capitalist consumerism in which young girls can produce themselves as tomboy subjects by wearing 'tomboy' clothing which is considered being 'cool'" (Robinson and Davies 2010, 26; see also Abate 2008, 223). Linked here is Jamie Skerski's argument that "[t]he dominance of tomboy chic threatens to re-define what tomboy identity signifies in the twenty-first century, transforming an enduring figure of gender rebellion into a wardrobe decision. Further, as tomboy fashion distances itself from overt masculinity in favor of accessorized femininity, it becomes a style based on conformity rather than resistance" (Skerski 2011, 477). *Annedroids* has not looked to market or merchandise its tomboy image or aesthetic, and although one might be left wondering if the tomboy is less commercially viable than her more predictably feminine counterparts (Tucker 2011), Skerski's findings make it clear that this is not the case.

7. Drawing on a "small sample of adult, working and lower-middle class, New Jersey-area lesbian, bisexual, and heterosexual women who identified as childhood tomboys" (Carr 2007, 439), Carr also foregrounds the role of heterosexual sexual and/or romantic interest as a reason for transitioning through or from earlier tomboy identities. In short, "tomboyism was generally seen as incompatible with heterosexual success" (Carr 2007, 443).

8. Perhaps unsurprisingly, Peggy Orenstein asks why "outgoing, outdoorsy activity and styles of dressing that are not over-feminized have to be labelled as boyish at all" (Orenstein cited in Tucker 2011), with the hope that we can "move towards thinking of these attributes as positive, not necessarily boyish" (Orenstein cited in Tucker 2011; See also Orenstein 2012).

9. Emily Ashby makes the point that *Annedroids* is not a "venue for fashion lines or the latest decorating trends; it's a place where beds are sometimes unmade, houses are modest, and neighborhoods include an unsightly junkyard that holds the keys to inspire the characters' greatness" (Ashby 2022).

10. Anne is made up and made over "with bright blue eye-shadow up to her eyebrows and a pink sequined beanie" looking "ridiculous rather than glamorous" at the big reveal (Carlson and Crowell 2018, 12).

11. One might suggest that although *Annedroids* does well to open up empowered representations of girlhood, it struggles to move beyond predictable stereotypes when

it comes to parental roles. Taking the following exchange from S3:E9 by way of an example:

> Anne: My dad and I don't really talk about anything, we just make things or fix things—sometimes we break things.
>
> Nick: My mum and I talk about everything—but we don't really do anything.

In this instance both parents are playing to gendered stereotypes. We see Nick with Anne's dad fixing up his mom's car, while Anne and Maggie talk and share confidences, as Anne begins to open up about her mother. Although a cursory glance at the scene in question leads us to assume that Annedroids offers little scope for progressive parenting representations, the fact that it is Anne's dad who works with, emotionally supports, and physically comforts Nick in a later episode when his own dad leaves demonstrates that these single parents are more than stereotypes (S4:E10).

12 Ostensibly, the female characters could be said to play directly into the television trope of the "tomboy and girly girl" when we find that the "'Girly Girl' will highly care about her appearance [and] pursue 'girly' interests" while "the 'Tomboy' will be into mechanics, house and/or building construction and/or renovation, or the like. She couldn't care less about her hair or makeup but is often an Unkempt Beauty anyway" (TV Tropes 2019).

13. The ASPIRES 2 project is a longitudinal research study looking at young people's science and career aspirations. Originally based at Kings College London, it has since moved to the UCL Institute of Education. See: https://www.ucl.ac.uk/ioe/departments-and-centres/departments/education-practice-and-society/aspires-2.

14. One might suggest that the lack of mother figures and the problematic representations of those mothers who are in the family home belongs firmly within the tradition of adolescent entertainment, as one way in which we can enjoy the trials and tribulations of the teen experience without the young characters or adolescent audience being impeded by a controlling or civilizing adult agenda. However, as I have suggested elsewhere, this is less about a lack of parental figures or guardians of authority, and more to do with an absence of mothers. As such, the lack of a maternal role has little to do with negotiating an adult agenda and much to do with removing the mother figure from the piece. Indeed, much adolescent programming makes it clear that fathers and male guardians are to be respected because they, and they alone, offer help, support, and direction for those teens under their care (Feasey 2012, 155–59). Moreover, in an article on television and the absent mother, I point to the growing popularity of the single father, or rather the popularity of the "missing mother," as it is seen to exist in children's literature (Vandenberg-Daves 2004), the Hollywood family film (Feasey 2015), the Disney franchise (Worthington 2009), mainstream animated features (Åström 2015), and fairytales (Woolf-Hoyle 2011; Feasey 2017, 227).

15. Toward the end of the final season, we are finally introduced to Anne's mom through a series of plot twists that involve evil robotic technicians and dastardly corporations. In the last episode of the show, the woman makes it clear, through a holographic form, that she has always loved Anne but has made the difficult decision

to put her scientific advancements above her maternal responsibilities in order to save the planet for her daughter and subsequent generations.

16. Anne is set a special assignment by Julie Payette, Governor General of Canada and former member of the Canadian Astronaut Corps.

17. Traci Craig and Jessica LaCroix state that "[t]omboy identity can gain women limited privilege to spaces for which masculinity is an unspoken requirement" and yet "[t]he temporary nature of the protections privileged to tomboys undermines the ability of tomboys to truly transcend the binary gender system" (Craig and Lacroix 2011, 450).

18. Anne wears more predictably feminine attire on three occasions in the show's history, and each exception goes some way to prove the rule that, in this case, Anne is a tomboy. When she dresses as Dorothy from *The Wizard of Oz* (1939) for a children's birthday party, it is a costume, not her own clothing, and the distinction is key. She attends the party and dresses up purely to allow her access to the dry ice so that she can embark on further scientific experiments while the celebrations are underway. The second noticeable feminine transformation is of a punky Rapunzel-like figure who appears in one of Nick's nightmares, and as such, this image was not of Anne's making. Lastly, in the final episode of the show when she wears a night-time insect attractor suit which doubles as a black ball gown for an end of year class dance, her dad wears the same outfit. In short, the dress is not associated with heteronormative femininity.

BIBLIOGRAPHY

Abate, Michelle. 2011. "Introduction: Special Issue on Tomboys and Tomboyism." *Journal of Lesbian Studies* 15 (4): 407–11.

———. 2008. *Tomboys: A Literary and Cultural History.* Philadelphia: Temple University Press.

Ahlqvist, Sheana Halim, May Ling Halim, Faith K Greulich, Leah E Lurye, and Diane Ruble. 2013. "The Potential Benefits and Risks of Identifying as a Tomboy: A Social Identity Perspective." *Self and Identity* 1 (5): 563–81.

Ashby, Emily. 2022. *Annedroids* TV Review. Common Sense Media.

Balay, Anne. 2010. "'They're Closin' Up Girl Land': Female Masculinities in Children's Fantasy." *Femspec* 10 (2): 5–23.

Beck, Sara L., Rebecca Hains, and Colleen Russo Johnson. 2017. "'PAL can Just be Themselves': Children in the US Respond to *Annedroids*' Genderless TV Character." In *Beyond the Stereotypes? Images of Boys and Girls, and their Consequences*, edited by Dafna Lemish and Maya Götz, 225–36. Göteborg: Nordicom.

Burn, Shawn Megan, A. Katherine O'Neil, and Shirley Nederend. 1996. "Childhood Tomboyism and Adult Androgyny." *Sex Roles* 34 (5): 419–28.

Carlson, Ashley Lynn, and Hope J. Crowell. 2018. "Achievements, Gaps and the 'Achievement Gap' STEM in Children's Programming." In *Women in STEM on*

Television: Critical Essays, edited by Ashley Lynn Carlson, 7–19. Jefferson, NC: McFarland.

Carr, C. Lynn. 1998. "Tomboy Resistance and Conformity: Agency in Social Psychological Gender Theory." *Gender and Society* 12 (5): 528–53.

———. 2005. "Tomboyism or Lesbianism? Beyond Sex/Gender/Sexual Conflation." *Sex Roles* 53 (1/2): 119–31.

———. 2007. "Where Have All the Tomboys Gone? Women's Accounts of Gender in Adolescence." *Sex Roles* 56: 439–48.

Clayton, Amy. 2010. "The Future of Feminism is Slayed: Tomboyism in Joss Whedon's *Fray*." *Red Feather Journal* 1 (1): 26–39. http://nebula.wsimg.com/deb4c88aa6241c946a010653b0e6c3d5?AccessKeyId=F0152308703B0C3D5115&disposition=0&alloworigin=1.

Craig, Traci, and LaCroix, Jessica. 2011. "Tomboy as Protective Identity." *Journal of Lesbian Studies*, 15 (4): 450–465.

Csikszentmihalyi, M. 2021. "Adolescence." *Encyclopedia Britannica*. February 20, 2021. https://www.britannica.com/science/adolescence.

Currie, Dawn H. 1997. "Decoding Femininity: Advertisements and Their Teenage Readers." *Gender & Society* 11 (4): 453–77.

Davies, Cristyn. 2008. "Becoming Sissy." In *Judith Butler in Conversation: Analyzing the Texts and Talk of Everyday Life*, edited by Bronwyn Davies, 117–33. New York: Routledge.

Devor, Holly. 1989. *Gender Blending: Confronting the Limits of Duality*. Bloomington: Indiana University Press.

Feasey, Rebecca. 2012. "Absent, Ineffectual and Intoxicated Mothers: Representing the Maternal in Teen Television." *Feminist Media Studies* 12 (1): 155–9.

———. 2017. "Television and the Absent Mother: Why Girls and Young Women Struggle to Find the Maternal Role." In *The Absent Mother in the Cultural Imagination: Missing, Presumed Dead,* edited by Berit Åström, 225–40. London: Palgrave Macmillan.

Francis, Becky, Louise Archer, Julie Moote, Jen de Witt, and Lucy Yeomans. 2017. "Femininity, Science, and the Denigration of the Girly Girl." *British Journal of Sociology of Education* 38 (8): 1097–110.

Gonsalves, Allison. 2014. "Physics and the Girly Girl—There is a Contradiction Somewhere: Doctoral Students' Positioning around Discourses of Gender and Competence in Physics." *Cultural Studies of Science Education* 9 (2): 503–21.

Götz, Maya, Diana Iulia Nastasia, and J. J. Johnson. 2018. "Girls Building Androids and Robots: Equality in STEM with the Media Program *Annedroids*." In *Androids, Cyborgs, and Robots in Contemporary Culture and Society*, edited by Steven John Thompson, 35–64. Hershey: IGI Global.

Halberstam, Jack. 1998. *Female Masculinity*. Durham: Duke University Press.

Holland, Samantha and Harpin, Julie. 2015. "Who Is the 'Girly' Girl? Tomboys, Hyper-Femininity and Gender." *Journal of Gender Studies* 24 (3): 293–309.

Kimmel, Michael. 2004. "Masculinity as Homophobia: Fear, Shame, and Silence in the Construction of Gender Identity." In *Feminism and Masculinities*, edited by Peter F. Murphy, 182–99. Oxford: Oxford University Press.

McDermott, Shawna. 2019. "The Tomboy Tradition: Taming Adolescent Ambition from 1869 to 2018." *Children's Literature Association Quarterly* 44 (2): 134–55.

"Meet Addison Holley!" *Justine*. 2019. https://justinemagazine.com/meet-addison-holley/.

Orenstein, Peggy. 2012. *Cinderella Ate My Daughter: Dispatches from the Front Lines of the New Girlie-Girl Culture*. London: Harper.

Paechter, Carrie. 2006. "Masculine Femininities/Feminine Masculinities: Power, Identities and Gender." *Gender and Education* 18 (3): 253–63.

Paechter, Carrie, and Sheryl Clark. 2007. "Learning Gender in Primary School Playgrounds: Findings from the Tomboy Identities Study." *Pedagogy, Culture & Society* 15 (3): 317–31.

Robinson, Kerry H., and Cristyn Davies. 2010. "Tomboys and Sissy Girls: Exploring Girls' Power, Agency and Female Relationships in Childhood Through the Memories of Women." *Australasian Journal of Early Childhood.* 35 (1): 24–32.

———. 2007. "Tomboys and Sissy Girls: Young Girls' Negotiations of Femininity and Masculinity." *International Journal of Equity and Innovation in Early Childhood*, 5 (7): 17–31.

Segel, Elizabeth. 1989. "The Gypsy Breynton Series: Setting the Pattern for American Tomboy Heroines." *Children's Literature Association Quarterly* 14 (2): 67–71.

Sentilles, Renée. 2018. *American Tomboys, 1850–1915*. Amherst: University of Massachusetts Press.

Siede, Caroline. 2014. "Amazon's *Annedroids* Effortlessly Dismantles Kid Show Gender Roles." *A.V. Club*. July 25, 2014. https://tv.avclub.com/amazon-s-annedroids-effortlessly-dismantles-kid-show-ge-1798270632.

Skerski, Jamie. 2011. "Tomboy Chic: Re-fashioning Gender Rebellion." *Journal of Lesbian Studies* 15 (4): 466–79

Stahl, Lynne. 2016. "Chronic Tomboys: Feminism, Survival, and Paranoia in Jodie Foster's Body of Work." *The Velvet Light Trap* 77: 50–68.

Stoller, Robert. 1968. *Sex and Gender: On the Development of Masculinity and Femininity*. New York: Science House.

Stockton, Kathryn Bond. 2009. *The Queer Child, or Growing Sideways in the Twentieth Century.* Durham, NC: Duke University Press.

Taryn. 2014. "Girls Can Build Robots Too! A Review of *ANNEDROIDS*." *tumblr*. https://scirens.tumblr.com/post/94212003078/girls-can-build-robots-too-a-review-of-annedroids/embed.

Thorne, Barrie. 1993. *Gender Play: Girls and Boys in School*. New York: Routledge.

Tucker, Eleanor. 2011. "Girls Will be Tomboys." *The Telegraph*. December 11, 2011. https://www.telegraph.co.uk/lifestyle/8935656/Girls-will-be-tomboys.html.

TV Tropes. 2019. "Tomboy and Girly Girl." *TV Tropes*. https://tvtropes.org/pmwiki/pmwiki.php/Main/TomboyAndGirlyGirl.

Chapter 8

Misnomers and Contemporizations

An Examination of the Tomboy Figure in the Duffer Brothers' Stranger Things

Erica Joan Dymond

As the premiere of the much-ballyhooed second season of *Stranger Things* approached, *Flavorwire*'s Moze Halperin excitedly informed readers of the addition of Sadie Sink's character, Max Mayfield. Seeming to anticipate confusion, Halperin explained that "there *can* be two tomboys on one show" (2016, emphasis in original). The words "two tomboys" immediately attract attention. While referring to Max as a "tomboy" is reasonable, labeling Eleven as such seems misguided. Nonetheless, Halperin is not alone in this assessment. For instance, *Playboy*'s Kate Leth reduces the second season's dynamic between Max and Eleven to "two tomboys vying for the slot of Token Girl" (2019). While the statement is problematic in general, this idea of "two tomboys" strikes a discordant note. Most remarkable is that countless critics and scholars render this same conclusion. Even noted essayist Lisa Selin Davis refers to Eleven and Max as "two tomboy*ish* characters" in her recent *Tomboy: The Surprising History and Future of Girls Who Dare to Be Different* (2020, 80, emphasis in original). Certainly, a cursory reading of Eleven's appearance may return this result; however, a comprehensive evaluation wholly excludes such a finding. In fact, to refer to Eleven as a "tomboy" disregards her years of neglect and suffering. Likewise, it does a disservice to those who identify as a "tomboy" and/or are invested in "tomboy culture." It is, by all means, short-sighted.

Similarly, while the second season *does* depict gender variance in the character of Max, she represents more a contemporary interpretation of the tomboy figure. Customizing her version of the tomboy to her own needs and desires, Max embraces the feminine as much as the masculine. She is not the rigid stereotype one might find in the film and television of the 1980s, but entirely her own person. Essentially, though her character is situated in a "tomboy" era (the 1980s), she reflects a time (now) where transcending the perceived parameters of one's gender rarely elicits a label or may simply be referred to as "gender expansive."

In both instances, the label of "tomboy" becomes a multifaceted issue that requires thorough unpacking. And, in the process of examining these two characters, as much is revealed about the world outside of narrative as inside.

ELEVEN: THE TOMBOY WHO WASN'T

A character's first moments on screen are critical. They serve as a permanent touchstone for viewers, providing definition and establishing expectations. In S1:E1 of *Stranger Things*, the Duffer Brothers opt for a quiet introduction to Eleven's character. The set-up for this scene begins with an undisclosed emergency at Hawkins National Laboratory. There is an inquiry about "the girl" with the response, "She can't have gone far" [00:21:04]. A cut brings viewers to the nearby forest. A close-up of small, bare feet suggests that this is "the girl" the scientists are seeking. As the feet approach the camera, they softly roll from heel to toe. They remain impossibly clean as they gingerly step through the detritus. Then, the right foot turns slightly on its side to minimize contact with the forest floor. In the initial few seconds of this scene, the delicate blocking employed by the directors shows Eleven's character as both careful and vulnerable. Next, a slow tilt up reveals Eleven's hospital gown and rests on her doe-eyed expression. From the autumnal hue of the pine needles surrounding her feet to the warm light on her face, Eleven's character is presented in the gentlest terms. Certainly, the Duffer Brothers could have offered a more dramatic scene. Since Eleven crawled through a small drainpipe to escape the lab (as noted in S1:E2), she could have been shown with her hands, knees, and feet caked in sediment. Likewise, given that she has been patrolling the forest for an undetermined length of time, her feet and ankles could be equally as layered in grime. Instead, she is depicted in a lightly stained hospital gown with select smudges on her person (most of which only become apparent when she is in Benny's Burgers). Even the single tear to her hospital gown appears to have been created with surgical precision. Here, a small swatch of fabric is missing from the front, bottom hem. The tear is far too clean to spark alarm. Only later, when the missing square of fabric is employed as a red herring in the search for Will Byers, does its actual purpose become clear.[1] Therefore, even the minimal distress that viewers see to Eleven's clothing is not intended to highlight the physical trauma of her escape, but to further the narrative. In essence, while it may be more practical to show Eleven's person covered in debris and her clothing in tatters, the directors elect for a quiet introduction. One that is deliberately soft and sympathetic. One that elicits compassion and concern from viewers. What becomes apparent in this introduction is then reiterated throughout the entirety of the show: Eleven's image is the result of exploitation and abuse. It does not reflect any aspect of the tomboy figure or of tomboy culture.

In fact, via exceptional storytelling and cinematography, the Duffer Brothers repeatedly underscore that Eleven has been denied her true gender expression: not that of a so-called "tomboy" but that of a gender-conforming child/young adult. S1:E3 provides evidence of the pain she has experienced in not being permitted to live authentically. Here, Mike has hidden Eleven in the Wheeler's basement. With the family gone, Eleven sneaks upstairs to Nancy's bedroom. When she opens Nancy's music box, Eleven stares at the plastic pirouetting ballerina. Mouth agape, Eleven tries to catch her breath as this feminine-coded object inspires intermittent pain and joy. She closes the box and then moves to a pinboard decorated with photos from Nancy's life. A point-of-view shot brings the audience to Eleven's perspective and an overview of the board. Seen in this collage is a masculine-coded photo of a young Nancy wearing a denim baseball cap, blue striped T-shirt, and denim overalls. However, when the POV shot focuses on a single photo, it is of Nancy as a child, playing on the beach. A tilt up moves from the happy girl in the one-piece swimsuit to a childhood photo of Nancy dressed as a tiara-wearing princess. A cut brings viewers back to Eleven's face. Her brow furrows, her lips quiver. Her pain is explicit as she sees the life that she was denied, one that is intensely feminine coded. A cut returns viewers to her perspective. Eleven remains on the same princess picture and then a pan to the right shows Nancy in her First Communion gown and (another) tiara. As the camera continues to pan right, viewers see close-ups of a rosette-ringed birthday cake, adolescent Nancy, and then photo strips of Nancy and Barb. The final cut of this scene reveals Eleven's twitching nose, shaking shoulders, and tormented face. The camerawork of this scene is telling—it skillfully shows Eleven moving through Nancy's childhood and into her young adulthood. The pictures illustrate milestones—ones that Eleven has been prohibited. More importantly, the photos that capture Eleven's attention are all feminine coded. Like the vaguely provocative photo of Nancy dressed like a bunny (presumably for Halloween), the previously mentioned masculine-coded photo has little relevance to Eleven. In this moment, the Duffer Brothers have a clear opportunity to address gender variance; nonetheless, the directors use this moment underscore that Eleven merely wants what Nancy has. As artistically suggested in this early scene, Eleven's authentic gender expression falls well within gender norms.

This sophisticated style of visual storytelling assists in clarifying Eleven's desire to lead a gender-conforming life. It is employed throughout the first season to leave no doubt about the torture she endured. The resulting tension between how Eleven is physically presented to viewers and her authentic gender identity creates a specter that haunts the first season. Still, Eleven's surface image is so striking that it seems to mislead both laypeople and critics into seeing an expression of gender variance. In an article for *College Fashion*, a staff writer describes Eleven's wardrobe change from the first season to the second as "[evolving] from tomboy to punk rockstar" (Dacie 2019, "*Stranger Things* Fashion: Eleven"). While this assessment is problematic in that it prioritizes one form of self-expression above another, it is also troubling in that it offers only the most cursory read of Eleven's appearance. Lest this label of "tomboy" be perceived as a simple gaffe, it is important to note that in a later article for *College Fashion*, this same writer uses similar wording to compare Max and Eleven: "Max has a distinct tomboy feel to her style, kind of like a less-edgy Eleven" (Dacie 2019, "*Stranger Things* Fashion: Max Mayfield"). Now, given the relaxed format of this online magazine, it may be sage to dismiss this classification of "tomboy" as flippant or even uniformed. However, in the academic collection *Uncovering Stranger Things: Essays on Eighties Nostalgia, Cynicism and Innocence in the Series*, this same "tomboy" label is repeatedly used. For instance, in his study on the depiction of the nuclear family in *Stranger Things*, author David Anthony Franklin references Eleven's "tomboy look" (2018, 177). Moreover, in this same volume, author Emily E. Roach nearly echoes the sentiments of the *College Fashion* writer when she offers a comparison between Eleven and Max: "Like Eleven in the first season, Max is introduced as something of a 'tomboy' albeit with fewer dimensions than Eleven" (2018, 142). All these instances are surprising since the Duffer Brothers invest in meticulously paced flashbacks that unravel Eleven's life of imprisonment and mistreatment. The directors heavily imply that her appearance is the result of both abuse (those who shaved her head and gave her a wardrobe of hospital gowns) and generosity (those who gifted her clothing and accessories). Nonetheless, since this "tomboy" perception is present in both the popular and academic spheres, Eleven's appearance requires explication.

The notion of the tomboy and of tomboy culture is strongly associated with exploration, expression, and preference. Each of these words indicate choice. However, Eleven has no choice in her appearance. Her shaven head is for the convenience of her captors. It serves as a constant reminder of her exploitation. Once free from their tyranny, Eleven allows her hair to grow. It is shown increasingly longer as the seasons progress. Likewise, every article of clothing in the first two seasons is either gifted to Eleven or stolen out of necessity: the oversized Benny's Burgers T-shirt (S1:E1), Mike's tan snap-front jacket (S1:E1-S1:E2), Mike's navy sweatshirt (S1:E2-S1:E4), Mike's gray sweatpants (S1:E2-S1:E4), Mike's green and yellow striped tube socks (S1:E4-S2:E3), Nancy's pink dress (S1:E4-S2:E3), Mike's blue jacket (S1:E5-S1:E7), Hopper's blue and tan plaid shirt (S1:E8-S2:E3), the hunter's black puffer jacket (S2:E2-S2:E3), the hunter's red and black cap (S2:E2-S2:E3), all of the clothes she wears when in Hopper's care, the "punk" outfit given to her by Kali (S2:E7-S2:E9). None of these items are of her choosing. They are merely the result of happenstance. Therefore, the elements that most define Eleven's "look" cannot be deemed "tomboy." To do so would misread her character . . . as well as disregard the spirit and purpose of the tomboy figure and tomboy culture.

When endeavoring to interpret Eleven's authentic gender expression, it is tempting to consult the makeover sequences of the first and second seasons. Certainly, Eleven registers satisfaction with both outcomes. In the first season, she seems soothed by the deeply feminine-coded ensemble created by the Hawkins friend group. This appears to provide further support for her being gender conforming. However, in the second season, she also seems to enjoy the quasi masculine-coded clothing provided Kali's Chicago crew. In fact, there are hints of tomboy culture in this outfit. However, the media's complicated history with "the makeover" reminds viewers to proceed with caution. Many of the 1980's teen films that inform the tone and style of *Stranger Things* contain deeply problematic makeover scenes.[2] For instance, works such as Howard Deutch's *Some Kind of Wonderful* and John Hughes's *The Breakfast Club* feature young women who are transformed to reflect conventional beauty standards. Once primped and polished, they are praised and rewarded; nonetheless, little of the external alteration reflects the actual character. And, after decades of makeover films like Amy Heckerling's *Clueless*, Robert Iscove's *She's All That*, Donald Petrie's *Miss Congeniality*, and Garry Marshall's *The Princess Diaries*, audiences are primed to see movie makeovers as disingenuous. Therefore, while the makeover scenes of the first two seasons deliver a satisfying tribute to the Duffer Brothers' favorite decade, savvy viewers enter these sequences prepared for their artificiality and seeking contemporary subtext—all of which is deftly provided.

Viewed holistically, the makeover sequence of S1:E4 offers a textbook lesson in sex, gender, and gender expression. While it reads as a playful moment, it is remarkably layered, often revealing as much about the Hawkins friend group as it does Eleven. It begins with the young men needing to sneak Eleven from Mike's basement to the A.V. room at Hawkins Middle School (to rescue Will from the Upside Down). Immediately, Lucas determines the venture as an impossibility because "there is no way we're going to get the weirdo in there without anyone noticing . . . I mean ... look at her" [00:17:29]. The three young men then quizzically gaze at Eleven. At this juncture, the friend group struggles to reconcile Eleven's outward appearance with her biological sex. They view her as "weird" only because they know her sex and understand that her masculine-coded appearance is not of her choosing. They never consider that she effortlessly passes as a boy/young man.[3] What is obvious to viewers is nonsensical to the friend group. To them, costuming Eleven in a pink baby-doll dress and synthetic platinum-blonde wig is more logical than her inconspicuous sweatpants, sweatshirt, and close-cropped hair. Here, the Duffer Brothers show the irrational barriers that sex and gender can create. This is a conscious choice on behalf of the artists, a coy wink at the knowing viewers.

As the makeover sequence of S1:E4 continues, it transitions to a montage. In an homage to the final scene of John Hughes's *Sixteen Candles*, Mike and Eleven sit opposite each other. The framing is tight and a gauzy sunlit curtain provides an ethereal backdrop. As Mike leans toward Eleven, she mirrors his gesture. He tenderly dusts blush on her cheeks. The cinematography of the sequence conveys a distinctly intimate tone. And, while the surface optics have potential for a queer reading, viewers are well aware that this entire scene exists so that Eleven's biological sex can be made evident. More than anything, this moment continues to emphasize the romantic narrative which commences the instant Mike meets Eleven. A cut then brings viewers to Lucas and Dustin methodically searching through bins and boxes. Here, the framing is looser and the interaction between the two is limited as each strives to locate (what they perceive as) gender-appropriate attire for Eleven. Superficially, these scenes seem to stand in contrast to each other: one is devoted to solidifying the love story, the other to completing a task. Nonetheless, as will soon be addressed, both are very much steeped in issues of gender.

After Lucas selects a pink baby-doll dress and Dustin chooses a blonde wig, a cut brings viewers back to Mike and Eleven. An over-the-shoulder shot shows Mike applying pink lip balm to Eleven and a reverse shot shows her earnestly looking in his eyes. Here, it is evident that Eleven is allowing Mike to shape her appearance.[4] The scored portion of this sequence concludes as the young men wait outside a closed door while Eleven changes. Now, several aspects of this brief montage require attention. Reflecting the long-held tradition of cinematic makeovers, Eleven does not have the privilege of exploring the bins of garments and accessories. She has no voice in what she will be wearing. Likewise, she is given no choice in makeup. In fact, Mike never explains what he is doing with the cosmetics. When he first touches

Eleven with the blush brush, she flinches. Even then, he does not pause to discuss the purpose of these products (the scored montage does not "allow" for dialogue); instead, he casts a "let's continue" nod and then a smile in her direction. As a result of her devotion to and dependency on Mike, she defers to him entirely. Ultimately, having created an entirely new appearance for Eleven, the young men have turned this masculine-coded version of Eleven into their idea of what a young woman looks like. It is one shaped by their environment as well as the media. And, one that denies agency.

As this first makeover scene concludes, it needs to be emphasized that what Eleven enjoys most about this new look is how it affects Mike. As Eleven emerges from the once closed-off room, her eyes remain firmly locked on Mike. She is seeking his response. She is not watching to confirm if she "passes" as a conventional young woman but if Mike approves of this alteration. When Mike sees Eleven, he physically registers her transformation: his shoulders jump, his eyebrows raise, and his eyes widen. To emphasize that Mike's reaction is paramount, rack focus is used to blur Lucas and Dustin into the background. Mike's face remains the only point of attention. When Mike declares Eleven as "pretty," she maintains his gaze and smiles [00:18:22]. Wearing Nancy's clothes and makeup, Eleven is seeking this precise word. In fact, the first notes of this makeover scene occur two episodes prior to the actual event. As Eleven tours Mike's home in S1:E2, she meanders to a collection of framed photos. She fixes on a portrait of Nancy. Nancy is wearing a soft-pink argyle sweater and has her wavy shoulder-length hair pulled forward. Her appearance is feminine coded. Seeming to study it, Eleven strokes the glass, smiles sorrowfully, and says, "Pretty" [00:15:39]. This word becomes imbued with meaning. It signifies the life that Eleven has been seeking. Now, in S1:E4, Eleven moves to the hallway mirror and inspects the results of the makeover. She whispers "pretty" with the slightest nod of confirmation [00:18:45]. While heartwarming and seeming to confirm Eleven's gender-conforming nature, the cinematic composition of this moment begs attention. The framing foregrounds Eleven's reflection but shows Mike directly behind her. This alludes to both the influence Mike has in this transformation as well as his stake in it. As with the previous rack focus, Dustin and Lucas have been eliminated from this moment, again, forwarding the romantic narrative. Much like Eleven's image (often labeled as "tomboy") in the first three episodes of the premiere season, this feminine-coded one cannot be considered a representation of Eleven's true gender expression. It is the creation of young men, influenced by juvenile love, and employed out of perceived necessity.

Clearly, it is (all too) easy to see the makeover scene of S1:E4 as reinforcing sexual and gender norms: turning the "tomboy" into the "pretty girl" thus resolving the potentially "problematic" romantic narrative. In fact, a writer

Figure 8.1 Eleven (left, played by Millie Bobby Brown) examines her makeover in the hallway mirror. Mike (right, played by Finn Wolfhard) is seen in the background of her reflection. *Stranger Things* S1:E4 (2016).

for the internet tabloid *BuzzFeed* sees this moment (along with others in the show) as particularly insidious:

> *Stranger Things* makes sure to scrub all possible traces of queerness from its characters ...[the show] champions the nerds and the weirdos, as so much of '80s pop culture did, but the writers temporarily put Eleven in a wig and make most characters seemingly straight as if to assure that their weirdness won't become unruly.[5] (Keating 2016)

Shortsighted, this statement seems to overlook the preposterous outcome of the S1:E4 makeover: a "normal" looking person has been transformed into a cartoon character by adolescent men. This is explicit commentary on a society that views women through a brutally narrow lens. Moreover, this statement also neglects the sequence's more subtly transgressive moments. A deeper examination reveals the young men as fearlessly entering a feminine-coded realm. When Mike applies Eleven's makeup, when Lucas holds the pink dress to himself, and when Dustin dons the blond wig, each young man is transcending the perceived boundaries of his gender. One might expect Lucas and Dustin to affect a feminine pose as they interact with these feminine-coded objects; societal expectations nearly obligate them to do so. Likewise, viewers may expect Mike to struggle with the cosmetics, insist that Eleven apply them to herself (to avoid revealing that he knows exactly how these products operate), or laugh with embarrassment. None of this happens. All fully entrench themselves in this potentially "emasculating" task. Therefore, as laypeople and critics erroneously view the show as exclusionary or even look to Eleven as an example of gender fluidity or evolving ideas of gender (too conveniently placing her in the role of "tomboy"), it is the show's young men who frequently reflect a more progressive, twenty-first century perspective.

Naturally, some viewers might turn to the makeover scene of S2:E7 for support of gender variance. However, like with S1:E4, S2:E7 offers little insight into Eleven's gender identity. In fact, the second season's makeover is a nearly uncanny echo of the first season's makeover but with a somewhat masculine-coded result. At the beginning of this episode, Eleven escapes her sequestration in Hopper's cabin to find her "sister" (fellow Hawkins National Laboratory hostage) Kali. Kali is a gang leader. Since she and her cronies embrace a punk lifestyle and aesthetic, Eleven is frequently teased for her rural (read: "uncool") appearance. Nonetheless, after demonstrating her value to the crew, Eleven is invited to participate in one of their "missions." With deference to the era of the makeover, Eleven is transformed to resemble a member of Kali's crew. This sequence begins with Eleven passively sitting while others actively alter her. Perhaps equally worrisome, as Dottie and Kali hold new clothes and cosmetics up to Eleven, her expression is one of bewilderment. No permission is asked, nothing is explained. Once again, Eleven has no agency. And, since she is a runaway under Kali's care (much like when she was under Mike's care), Eleven is allotted little room for protest. A series of close-ups then show Dottie's hands combing and sculpting Eleven's hair, carelessly smudging a kohl color onto Eleven's eyelids, and finally patting a crimson hue onto Eleven's lips.[6] When Dottie is done, she spins the chair to face Kali, Mick, Axel, and Funshine. Dottie stands, arms crossed, admiring her creation. She does not offer Eleven a mirror to inspect her new look or to voice an opinion. Eleven remains entirely unconsulted. Nonetheless, Kali nods in approval and the others smile in agreement. When Dottie proclaims her artistry as "bitchin'," Eleven parrots this word [00:23:43]. This "bitchin'" is an echo of the first makeover's "pretty" except here Eleven's eyes narrow as she tries on this new bit of slang. In this case, even the description of Eleven's look is not of her choosing . . . or in her vocabulary. As the gang begins their departure, a Tarantino-esque slow-motion shot allows ample time to assess Eleven's clothing. An oversized black blazer, plain black shirt, and pegged denim pants all provide a more masculine-coded appearance. And, while she appears comfortable with this outfit, viewers are aware that this is the work of Dottie and Kali.[7]

In S2:E7, akin to the makeover of S1:E4, Eleven has no choice in her appearance. However, unlike the makeover of S1:E4, there is no perceived need for this change. The Hawkins friend group assumes that for Will to be saved from the Upside Down, Eleven *must* undergo a temporary physical transformation. The young men believe they are briefly changing Eleven out of necessity. Conversely, Kali's group merely wants Eleven to be visually complementary to their gang. The makeover of S2:E7 is one belonging, but on a mostly aesthetic level. While it is intended to be more permanent and initiate Eleven into Kali's ersatz family, it also disregards her true desires. Nothing of Eleven's gender expression is to be found here.

While both the makeovers of S1:E4 and S2:E7 reflect the sensibilities of those who performed them, the "makeover" of S3:E2 offers a genuine glimpse of Eleven's true gender-expression. The sequence opens with Max and Eleven exiting a bus in front of the Starcourt Mall. Correctly deducing that Eleven has never been shopping, Max says, "I guess we're going to have to try everything" [00:25:29]. Max's comment reveals a desire to guide, not dictate. She puts this into action as the two tour The Gap. When Eleven stops in front of a trendy paint-splatter shirt, Max inquires, "Do you like that?" [00:26:00]. A short but needed exchange commences:

> Eleven: How do I know . . . what I like?
>
> Max: You just try things on. Until you find something that feels like you.
>
> Eleven: Like me?
>
> Max: Yeah. Not Hopper. Not Mike. You. [00:26:03–00:26:28]

While the scene ends here, the moments that follow serve a valuable function. As Max's advice trails away, the Duffer Brothers cut to a quiet establishing shot of Melvald's General Store. Then, another cut offers a close-up of a textbook collection spread over the glass case of a checkout counter. A slow pan reveals that the titles are related to electromagnetic theory. Finally, a tilt up shows Joyce. The shot lingers as she silently considers the material. This fairly dormant stretch of time allows Max's empowering words to be weighed. And, of equal importance, this break from the mall sequence removes any sense of urgency. As Max and Eleven enter into this makeover, there are no extenuating circumstances. This is not the rescue mission of Season One or the attempted indoctrination of Season Two. This is simply Eleven exploring her options and finding her personal aesthetic.

After a considerable break, a transition in S3:E2 returns viewers to the young women continuing their shopping trip. A 1980s style fashion montage commences. First, Eleven is shown in a pair of high-waist yellow pants, splatter shirt, and suspenders. Though the ensemble is cluttered, Max nods with encouragement: the only input she provides is to correctly position Eleven's beret. The same can be seen when Eleven tries on a loose-fitting splatter-shirt and skirt. Max merely offers a wide belt to pull the outfit together (both literally and figuratively). And, Max's accommodating approach is clearly effective. Unlike the makeovers of previous seasons, Eleven is shown as laughing and smiling throughout the experience. As a writer for *SyFy Wire* notes, "She's given the chance to play around with fashion instead of relying entirely on the functionality of it" (Fiske 2019). Moreover, while a traditional montage might feature Max helping Eleven within the privacy of the dressing room or even tossing clothes over the fitting room door, here viewers see Max investing downtime in shopping for herself. Unlike the makeovers of S1:E4 and S2:E7, Max's focus is not crushingly fixed on Eleven. Max is, largely, present for support and consultation. All of this provides Eleven with the agency she repeatedly has been denied. And, as Eleven walks the mall halls in her new bold-print jumper, she appears confident and gleeful. The big Gap bag seen in her hand provides the clothes for Season Three: age appropriate, trendy, and feminine coded. All were selected by Eleven. None are the product of coercion or even suggestion.

In 2016, *Bustle*'s Allie Gemmil introduced Eleven's character to readers: "She is tough. She is tender. She is a tomboy with a heart of gold." Gemmil was partially correct. Eleven is tough and tender, but she is not a tomboy. This surface read neglects choice—which is the lynchpin of "tomboy culture." Had Gemmil waited until the release of Season Two, she could have noted the same about Max Mayfield—in that case, she (very nearly) would have been correct.

MAX MAYFIELD: THE TOMBOY WHO (VERY NEARLY) WAS . . . FOR AWHILE

Introduced in the second season, Maxine Mayfield (also known as "Max," "Mad Max," and "MADMAX") becomes something of a proxy for the secreted Eleven. In fact, the storyline similarities are unmistakable. Both young women are outsiders. Both are products of abuse. Both (initially) cause strife within the friend group. And, both (ultimately) find a sense of belonging in Hawkins. However, whereas Eleven is incrementally revealed as gender-conforming, the second season's Max has many of the traits commonly associated with the tomboy figure: she prefers the company of male-identifying peers, enjoys masculine-coded activities, and displays a slightly more aggressive personality (Bailey et al. 2002, 339–40). Moreover, in her debut season, she often selects clothing that is masculine coded. In fact, Max's wardrobe consists mostly of hooded sweatshirts, track jackets, striped tees, and denim pants. Not merely an aesthetic choice, her clothing is a practical complement to her passion for skateboarding. It allows her a better range of motion as well as provides a minimum of protection against minor accidents. In essence, her attire and activities are congruous. This lends credence to her "tomboy" label. Nonetheless, while many aspects of Max are masculine coded, there also seems to be an attempt to visually mitigate some of the harsher facets of her tomboy persona. At this juncture in the show's development, this may have been necessary.

The first season of *Stranger Things* is defined by separation and loss. It is an emotionally taxing eight episodes. As the second season begins, viewers are eager to see the friend group reunited and merry. However, Max prevents the fruition of these desires. Through no fault of her own, she immediately provokes the ire of Mike as well as sparks friction between Lucas and Dustin. Certainly, this mirrors the tension that Eleven created in the first season and seems to underscore Max as her surrogate. However, Max's character carries an additional burden. She unwittingly interferes with the fabled love story between Mike and Eleven. In fact, even before *Stranger Things 2* went into production, fans vehemently opposed the addition of Sadie Sink's character to the cast. An interview with *W* magazine reveals that that the performer needed to leave social media as a result of the Instagram backlash declaring "that Sink's Max would ruin the show by splitting up Mike and Eleven" (Eckardt 2017). Undoubtedly, the Duffer Brothers understood that Max's character would be a challenge for viewers to accept. Therefore, by retaining the softer aspects of Sink's natural appearance, the writers/directors created a visually gentler character, one to whom resistant viewers may be more receptive. However, and most essentially, in doing so, the Duffer Brothers also committed to a more contemporary portrayal of the so-called "tomboy."

Max's long, red, wavy hair might be her most notable feature. In Season Two, it is typically loose, pulled forward, and framing her face. While this seems to reflect her "carefree" California upbringing, it is also strikingly feminine coded. Moreover, the same gentle notes can be found in the pale-yellow T-shirts and sweaters in which she is frequently seen. Her character is granted tremendous warmth by this luminous, somewhat feminine-coded color. This select softness renders Max as multidimensional, preventing her from being a rigid stereotype. She is not the shorn, gruff-looking, grease-stained tomboy of the 1980s films that inspired *Stranger Things* but a more contemporized version of a so-called "tomboy": one which reflects a twenty-first century perspective where gender expression can be both fluid and expansive. While exploring masculine-coded pursuits and aesthetics, Max also preserves feminine-coded ones: all are of her choosing. It is this precise hybridization that initially makes Max fascinating (to Dustin and Lucas) as well as threatening (to Mike and Eleven).

While Eleven's first moments on screen reflect her tortured life and gentle spirit, Max's first moments exhibit her new-school tomboy nature. Here, in S2:E1, the set-up for her entrance is a tribute to John Hughes's *Ferris Bueller's Day Off*. At Hawkins Middle School, Mr. Clarke delivers a lecture on the human brain. Though he is a considerably more dynamic teacher than Ben Stein's Mr. Lorensax, a reverse shot shows students paralyzed by boredom. A series of amusing cuts now commences. Echoing the Hughes film, each cut depicts individual students intellectually removed from the teacher's lesson. The first cut shows a male student boldly receiving an illicit note and then using a broad gesture to pass it to the young man behind him. The next offers a ridiculously dead-eyed, gaped mouthed, young woman absentmindedly operating a paper fortune-teller. The final cut shows a female student slouched in her chair, blowing a pink bubble. Like the Hughes's classic, the teacher disregards this flagrant behavior and persists with his lecture. And, like the original, the loud popping of the pink bubble signals a change. In *Ferris Bueller's Day Off*, the popping occurs a few seconds prior to a scene transition. Here, it happens just as the principal escorts Max, a transfer student, into her new classroom. The first few minutes of this overall scene do more than honor a legendary director: they establish tone.

When Max enters Mr. Clarke's classroom in S2:E1, she walks into a "teen comedy." The Duffer Brothers create this playful atmosphere as a buffer. It dilutes Max's abrasive attitude, informing viewers that she is not the new villain of the season. This is important since in her first seconds on screen, Max exudes exasperation. As she swiftly crosses the classroom in an attempt to reach the one empty seat in the back corner of the room, her expression is one of annoyed determination. Her flaming red track jacket seems to only telegraph her agitation. Then, when Mr. Clarke demands that she return to the front of the room for a formal introduction, Max does not attempt to conceal her annoyance. She stops midstride, dramatically inhales, and rolls her eyes. While Mr. Clarke does not witness this, viewers do. It is clear that Max is not performing a polite, first-day-at-a-new-school show. This leaves viewers to wonder what may follow if this is potentially Max's best behavior. When Mr. Clarke affably says, "Come on up. Don't be shy," he is misreading the situation [00:15:36]. Max is not shy; she is frustrated by the teacher's arguably cliché request. That she ultimately capitulates demonstrates that though she is transgressive, she is not self-destructive. As Max stands by Mr. Clarke's desk, a medium-shot shows her shifting with mortified impatience. Her silent struggle turns vocal only when Mr. Clarke introduces her as "Maxine":

> Mr. Clarke: Class, please welcome, all the way from sunny California, the latest person to join us on our curiosity voyage, Maxine.
>
> Max: It's Max.
>
> Mr. Clarke: Sorry?
>
> Max: Nobody calls me Maxine. It's Max. [00:15:41–00:15:50]

This is a key moment. Foremost, the truncated "Max" is a masculine-coded name. This name ties so closely to Max's identity that she is willing to prolong her agonizing stay in front of the class to "correct" Mr. Clarke. Secondly, when Max reveals her preferred name, a medium shot of Dustin shows his perpetually jovial face turn to shock. He instantly recognizes this moniker. This is the name of the person ("MADMAX") who has been topping the leader boards at the arcade, besting Dustin's previous achievements in *Dig Dug* and *Centipede*. Astonishment is also clear in Lucas's voice when he reverentially whispers, "MADMAX" [00:15:55]. The Hawkins friend group wordlessly consults with each other and then stares in awe. Here, the power that Max (more specifically, her masculine-coded accomplishments) has over the young men is evident. Having met her obligation to Mr. Clarke, Max offers no more. She does not politely wait to be released. Instead, she boldly proceeds to the selected chair, sits, crosses her arms, and then matches the gaze of the friend group (who have fully turned in their seats to better observe her). Bristling with aggression, these first few moments are tempered both by the previously established comedic tone *and* the cinematography of the final shot. Here, as Max stares back at the Hawkins friend group, marmalade light pours through the adjacent window. It dramatically illuminates the right side of her face and hair, lending her seemingly intimidating character tremendous warmth. Moreover, that the light only affects one side of her person seems indicative of Max's "warm side." Made visible here, this duality provides the tension that makes her character remarkable: she is tough but tender, courageous but tormented, distant but gracious, independent but vulnerable, masculine but feminine.

Figure 8.2 Max (center, played by Sadie Sink) selects her seat and warm light from the window illuminates her left side. *Stranger Things* S2:E1 (2017).

As S2:E1 continues, viewers are returned to Max as she skateboards outside of Hawkins Middle School. A close-up of the board's pink and pimento deck reveals matching pink bushings. Like this feminine-coded color on a masculine-coded object, the conspicuous yin and yang sticker that decorates the board alludes to Max's duality; or, better expressed, the wholeness of her character. In this dynamic shot, Max is shown as a confident figure seemingly performing tricks for her own amusement. To contrast to this vibrant portrait, the Duffer Brothers intercut the Hawkins friend group statically observing Max from behind a chain-link fence. For the second time in mere minutes, they are depicted as assessing this young woman *en masse*. That they believe they are covertly watching her is problematic. Moreover, alarm resounds in the phrase Dustin uses to refer to Max: "the target" [00:21:09]. Given that they know both her birth name and her preferred name, the tone is inappropriate, if not predatory. Nonetheless, as with many aspects of the show, the writers have prepared a satisfying resolution to this concern. A cut brings viewers back to Max as she picks up her board and moves to a side door. Any worries that viewers may have about the treatment of this character are allayed by her next move. Before she enters the school, Max discards a folded piece of paper into a trash bin. It is quickly retrieved and eagerly unfolded by the friend group. In large letters, it reads, "Stop spying on me [*sic*] creeps!" [00:21:35]. Though she has been granted a minimum of screen-time at this point, Max is shown as bold, observant, and self-sufficient. She began as the "target" but has defeated the friend group yet again. She has both exposed and shamed them. And, instead of an instantly gratifying, direct confrontation that would allow the young men to deny their misdeed, Max elects for a more effective, irrefutable approach. As the young men hold Max's note, they also hold tangible evidence of their misbehavior. While the message is direct and explicit, the delivery method is subtle and controlled. Yin and yang.

Contrary to the stereotype of the ostracized tomboy, Max is a person to whom others are drawn. In S2: E2, even after being revealed as "creeps," Dustin and Lucas attempt to stumble and joke their way to procuring her friendship. Nonetheless, Max remains unconvinced. The adolescent theatrics of the young men have little effect on her. Having eschewed the forced politeness instilled in many young women, Max makes no attempt at congeniality. Dustin panics as he senses Max's impatience with his ramblings. Wanting her to "trick or treat" with the Hawkins friend group, Dustin suggests that they can keep her protected from alleged bullies as well as lead her to the most candy-rich areas of town. Here, Max become aggressively animated. She cannot be made fearful by vague threats of violence, and she cannot be bought with suggestions of lowly sugary treats. It is their deceitfulness that provokes her ire. Refusing to reward this poor behavior, Max walks away from the young men without committing to their plans. As she disappears down the school hall, Dustin twice yells out the meeting place and time. His distress is clear. This interaction again demonstrates the power Max wields as well as her independence. Karen M. Walsh says of moments like this:

> Although the boys initially see Max as nothing more than a potential love interest, she refuses to be reduced to that. Therefore, she actively teaches them to treat women better . . . Max reminds the boys that she is their equal and that she is not a prize to be won. (2019, 230–31)

So, while Max was willing to listen to their proposal, her friendship is not readily or easily procured. As the depiction of her skateboarding solo during recess suggests, while Max may be new to the area, she is not desperate for companionship. She will accept their friendship, but on her own terms.

As S2:E2 continues, night falls. The Hawkins friend group is shown beginning their Halloween adventure. There is visual and contextual harmony in their matching outfits: each young man portrays a scientist/parapsychologist from Ivan Reitman's *Ghostbusters*. Likewise, as they walk side by side and discuss the merits of nougat-based candy, a deep sense of camaraderie emerges. However, the Duffer Brothers soon shatter this amiable tableau with a jump scare. A person brandishing a large (plastic) knife and dressed in a Michael Myers costume steps in front of the friends. While Lucas's high-pitched screams exacerbate the fright within the show, a jarring non-diegetic sound effect startles viewers. Sharing this moment of fear with the young men, the audience is momentarily positioned against this masked figure. Nonetheless, the wavy red hair protruding from the mask quickly breaks the illusion of danger. Max reveals herself to the young men and much of the scene's tension is alleviated. Here, Max's tomboy nature is clear. Not only does she outfit herself as a sadistic male figure from horror cinema, but she uses the power behind this violent image to momentarily frighten others, including viewers. However, no malice is intended. In fact, critics like Jamie McDaniel view this moment as Max's unofficial entrance into the friend group, as a playful trick that showcases her tomboy nature (2019, 205). Now, while Max may be attired in a male-coded costume and playing a heart-pounding prank, her feminine-coded hair, deliberately left down by the directors, lessens the effect of this aggressive choice. This softness is critical to quickly regain the trust of both the Hawkins friend group and viewers.

For the young men and the audience, the adrenaline of the aforementioned jump scare of S2:E2 has barely dissipated when Max emasculates the young men: "Holy shit! You should have seen the look on your faces. And, you [Lucas]? Who screams like that? You sound like a little girl" [00:34:54]. Considering their marginalized position in their small town's social hierarchy, it would not be unwarranted for the young men register to hurt or anger at such thoughtless comments from someone they regard as a new friend. Moreover, the group has never weaponized Max's masculine-coded traits against her. Here, viewers must take their cue from the friends. Perhaps because they have faced true terror and emerged victorious (as their *Ghostbusters* costumes suggest), most remain unfazed by Max's barbs. In fact, Will, Dustin, and Lucas watch in awe as Max strides far ahead of them, assuming a leadership position. And, now her trademark softness reemerges. She turns with a warm smile, proclaims to have found the candy-rich area of town, and asks if they are following her. She concludes her invitation with a genuine giggle. The camera remains in a fixed position as Dustin and Lucas run off screen, trailing Max and shrieking with delight. This shot plainly shows their eagerness to join her, to quite literally run after her. A beat passes and Will follows. So, while it is accurate to note that Max's "slasher-style" introduction is alarming (in every sense), moments later, viewers see that her value has only increased. Her ability to sharply taunt but then act with kindness is a successful combination. Only Mike remains unconvinced. He stays on screen for viewers. He is depicted as dejected and issues an audible sigh before trudging off screen to end the scene. Like with some viewers, Max will have to try harder to win him over.

When a cut in S2:E2 transitions to the Hawkins friend group continuing their Halloween festivities, the dynamics have shifted. Lucas, Max, and Dustin now walk in the foreground. Max is positioned between the two friends, visually disrupting the continuity of the *Ghostbusters* themed costumes. First, the optics of this "villain" wedged between two "heroes" underscores Mike's (and some viewers') uncertainty of Max. But, more importantly, it also suggests she will momentarily disturb this camaraderie as she becomes the love interest of both young men. In fact, the clever directing of this scene allows the first sparks of attraction to be noted. Here, ever since the jump scare at the beginning of this sequence, Max wears the Michael Myers mask pushed atop her head. This allows for a note of femininity since her red hair spills over her shoulders and the (presumably) cool air has given her a rosy glow. Smiles fill the screen and giddy giggles abound as the young men experiment with Valley Girl slang. Were Max to remain faithful to her costume and keep her mask down, the juvenile flirtations seen in this moment would have been lost: concealed literally behind a rubber mask and figuratively behind the masculine coding of said mask. As depicted here and as constructed by the writers, Max is actively pursued by two young men (Dustin and Lucas). This is something of a rarity—if not a *coup*—for the tomboy figure as depicted in media.[8]

At this point in the series, it is convenient to perceive the Duffer Brothers as forcefully portraying Max as heterosexual. In fact, some critics view the construction of Max's character as a denial of inclusion. One scholar notes:

"The new additions of Billy and Max in the second season create somewhat frustrating character dynamics that hint at queerness that is never fully explored" (Roach 2018, 142). Though the sentiment is understandable, this statement is problematic. If the scholar is implying that Max's character should have been rendered as non-heterosexual, this would be a fundamental misread of the tomboy figure since it fails to observe the distinction between gender expression and sexual identity. Dr. Ritch C. Savin-Williams, licensed clinical psychologist and Professor Emeritus of Developmental Psychology at Cornell University, explains: "There is no direct connection between tomboyism and lesbianism . . . That is, a gender expression among girls that has been labeled as 'tomboy' has been unhitched from any particular sexuality" (2016). Likewise, if the scholar is implying that Max should have been portrayed as non-cisgender, this too is troubling since it disregards the manner in which tomboy culture allows cisgender girls and young women to explore the totality of the world more freely. In "Tomboy as Protective Identity," Traci Craig and Jessica LaCroix state that the "tomboy identity gives girls and women protected access to spaces typically denied to [them] in our gender segregated world" (2011, 456). Certainly, monitoring media for inclusion is essential; however, it is also important to recognize that Max's portrayal as "desirable" is an advancement in itself. In fact, this construction of her character reflects a decidedly contemporary perspective. Max's gender non-conforming tendencies (i.e., her tomboy qualities) are depicted as inconsequential to her overall attractiveness. The 1980's pop-culture that shapes the *Stranger Things* universe dictates that a makeover must occur to show the tomboy as a capable of a feminine-coded appearance and, therefore, worthy of male attention. Nonetheless, the Duffer Brothers reject this notion. At no point in the current seasons does Max ever receive a makeover. As the Duffer Brothers loudly indicate, she does not need one. Showing gender variance as an attractive quality *is* inclusive, progressive, and long overdue.

Extending beyond those with romantic interest in her, Max's influence on the Hawkins friend group is undeniable. This is made evident in S2:E3 when Dustin invites Max and the crew to the AV room. There he introduces them to D'Artagnan, an adolescent demogorgon. As Dustin sets D'Artagnan in Max's hand, she does not attempt to mask her feelings with a masculine-coded, stoic reaction. She cringes and says, "Oh God, he's slimy!" [00:21:40]. Max's influence becomes clear as she passes the creature to Lucas. Mirroring Max's facial expression and actions, he says, "Ugh, he's like a living booger" and then equally as hastily passes it onto Will [00:21:41]. Will does likewise, distorting his face in revulsion and handing it off to Mike. Mike, who is unimpressed with Max, then quietly and critically examines the creature. At this point, the chain is broken. While Mike's critical study of D'Artagnan underscores him as the group's leader, Max's power over the group warrants attention. This new-school tomboy who embraces both the masculine and the feminine is setting the tone for the friend group . . . even going so far as to elicit feminine-coded responses from three of the young men. This is remarkable since it continues to elevate the tomboy from the role of outcast to one of influence. However, it is this precise influence that fuels Mike's frustration.

The discord between Max and Mike is later explored in S2:E3. Seeking the now-escaped D'Artagnan, the Hawkins friend group splits up to scour the school. Max uses this moment to open a private dialogue with Mike. In this moment, Max's new-school tomboy qualities become amply evident. Foremost, Max's desire for a one-on-one conversation with Mike is laudable. It shows her sincere desire to understand how she can improve their relationship. Moreover, it also avoids the potential dramatics or victimization that could occur if the other friends were present. This is a mature choice. Nonetheless, as Mike attempts to dodge her earnest inquiries, Max steps on her skateboard and obstructs his progress. This form of physical confrontation is decidedly less mature. This same pattern is repeated just seconds later. Knowing Mike's value to the group, Max tries to win his favor by referencing one of his favorite pastimes: *Dungeons & Dragons*. She offers to become "the party's" "zoomer" [00:42:29]. Given that a "zoomer" is not an actual character class, Mike remains uninterested. Not seeing the desired results, Max hops on her skateboard and begins to circle Mike. The scene now assumes a somewhat predatory tone. A point-of-view shot shows Mike's perspective. Since Max is on her skateboard, she towers over Mike. Likewise, she undoubtedly has power over him since he admits that she is making him "dizzy" [00:43:00]. Now, while her behavior has the potential to be read as physically aggressive, several aspects of this moment seem to undercut this interpretation. The more antagonistic her actions become, the more Max's expression softens. Likewise, her face-framing red hair and pale-yellow shirt lend her a very real radiance. But, perhaps more importantly, Max is admitting that Mike holds the key to her happiness. She is *asking* for admission to their "party." It is here that Mike's expression, too, visibly softens. Having seen this unmistakable break in Mike's steely facade, Max seizes the opportunity. As she continues to circle him, she inquires, "Am I in or out?" [00:43:05]. The framing of her question leaves no room for debate. This is reflective of Max's assertive personality. And, when Mike breaks into a smile, that smile is returned by Max. Unfortunate for Max, this moment is interrupted by Eleven and the resolution to S2:E3 is postponed until S3:E9—when Max reveals that being a "zoomer" extends to her use of her brother's Camaro Z28. Even so, her direct confrontation of Mike combined with her affable personality seems to have had positive results. Her new-school tomboy nature eventually wins over Mike and even those reluctant viewers. In fact, after the release of Season Two, the film industry website *IndieWire* ranked all twenty-nine characters. Max achieved a respectable ninth place—besting Mike, Will, and even Bob. The writers note: "She skateboards! She plays video games! She takes no guff! Max didn't get as much to do as the boys during Season 2, but her special skills made her an invaluable asset to the party, even if they were initially reluctant to induct her" (Miller et al. 2017). However, for all of this excitement and praise, the series was about to lose its tomboy.

The second season's conclusion finds the Hawkins friend group preparing for the 1984 Snow Ball. Here, viewers are presented with a quiet hint of Max "aging-out" of tomboyism. While there is no "Snow Ball makeover," there is a scene with Max's mom styling the young woman's hair. She pins back an accent braid with a large barrette. Watching her mom in the mirror, Max seems uncertain. But once the barrette is placed, there is a moment of acceptance ... which is instantly destroyed when her mother says, "See? Pretty" [00:48:20]. Undoubtedly, "pretty" is a loaded word in the world of *Stranger Things*. For Eleven, being called "pretty" represents acceptance and "normalcy." It holds the hope of the gender-conforming life Eleven wishes to lead. However, for Max, it sounds like a soft nudge toward the gender conformity that she has (previously) expressed little interest in. "Pretty" also seems to imply that previous to this new hairstyle, Max's hair was not "pretty." While her mother's comment (justifiably) elicits Max's eye-rolling annoyance, Max never removes the barrette. It is clearly spotted throughout the Snow Ball 1984 sequence and seems to provide the slightest indication to the changes that will occur in Season Three.

When Max returns in S3:E1, approximately seven months have passed. Her shift toward the feminine is evident. Her hair is chicly layered, deeply parted on the side, and lightly moussed to accentuate her curls. Sarah Hindsgaul, lead hair stylist for *Stranger Things 3*, confirms the reason for this alteration, "[When Max arrived in Hawkins] she was very skater, very relaxed, very tomboy, middle-parted [hair], very 'I don't care at all' . . . But this year [Max and Eleven] are figuring out boys and all that comes with that" (Gardner 2019). In addition to Max's new hairstyle, she has adopted a fresh fashion sense as well. Loose track jackets and denim pants are replaced with form-fitting, brightly striped T-shirts and shorts. Of this development, Senior Style Editor for *Seventeen* Kelsey Stiegman proclaims, "Max breaks free of her trademark tomboy persona by wearing basically every single color in the rainbow all at once" (2019). Though the focus on Max doffing her tomboy appearance may seem disheartening to those who identify as tomboys, are invested in tomboy culture, or even those championing more visibility for those who identify as non gender-conforming, it is also fair to note that the Duffer Brothers are acknowledging a common behavior called "gender intensification." In "Tomboys and Cowgirls: The Girl's Disidentification from the Mother," Dianne Elise explains that the "tomboy is pulled back into the heterosexual demand for femininity at adolescence" (1998, 150). Given Max's age—thirteen in Season Two and fourteen in Season Three—her behavior seems to reflect this transition (for girls/young women who identify as heterosexual).

This change in Max only seems to deepen as her relationship with Eleven strengthens. In Season Three, a profound friendship blooms between Max and Eleven. They soon become inseparable. As a duo, they indulge in deeply feminine-coded activities like paging through teen-idol magazines, shopping at the mall, visiting the bathroom together, having sleepovers at each other's houses, and even getting "glamour shots." As the pair grows closer, Max's skateboard is replaced with the two walking to destinations and even sharing a bike. By S3:E4, visual signs of their connection become apparent. Here, while each young woman sits beside her love-interest, viewers note that Max and Eleven share the same hairstyle and hair accessory: a high ponytail held in place by an eye-catching, brightly colored Scrunchie. This is an undeniable signal of their connection and their investment in feminine-coded pursuits. In this same scene, viewers also see the first appearance of a lilac color in Max's wardrobe. Her light-purple sleeveless hoodie is unmistakably feminine coded, underscoring this act of gender intensification.

Lilac deepens into aubergine as the third season concludes. Three months have elapsed since the trials of summer. Max and her (on-again, off-again) boyfriend Lucas are shown helping the Byers family pack their belongings. She wears a form-fitting, dark purple, V-neck sweater with multi-colored stripes across the bust. Her hair is French braided into pigtails and held by translucent yellow, flower-shaped elastics. By all means, the look shows an investment of time and is very much feminine coded. Reflecting on S2:E1 to this moment in S3:E8, it would seem that the directors capture a snapshot of tomboyism—one with, as is common, something of an expiration date.

Now, while Max may have left her track jackets in Season Two and her skateboard early in Season Three, the directors make it clear that her tomboy years were not wasted. After Eleven is attacked by the Mind Flayer in the penultimate episode of Season Three (S3:E7), Nancy attempts to administer first aid. She nearly makes a critical error, but Max intervenes: "First we need to stop the bleeding, then clean, then disinfect, then bandage. I skateboard. Trust me" [00:18:20–00:18:25]. Here, the directors show the knowledge Max gleaned as a tomboy is critical to the life of another. And, while the skateboard never reappears (in this season), Max retains the fortitude, bravery, and resolve that she has shown throughout the series. Her clothes and appearance may have changed, but she has not. Undoubtedly, tomboyism has expanded and enriched her world.

CONCLUSION

In a conservative-leaning article written for *The Telegraph*, Peter Walker says that "lead characters such as Katniss Everdeen in *The Hunger Games*, Tris Prior in the *Divergent* series, [and] Eleven in *Stranger Things* have sparked a revival of strong tomboyish females [*sic*]" (2017). It seems only fitting that this misread of Eleven's character would appear in a piece that accuses these same figures as spawning a revolution of young women who desire to "swap genders" (Walker 2017). As evidenced here, Eleven's erroneous "tomboy" label demonstrates how one's exterior can be so influential that it suspends critical thinking. It serves as the most basic of admonitions: a character (or a person) must be assessed holistically, and not by her/his/their most obvious attributes.

Likewise, it is fair to see Max as a tomboy. She shares a number of traits with this iconic figure. However, it may be more accurate to say that the Duffer Brothers have constructed a more modern character in Max. By embracing both the feminine and masculine, she becomes profoundly current. She is not a rigid stereotype but a person entirely of her own design. Not only does she demonstrate the fluid nature of gender expression, but she is shown as making it attractive/desirable. Here, she is not the lonely outcast of 1980s teen films. She is a magnet to whom others are drawn. She is, indeed, admirable. That alone, is a massive triumph for this figure.

In *Stranger Things*, viewers are presented with complex concepts pertaining to sex and gender. While the series may be set in the conservative 1980s, the sentiment is entirely progressive. This blend of nostalgia and modernity creates compelling drama as well as relevant social commentary. The characters offered by the Duffer Brothers challenge notions of sex and gender. Observing how this is navigated by those inside the narrative as well as outside provides tremendous insight. It shows how far society has evolved . . . and how much work still needs to be done.

NOTES

1. This occurs in S1:E2 when Mr. Clarke finds the fabric caught on the drainpipe and assumes it must be from Will [00:35:10].

2. In *Stranger Things: Worlds Turned Upside Down: The Official Behind-the-Scenes Companion*, Gina McIntyre explains, "For the brothers, the 1980s setting was essential to the premise. Not only was the show a love letter to the films that had influenced

them growing up, almost all of which took place in that decade, but it was also vital to the plot" (2018, 22).

3. In fact, in a piece on Millie Bobby Brown, *W* magazine stated that "thanks to her cropped 'do, she sometimes gets mistaken for a boy and has even adopted the alter ego Jon for such occasions" (Lawrence 2016).

4. Not only is Eleven striving to please Mike as a result of her attraction to him, but because he is giving her refuge. The power that he wields over both her happiness and her wellbeing must be acknowledged in this moment of Eleven's passivity.

5. Keating submitted this assessment prior to the inclusion of the third season's Robin Buckley (who identifies as a lesbian). However, this author *does* seem to overlook allusions to Will Byers as being a member of the LGBTQIA+ community. Here, it is important to note that in the show's original pitch, the following describes Will's character: "Will Byers, twelve, is a sweet, sensitive kid with sexual identity issues. He only recently came to the realization that he does not fit into 1980s definition of 'normal.' His innocent choices, such as his colorful clothes, prove a constant source of bullying" (Bacon 2019).

6. It warrants noting that the technical reason behind Eleven's precise hairstyle is to highlight her significant talents. In an interview with *Entertainment Weekly*, Sarah Hindsgaul (lead hair stylist for *Stranger Things 2*) states, "The whole thing with the makeover, that's finally the time for her to start kicking ass and saving everybody, and I wanted to make sure we could see her face for that as much as possible. I wanted to bring it all out so it could all be in her acting and there's nothing hiding her—like she's opening up completely and now she's completely available. So that's how we came up with the slicked-back thing" (Schwartz 2017).

7. However, one element of the outfit was, apparently, chosen by Eleven. In an interview with *E! News*, costume designer Kim Wilcox reveals that Eleven kept her own socks so "she's becoming part of the tribe, but she's doing it in her own way" (Bricker 2017). Given that this is not common knowledge and barely perceptible, it carries negligible weight.

8. Alex Hirsch's *Gravity Falls* also includes a positive example of tomboy figure (Wendy Corduroy) who is the love interest of two young men (Dipper Pines and Robbie Valentino).

BIBLIOGRAPHY

Bacon, Thomas. 2019. "*Stranger Things* Original Plan Confirms Season 3's LGBT Reveal." *Screen Rant*. August 18, 2019. https://screenrant.com/stranger-things-season-3-will-byers-gay-confirmed/.

Bailey, J. Michael, Kathleen T. Bechtold, and Sheri A. Berenbaum. 2002. "Who are Tomboys and Why Should We Study Them?" *Archives of Sexual Behavior* 31 (4): 333–41.

Bricker, Tierney. 2017. "Everything You Need to Know About Eleven's Bitchin' Makeover in *Stranger Things* Season 2." *E! News*. October 30, 2017. https://

www.eonline.com/ca/news/889975/everything-you-need-to-know-about-eleven-s-bitchin-makeover-in-stranger-things-season-2.

Craig, Traci, and Jessica LaCroix. 2011. "Tomboy as Protective Identity." *Journal of Lesbian Studies* 15 (4): 450–465.

Dacie. 2019. "*Stranger Things* Fashion: Eleven." *College Fashion*. June 23, 2019. https://www.collegefashion.net/inspiration/stranger-things-eleven-fashion/.

———. 2019. "*Stranger Things* Fashion: Max Mayfield." *College Fashion*. July 7, 2019. https://www.collegefashion.net/inspiration/max-stranger-things-style/.

Davis, Lisa Selin. 2020. *Tomboy: The Surprising History and Future of Girls Who Dare to Be Different*. New York: Hachette.

Duffer, Matt, and Ross Duffer. 2016. *Stranger Things*. Streaming: Netflix. Directed by Matt Duffer, Ross Duffer, et al. United States: 21 Laps Entertainment.

———. 2017. *Stranger Things 2*. Streaming: Netflix. Directed by Matt Duffer, Ross Duffer, et al. United States: 21 Laps Entertainment.

———. 2019. *Stranger Things 3*. Streaming: Netflix. Directed by Matt Duffer, Ross Duffer, et al. United States: 21 Laps Entertainment.

Eckardt, Stephanie. 2017. "Unraveling the Mystery of Sadie Sink, *Stranger Things*' Infatuating Skater Girl Max in Season 2." *W*. October 27, 2017. https://www.wmagazine.com/story/who-is-sadie-sink-actress-max-stranger-things-season-2.

Elise, Dianne. 1999. "Tomboys and Cowgirls: The Girl's Disidentification from the Mother." In *Sissies and Tomboys: Gender Nonconformity and Homosexual Childhood*, edited by Matthew Rottnek, 140–52. New York: New York University Press.

Fiske, Alyssa. 2019. "*Stranger Things* Turned the Makeover Trope on its Head." *SyFy Wire*. July 22, 2019. https://www.syfy.com/syfywire/stranger-things-turned-the-makeover-trope-on-its-head.

Franklin, David Anthony. 2018. "Half-Lives of the Nuclear Family: Representations of the Mid-Century American Family in *Stranger Things*." In *Uncovering Stranger Things: Essays on Eighties Nostalgia, Cynicism and Innocence in the Series*, edited by Kevin J. Wetmore Jr., 174–82. Jefferson: McFarland.

Gardner, Abby. 2019. "All the Hidden Messages in the Hairstyles on *Stranger Things*." *Glamour*. July 20, 2019. https://www.glamour.com/story/hairstyles-hidden-messages-stranger-things.

Gemmil, Allie. 2016. "The 13 Best Eleven from *Stranger Things* Memes That Prove How Much Fans Love Her." *Bustle*. August 26, 2016. https://www.bustle.com/articles/180907-the-13-best-eleven-from-stranger-things-memes-that-prove-how-much-fans-love-her.

Halperin, Moze. 2016. "Millie Bobby Brown Is Reportedly Returning to *Stranger Things*, Because the Duffer Brothers Aren't Idiots." *FlavorWire*. August 31, 2016. https://www.flavorwire.com/593077/millie-bobby-brown-is-returning-to-stranger-things-because-the-duffer-brothers-arent-idiots.

Keating, Shannon. 2016. "Hollywood's Problem with Unfeminine Girls." *BuzzFeed*. August 12, 2016. https://www.buzzfeed.com/shannonkeating/stranger-things-and-compulsory-femininity?utm_term=.mgDEJarY7#.hqNk7PGQ1.

Lawrence, Vanessa. 2016. "Like Eleven, Millie Bobby Brown Can Be Very Badass." *W*. October 3, 2016. https://www.wmagazine.com/story/like-eleven-millie-bobby-brown-can-be-very-badass.

Leth, Kate. 2019. "How *Stranger Things* Appears to Fix Its Smurfette Problem." *Playboy*. March 21, 2019. https://www.playboy.com/read/stranger-things-eleven-max-season-3.

McDaniel, Jamie. 2019. "Growing Up in the Upside Down: Youth Horror and Diversity in *Stranger Things*." In *The Palgrave Handbook of Children's Film and Television*, edited by Casie Hermansson and Janet Zepernick, 205–22. Cham: Palgrave Macmillan.

McIntyre, Gina. 2018. *Stranger Things: Worlds Turned Upside Down: The Official Behind-the-Scenes Companion*. New York: Del Rey.

Miller, Liz Shannon et al. 2017. "All the *Stranger Things* Characters, Ranked from Worst to Best." *IndieWire*. November 3, 2017. https://www.indiewire.com/2017/11/stranger-things-characters-best-worst-1201893638/2/.

Roach, Emily E. 2018. "AIDS, Homophobia and the Monstrous Upside Down: The Queer Subtext of *Stranger Things*." In *Uncovering Stranger Things: Essays on Eighties Nostalgia, Cynicism and Innocence in the Series*, edited by Kevin J. Wetmore Jr., 135–45. Jefferson: McFarland.

Savin-Williams, Rich C. 2013. "Do Tomboys Grow Up to Be Lesbian?" *Psychology Today*. November 16, 2013. https://www.psychologytoday.com/us/blog/sex-sexuality-and-romance/201611/do-tomboys-grow-be-lesbian.

Schwartz, Dana. 2017. "Inside Eleven's Punk *Stranger Things 2* Makeover." *Entertainment Weekly*. November 2, 2017. https://ew.com/tv/2017/11/02/stranger-things-2-hair-interview/.

Stiegman, Kelsey. 2019. "Here's Where to Shop All of Max's Best Outfits from *Stranger Things 3*." *Seventeen*. August 2, 2019. https://www.seventeen.com/health/a28589137/max-outfits-stranger-things/.

Walker, Peter. 2017. "Popularity of Tomboys is Encouraging Girls to Swap Gender, Says NHS Psychologist." *The Telegraph*. May 8, 2017. https://www.telegraph.co.uk/science/2017/05/08/popularity-tomboys-encouraging-girls-swap-gender-says-nhs-psychologist/.

Walsh, Karen M. 2019. "Maxine 'Mad Max' Mayfield." In *Geek Heroines: An Encyclopedia of Female Heroes in Popular Culture*, edited by Karen M. Walsh, 229–31. Santa Barbara: Greenwood.

PART IV

THE VIRTUAL WORLD: THE TOMBOY IN VIDEO GAMES AND ON THE INTERNET

Chapter 9

Beyond Good and Evil ... and Gender and Humanism? Exploring Jade as a Posthuman Protagonist

Poppy Wilde

In the following chapter, I will analyze the figure of the tomboy through the main protagonist, Jade, from the 2003 videogame *Beyond Good and Evil,* directed by Michel Ancel and produced by Ubisoft. I explore the ways in which humanist history has capitalized on binary categorizations to privilege certain subject positions over others, enacting a patriarchal society that creates clear differences between "masculine" and "feminine" traits. By outlining a posthuman perspective, I demonstrate the ways in which posthumanism seeks to move toward postdualistic perspectives, including those of gender. "Tomboyism can be seen as a resistance to narrow and strict gender delineations" (Jones 1999, 132) and offers a non-normative site of gender performance. This resistive action against binary gender performances therefore allows a consideration of tomboy-as-posthuman-subjectivity. In *Beyond Good and Evil*, Jade embodies this subjectivity, and through my analysis of the game, I demonstrate the various ways in which Jade encapsulates both stereotypically "feminine" and stereotypically "masculine" traits and remixes them to create an alternative gender performance that defies clear categorization.

There is a tension in the term "tomboy"; if binaries such as masculinity and femininity are deconstructed through posthumanism, can such a classification as "tomboy" exist? As Carr notes, the tomboy "is associated with both the subversion of gender roles and the perpetuation of an oppressive, dichotomous gender system" because it is specifically linked to socially constructed notions of gender (1998, 531). However, I believe the "tomboy" as a subversion of gender roles allows us the opportunity to explore how texts such as *Beyond Good and Evil* embody a postdualistic configuration of the "human."

HUMANIST HISTORIES, POSTHUMAN POSSIBILITIES

Humanism operates in a variety of ways to construct a particular mode or model of the human and its corresponding place in the world. This is based centrally around the idea that humans are the most important creatures on earth; autonomous creatures, in control of their own lives and free to make their own choices. Within that ideological construction, humanism favors specific attributes: the rational mind, self-control, and self-responsibility. These foundations of humanism, as I will explain below, have enacted specific categorizations that enforce dualistic binaries. These binaries serve to separate the "self" from the "other" in ways that dominate much of how humanistic, neoliberal societies see the world today.

THE BREAKDOWN OF GOD

Following a history of deeply religious belief, the Enlightenment period signified a cultural shift wherein key philosophical thinkers attempted to dispose of God, arguing, for example, that "[e]nlightenment is man's emergence from his self-imposed immaturity" (Kant 1784), which is to say, the "immaturity" of allowing others to think for them and determine their actions. Through this "enlightenment," then, humans no longer needed to defer to God, but instead occupied god-like positions themselves; with no competing species and no higher power, an anthropocentric worldview was adopted. Accordingly, humans saw themselves as the center of all things and saw the earth, animals, and machines as there to do our bidding. This historical shift has allowed humans to shape the earth in ways that suit them, to see machines and objects as subordinate, and to enforce control and power over other animals, deciding their status and fate.

HUMANS AS AUTONOMOUS

The viewpoint that human beings are in control of others leads to the notion that they are also in control of their own destiny: the significance of "free will," autonomy, and individuality are therefore paramount and integral to this view of the human. Braidotti (2013) highlights humanism's assertion of the singularity and individuality of human existence; the belief of being in control suggests that each of us operates in isolation and that we are self-reflexive, self-managed, and self-made. This view is enforced and embodied through a series of binary understandings—nature/culture, body/mind, material/immaterial, human/machine, human/animal—and gender has often been included in this list, with a binary consideration of male/female. In the same way that human is privileged over animal, each binary has an implicit hierarchy, which Derrida refers to as a "violent hierarchy," wherein "one of the two terms governs the other [. . .] or has the upper hand" (1981 [1972], 41). These violent hierarchies create relationships of subject over object, controller over controlled.

FAVORING THE RATIONAL MIND

What was deemed to place human beings above the others of this world—earth, animal, machine—was their ability to think. This position is linked with Descartes's famous quote: "I think, therefore I am" ([1637] 1924, 31). Descartes argued that it was not his ability to feel that made him human, but his ability to think. Descartes utilized this idea to draw a strict divide between humans, animals, and machines, which contributed to anthropocentric hierarchies of thought. However, this also created hierarchies among "humans" and this idea has specific ideological roots. If the human thinker can be placed above everyone and everything else, then not only are nonhuman "others" categorized as less important but an immediate hierarchy within humans is also implied. Of course, this hierarchy favors those in power. After all, who are the thinkers other than the educated, and who can be educated other than the male, the powerful, the wealthy—the white, able-bodied, upper-class human? This is therefore a double-edged sword—by valuing only those who were white, masculine, able-bodied, etc., any other subjectivities were "othered"—made *less than*. By then denying certain groups access to that which was valued, such as education, as well as basic rights such as land-ownership and the right to vote, that othering was perpetuated. Humanism, therefore categorizes the *subhuman* as much as the human—denying full "humanity" to some, and therefore alienating them from the "norm."

Because humanism privileges the rational, thinking mind, women, historically seen to be creatures more of the body than the mind, were, and still are, unsurprisingly, disadvantaged, as are others who were already oppressed: people of color, people with disabilities, and members of the LGBTQIA+ community, for example. By enforcing these categorizations and embedding these ideologies within the political and social understandings of the day, a variety of humanistic dualisms were applied and enhanced. This version of humanism privileges the male, rational, thinker, restricting the female to the realms of the irrational, emotion, and feeling.

POSTHUMAN POSSIBILITIES

Posthumanism, in its essential form, argues that, due to the above issues of anthropocentrism, exclusivity, and the privileging of certain traits and qualities over others, the category of the "human" is based on historically flawed assumptions about the nature of being human. By highlighting the ideologies that have underwritten humanism, posthumanism has suggested that the full rights of the "human" have only ever been accessible to a select few, as "[s]exism, racism, classism, ageism, homophobia, and ableism, alongside other forms of discrimination, have informed the written and unwritten laws of recognition as to who was to be considered human" (Ferrando 2019, 4). As such, the "human" is in need of redefinition (see Braidotti 2013).

The sexism that Ferrando mentions is apparent in the ways in which women have historically been ostracized from prominent positions in society, which continues in contemporary culture. Toffoletti argues that "woman is aligned with nature, irrationality and the body, in direct opposition to culture, reason and the mind, she cannot occupy the position of the human subject. Woman is never 'fully' human" (2007, 19). The category of "human" is a political issue, as it draws boundaries between rights and expectations and therefore creates hierarchies and, accordingly, prejudices and discrimination. Posthumanism seeks to address these issues and disrupt many of these taken-for-granted assumptions about what it is to be "human" with regards to notions of control, individuality, and agency.

Before shifting my focus to the specifics of posthumanism and gender in the next section, it is worth spending some more time working through posthumanism's aim in deconstructing humanism's categorizations, binaries, and implicit hierarchies. Rather than limiting the remit of posthumanism to consideration of binaries and boundaries between humans, by opening up conversations around the anthropocentric ideologies of humanism, posthumanism makes apparent the ways in which "others" are involved in a complex entanglement with humans, and it is only through these "others" that humans can come to be. Much of the work of posthumanism is also, therefore, post anthropocentric, as in questioning, dismantling, and disrupting these demarcations, we can see how they were initially formed from an anthropocentric worldview, privileging what were perceived to be human attributes above those of animals, machines, and nature.

The critique of the "control" that the liberal humanist subject is supposed to possess is about considering how much humans are shaped by that which is apparently "outside" or apart from them. Viewing "others" (animals, machines, nature, and so on) as of equal importance to the human is the first step; however, much critical posthumanism is concerned with more radical interventions that look to our entanglements and the complex ways in which we intra-act with entities around us in order to form subjectivity. Rather than considering the self as individually constructed and made, posthumanism instead looks to the boundaries of the human as porous, in constant flux, or undefinable (see, e.g., Hayles 1999; Barad 2007). For example, Pepperell's work suggests that the human is a "fuzzy-edged" entity, and he points out the exchange of liquids, gasses, food, sound, heat, and so on, that the human relies upon to live, stating that "[b]ecause of this perpetual exchange between the living human organism and its surroundings, there can be no fixed state of a living human" (2003, 20).This can radically alter the concept of the human from a supposedly autonomous being to a "non-unitary" subject—if we are in constant negotiation with "others" around us, where does one end and one begin? As Gane states, the posthuman is "a new culture of transversalism in which the 'purity' of human nature gives way to new forms of creative evolution that refuse to keep different species, or even machines and humans, apart" (2006, 432). This is what Elaine Graham refers to as "a dissolution of the 'ontological hygiene' by which for the past three hundred years Western culture has drawn the fault-lines that separate humans, nature and machines" (2002, 11). Barad (2007) uses intra-action rather than *inter*action to theorize that entities are not ontologically distinct prior to their encounter, but that it is through their intra-action that distinct agencies emerge.

Rather than considering the gamer as "in control" of the avatar, I have instead previously theorized the ways in which the avatar-gamer is an example of posthuman subjectivity (Wilde and Evans 2019; Wilde 2020). Through the intra-action of avatar and gamer, alongside specific other entities (e.g., computer, game, etc.), a specific form of subjectivity is able to emerge. This allows an empathetic experience, whereby the avatar-gamer embodies a "posthuman subjectivity, recognizing that there is no primary subject, and instead demonstrating the ways in which feelings emerge through a network of intra-acting forces" (Wilde 2018). This experience is affective and, through the avatar-gamer assemblage, the binary between "self" and "other" is disrupted in favor of an understanding of subjectivity as emergent and entangled. Yet, as previously mentioned, beyond disruptions of self and other or human and machine, posthuman thought is evident in other postdualisms, such as those that move beyond the binary of male and female. The focus of this chapter, the "tomboy," is one such postdualism.

POSTHUMANISM: QUEERING GENDER NORMS

A heteronormative society suggests (cisgender) heterosexuality as the norm and enforces the binary opposition of male/masculinity and female/femininity. As Schilt and Westbrook explain, "[h]eterosexuality—like masculinity and femininity—is taken for granted as a natural occurrence derived from biological sex. [. . .] The taken-for-granted expectation that heterosexuality and gender identity follow from genitalia produces heteronormativity" (2009, 443). By considering these gendered positions as intrinsic, biologically determined "facts," an argument for a heterosexual society is made that each gender is specific, rigid, and requires the "balance" of the other. This "taken-for-granted" ideological stance fits in with the aforementioned presumptions that humanism espouses, capitalizing on binary gender distinctions as outlined above by relegating each gender to specific roles. From this perspective, as Braidotti argues, breaking down the unitary subject of humanism allows more possibilities for cultural inter-mixity, including recompositions of genders and sexuality, and the posthuman condition must work with these (2013, 54). Braidotti maintains that these opportunities are productive, and part of this productivity is evident in the ways in which alternative conceptions of subjectivity have been defined through posthumanism. If we are all composite subjects, formed of the intra-relations between our bodies and others, including society and nature, then gender is similarly constructed, formed of specific ideological and discursive enactments. This links to the idea of "doing gender" as proposed by West and Zimmerman (1987), which considers gender as emergent and based on social interaction rather than as individually defined. Butler argues that "[g]ender is the repeated stylization of the body, a set of repeated acts within a highly rigid regulatory frame that congeal over time to produce the appearance of substance, of a natural sort of being" (1990, 45). Butler explains that "doing gender" is based on a series of expected practices and that the repetition of these practices and their associated gender (i.e., that women repeat feminine practices and men repeat masculine ones) suggests that these are innate and normalized, rather than socially constructed performances. In the same way, we create ourselves as intelligible, gendered subjects through a process of actions, but these actions are performative—there is nothing preceding them and only the actions themselves enable the subject position to emerge.

This aligns with Barad's work on performativity vs. representation. Where representation suggests the "thing" to be represented preexists the representation, a performative analysis argues that it is through performance that that thing *comes to be*. This is therefore a posthuman view, as it does not separate representation and represented, but argues that it is precisely through the embodiment or enactment of something that it is formed. Barad's posthuman approach thereby disrupts the binary of "material" and "discourse" by instead arguing that all observable phenomena are an entanglement of the two—they cannot be meaningfully separated. For Barad, "[b]odies are not objects with inherent boundaries and properties; they are material-discursive phenomena" (2007, 153). As such, gender is a material-discursive "phenomenon" that enforces specific subjectivities through performative "norms." By material here, I mean the materials and material surroundings that categorize gender, rather than merely the biological body which categorizes biological sex, not gender identity. As Barad's work suggests, we cannot meaningfully separate the body from the societal expectations and understandings that inform our interpretation of it. Moreover, we are held to account for our gender performances and are rewarded for normative gender practices, while deviation brings the risk of threats, punishment, judgment, or shame. This is important to note once again when considering the ideological stance that has empowered a patriarchal system by enforcing certain subjectivities through societal expectations that demure, passive, and deferential is the correct way for women to behave. As Haraway suggests, gendered consciousness is forced upon us by the historical social reality of the patriarchy (2016, 16; see also Butler 1990).

From this perspective, the consideration of non-binary genders and alternative gender performances are key to posthumanism's aim of deconstructing humanist notions and moving to postdualistic perspectives (see Ferrando 2016). In the same way that posthumanism resists the binary thinking of human/animal, human/machine, nature/culture, and mind/matter, the male/female binary should be challenged too. Yet the possibilities for posthumanism, fighting against an entrenched humanistic, hierarchical, and patriarchal history, have not yet been fully explored. As Braidotti states, "we need to experiment with resistance and intensity in order to find out what posthuman bodies can do" (2013, 99).

Holland and Harpin suggest that "tomboys challenge the gender binary by their very presence," (2015, 306) and we might therefore consider the figure of the tomboy to be what is needed in a (posthuman) revolution "which queries and queers the ways that the options are articulated and policed" (Halberstam and Livingstone 1995, 19). It could be argued that the term tomboy is in itself regressive—that it suggests that any girl/woman displaying masculine traits must be set apart and somehow "othered" with this term or that it suggests a form of gender determinism. Others have noted that the tomboy depends on "stereotypical notions of femininity and masculinity" (Carr 1998, 528), suggesting that it is akin to calling "a girl a quasiboy just because she liked to dress comfortably, play sport, climb trees, go on adventures" (Thorne 1993, 113). However, the tomboy offers an experimental resistance to the presupposed gender binary—not just to femininity—as the "tomboy identity leaves room for a person to articulate an identity that does not conform strictly to a binary gender construction" (Craig and LaCroix 2011, 452). Tomboyism has often been considered as an "active resistance" and rejection of femininity, although this can become problematized through the equally dualistic idea of "choosing masculinity" and conforming to masculine roles (Carr 1998, 540). This work is problematic in that it draws on certain ideas of "normal" tomboyism and refers to a gender binary rather than a spectrum. I reject this dichotomous view, instead arguing that the tomboy figure is neither placed entirely in opposition to femininity nor seen to "reject" or "choose" either male or female gender roles; instead, it breaks down such binaries by blurring and borrowing across a spectrum of gender identities. The version of the tomboy I present in this chapter encapsulates a hybridity of gender identities and therefore represents an embodiment of posthuman subjectivity.

For the purposes of this chapter, I suggest that, as per Kroker, "there are always gender drifters who remix, recombine, and resplice the codes of gender performance" (2012, 3) and that the tomboy is one embodiment of this that may therefore allow alternative "codes of gender"—or, indeed, the total abolishment of them—to arise. In order to analyze this emergence, I must draw upon stereotypical, gendered understandings of specific traits (e.g., masculine or feminine) to demonstrate how they are remixed and applied through the "tomboy" character of Jade in the videogame *Beyond Good and Evil.* While this may be problematic in the re-codification of heteronormative assumptions about gendered traits (a tomboy cannot be a tomboy without some "subversion"), it is my aim that the use of "tomboy" can here signify an embodiment of posthuman gender. I suggest that the adoption of multiple modes of gender performance allows the deterritorialization of certain behaviors or performances as belonging to a binary categorization, reterritorializing them instead as a posthuman entanglement.

This is not in any way to suggest that identification as a tomboy is the same as identification as non-binary, but to instead demonstrate how a particular "representation of the tomboy" functions to blur, blend, and borrow from previously opposing categories to create new discourses that might allow further uptake of other non-binary expressions or identifications. I do not think one has to explicitly identify as non-binary in gender identity to enact and embody a non-binary subjectivity. However, before beginning my analysis, I wish to very briefly provide some historical context to the portrayal of gender in videogames and the ways in which such portrayals have been subject to attempts at queering them.

GENDER PORTRAYALS IN VIDEOGAMES

Videogaming has an unfortunate history of being considered a "masculine" activity, with an industry that has ostracized women and created a situation whereby "games were developed by males for males" (Hartley 2002, 93). While it is beyond the scope of this chapter to give a full history, it is important to note that the representation of women in videogames is undoubtedly linked to the lack of women *behind* videogames. This problematic, gendered history has continued to the present day, and issues of gender diversity and representation are still evident. Women in videogames generally lack diversity in terms of character type and are underrepresented, oversexualized, and underclothed; attention is focused on hyperfeminine representations of female bodies (Friman 2015, 11; Beasley and Standley 2002, 289; Downs and Smith 2010, 723–724). Moreover, videogame culture is "an extraordinarily sexist affair" (Hoofd 2018, 230); flagrant sexism is evident outside of the games, most notably through the 2014 culture war of #GamerGate. This was a predominantly online harassment campaign that saw female game designers and critics, including Anita Sarkeesian, attacked for their commentary on female representation and their desire for a more balanced gender portrayal. During #GamerGate, several women in the videogame industry were viciously trolled and doxxed online, receiving death threats that led to the need for police protection and the cancellation of public appearances. These issues, of course, only served to highlight the toxicity of certain gamer cultures.

Suffice it to say that in gaming, the female figure has often failed monumentally to present a "revolutionary" representation of gender politics. From damsels in distress to sexualized others, there is concern that the repeated exposure to these characters will "begin to develop scripts about gender stereotypes" for players; in other words, players may begin to develop expectations about gendered behaviors (Downs and Smith 2010, 723). For example, some games portray hypersexualized women who will respond positively to groping (e.g., *Grand Theft Auto V*); it is therefore vital that problematic portrayals of gender and sexuality in videogames are addressed and more diverse characters, options, and imagery are introduced.

Yet videogame players have not always settled for the game-led gendering of avatars, and there are a variety of ways in which certain players have attempted to queer both avatars and play. Aesthetically non-normative gender types in *World of Warcraft* are often chosen by those who wish to disrupt traditional notions of femininity (Sundén 2012, 177), and similar activities are seen being performed by female players in *Everquest* (Taylor 2006, 97). Videogames can, for some, operate as a space to articulate different forms of femininity and identity that are not available to them in offline scenarios

(Eklund 2011, 339), whereas for others it is the practice of gaming itself that allows female gamers to take pleasure in the opportunity to challenge gender norms by exploring their own aggression through game combat (Royse et al. 2007).

As a female gamer, I find it refreshing to see examples of games where female characters offer a portrayal removed from the male gaze—that is to say, removed from the position of the passive woman, objectified and "displayed as sexual object" (Mulvey 1999, 837). Instead, the emergence of more female characters as active protagonists in their own adventures, with careers and relationships of their own, allows for a more diverse cast that defies prejudiced representation. Yet, while I hope that the videogame industry will continue to offer alternative modes of gendered performance, the subject of this chapter is nearly twenty years old: the 2003 Ubisoft action-adventure videogame *Beyond Good and Evil*.

I draw on this game because *Beyond Good and Evil* is notable in the study of tomboy cultures, as gender seems, for the most part, neither here nor there within the game—and not just where Jade is concerned. While Jade's femininity does not exclude her from being a figure of strength or intelligence, her masculinity does not exclude her from being caring. Although the game did not enjoy massive commercial success, this does not limit its relevance as a subject of study, as in some ways this creates a subcultural status, much like the tomboy figure. A variety of subcultural theorists have explored how participants in subcultures "challenge and reinforce social norms surrounding gender and sexuality" (Haenfler 2013, 14). We might consider tomboyism as a form of "resistance" and "deviance"—traits which are commonly attributed to subcultural groups. A videogame such as *Beyond Good and Evil*, which embodies similar values and fails to achieve commercial success, becomes potentially subcultural through "resistance to 'mainstream,' dominant, or hegemonic culture" (Haenfler 2013, 17).

Another reason for the choice of *Beyond Good and Evil* for this analysis is that its plot (explored below) links to Proehl's suggestion that tomboy narratives "subvert gender and sexual norms, center on the experiences of a female protagonist, and appeal to emotion in order to advocate for social justice and equality" (Proehl 2018, 2). While Proehl's focus is on literature, this categorization seems to fit the narrative of *Beyond Good and Evil*.

BEYOND GOOD AND EVIL: BACKGROUND AND PLOT

Beyond Good and Evil takes place in the fictional world of Hillys, where humans co-exist with humanoid, anthropomorphized animals. The story follows Jade, our hero, and her trusty sidekick/uncle/boar-like humanoid creature Pey'j as they attempt to uncover secrets pertaining to the ongoing alien invasion of the DomZ. The DomZ capture Hillyans and either drain their life force and convert it into power or force them into servitude by implanting them with alien spores. Jade is a photojournalist and looks after a variety of children from different species who have been orphaned in the alien invasion. Interestingly, this in itself correlates with Proehl's work on tomboy narratives, which suggests that "they [tomboys] express sympathy for other marginalized individuals" (2018, 7), with a key trope of tomboy narratives being "the formation of surrogate families" (2018, 8). The game utilizes Jade's career as a way for her to gather funds—her initial task is to photograph the various species of Hillys and send the images to a science museum. Playing as Jade, the gamer can therefore explore the world of Hillys, taking these photos, engaging in mini games, and exploring different landscapes. However, the main thrust of the story comes when Jade is approached by someone who wants photos of a DomZ creature. Jade-player[1] ends up fighting the creature to escape it, thereby revealing the true task; this was a test from the secret chief of the IRIS Network, an underground resistance movement. He reveals that the military control of Hillys, the Alpha Section, has been possessed by the alien DomZ force. The IRIS Network chief asks Jade to undertake the important task of investigating the DomZ/Alpha Section because the IRIS lead investigator, Double H, has been captured. Throughout the game, Jade-player therefore explores, investigates, and captures images of areas she has infiltrated. There are mini puzzles as well as battles within the game, and finally, Jade-player helps to overcome the DomZ invasion and rescue their victims. The game is played in the third-player style; the player works with Jade's avatar, with some elements of the game involving the direction of Pey'j or Double H.

POSTHUMANIZING JADE: TOMBOY AESTHETIC, RELATIONSHIPS, SKILLS AND PROFESSIONS

Aesthetic Embodiment and Relationship Roles

Jade presents as a "tomboy" within the game as she disrupts certain gendered expectations, initially through her aesthetic. Jade is depicted with cropped hair and baggy trousers, and Pinckard and Fernández-Vara suggest that Jade acts as a "counter" to the "hyper-gendered female representation of characters such as Lara Croft" (2015, 3). The cropping of Jade's hair contrasts Croft's swinging ponytail which, though practical, being pulled back from the face, still embodies the long hair closely associated with femininity. Jade's hairstyle, therefore, borrows from stereotypically masculine styles. Jade's body-type is far from atypical for videogames; she has a disproportionately small waist that is revealed by a short tank top. However, she does not boast an overlarge cleavage and most of her skin remains covered, thereby again countering the hypersexualized image of many female videogame characters. Sarkeesian explains:

> She actually looks the part of the active, practical young woman of color[2] who has a job to do . . . [W]omen in games are often depicted in wildly impractical, sexualized clothing designed to make them appealing to straight male players. But Jade isn't designed to fulfil someone else's fantasy. The midriff top is a little silly, but for the most part, she looks like someone who is dressed to accommodate her own needs. I mean, you don't get much more practical than cargo pants. (2015)

This focus on practicality aligns with Craig and LaCroix's (2011) suggestion that although tomboys' clothing may be seen to be more masculine, it may have much more to do with function than form (452). This also allows us to understand the power of gendered clothing to be restrictive or empowering of certain behaviors (see, e.g., Bratta 2015).

Eklund has explored the ways in which the avatars in *World of Warcraft* are "in many ways stylized for us, prefabricated with assumptions about gender and sexuality" (2011, 338); however, the assumptions about Jade's gender and sexuality are outside of the heteronormative stereotype. Buikema explains how these stereotypes are embedded from birth. She argues that as soon as a child is born, the naming of that child as "girl" or "boy" enacts certain meanings, connotations, and semiotic signifiers: "[t]he girl's domain is pink; she is sweet, passive, physical, spontaneous, beautiful, etc. Conversely, the boy is approached with an entirely different set of terms: sturdy, smart, resourceful, etc." (2018, 90). While this is often not the case in videogames, which often transcend girlish pinkness for a sexualized red instead, Jade, in contrast to this, is fully decked out in her namesake color—her combat trousers, jacket, headband, and even her lipstick are green. By incorporating lipstick but twisting expectations (by making it masculine green rather than feminine pink), Jade plays with feminine traditions of make-up and ultimately appropriates them for her own benefit, using lipstick not as an expression of femininity so much as an expression of "Jade." Moreover, she immediately proves herself to be sturdy, as she is thrown into battle with alien invaders early in the game and is continuously depicted as smart and resourceful.

In their analysis of twelve videogames, Jansz and Martis noted the ways in which "quite a few women became leaders in the games, but they continue to be presented in a sexualized way. As a result, these powerful women are depicted as sex objects as much as their powerless predecessors were" (2007,

147). However, this is not the case for Jade. This is notable not only through her aesthetic, but also in the way in which she relates to other characters around her. It is worth mentioning that another act of queering in *Beyond Good and Evil* is the lack of romantic discourses within the game. Sexuality is often brought into debate in studies around tomboys, linking the tomboy figure with a rejection of sexual desire/heterosexual desire/being the object of desire. Skersi, for example, posits that "the tomboy in popular culture is often signified by her refusal to view herself through the male gaze or participate in heterosexual mating rituals (the school dance, for instance)" (2011, 23), but as mentioned above, it is not only Jade who refuses to see herself through the male gaze—the male gaze is mostly lacking as a framework through which anyone is considered in the game. Friman argues that the portrayal of female characters as objects of romantic or sexual desire in videogames not only reduces the characters to gender stereotypes but also reinforces "an implied demand for a heterosexual male player" (2015, 23). However, Jade queers this expectation as her relationships are based on friendship and familial love rather than romance or desire. This is, in itself, a radical act. Despite Jade's sidekicks taking the form of two males—Pey'j and Double H—neither view her as subservient, and despite their apparent superiority (Pey'j as her uncle, and Double H as her predecessor), both defer to her strength and abilities, with no sexual objectification or gendered discrimination evident. This in itself renders Jade's sexual identity androgynous, thus enhancing her tomboy status (Creed 1995, 98).

In the opening sequence, although we see Pey'j drop in as a rescuer when Jade gets caught by the alien, he then throws her Daï-jo staff to her, saying, "Free yourself, Jade. I'll create a diversion." As Sarkeesian (2015) notes, "[h]e assists her but doesn't rescue her. He knows that even in this situation, she's far from helpless, and the fact that Pey'j treats her as a capable partner encourages us to see her that way, too." Other characters also continually reference Jade's capabilities, with members of the IRIS Network praising her achievements: "Friends . . . I believe Jade has just shown us an amazing demonstration of courage," "Nice work, kid . . . ," "Jade, your last report from the factory had a large impact on the population. The Hillyans have spontaneously shown their support," and "You've done an incredible job." These affirmations come from male humans as well as females from other species, thereby demonstrating the ways in which her work is acknowledged and seen as important, active, and integral to the underground IRIS Network.

Elsewhere in the game, Jade-player ends up first taking on Double H's job and then later rescuing him. Although he was the former lead reporter for the IRIS Network's investigation into the DomZ's take-over of the Alpha Section, the (male) IRIS Network chief sees no issue in replacing Double H with a young woman (after, of course, the aforementioned test). Jade, notably, unlike Double H, does not get captured by the DomZ, thereby demonstrating a higher level of skill than her male counterpart.

Double H is presented in stereotypically masculine ways—he is large and taller than Jade but also heavy built, with almost impossibly broad shoulders, a chiseled jaw, and an armored suit that also operates as a hovercraft. Relying on her small, slight, and stereotypically "feminine" frame, Jade-player is able to creep undetected past guards and into tunnels to infiltrate the area in which Double H is being kept prisoner and release him from the suspended sleep through which the DomZ were draining his energy. Upon his release, Double H drops to the floor at Jade's feet and displays his disorientation (and memory loss) while stating, "[a]nother 10 minutes and I'd have been a goner . . . I owe you my life," then exclaiming, "AT YOUR SERVICE, JADE THYRUS!" as he lowers his visor and jumps to attention. Double H immediately displays stereotypical masculinity through his strength (he breaks down a metal grid keeping them captive), demonstrating the need for both "masculine" and "feminine" traits for mutual survival. Where Double H was reliant on Jade's stealth, Jade-player is reliant on Double H's strength for the escape to be complete. However, Double H then follows this by falling down a large ravine, immediately undermining his own capability. Jade-player is then forced to continue alone, battling further DomZ aliens in order to save Pey'j, who was captured in the rescue mission. Pey'j greets her gratefully, saying, "Thanks Jade, I'd have ended up on a silver platter with an apple in my mouth if it wasn't for you" (referring to his pig-like species).

Furthermore, elsewhere in the game, Double H's aforementioned size works against him when he cannot enter or navigate certain spaces that Jade can. He exclaims: "Too tight for me! I'll cover your rear, Miss Jade!" In this way, Double H's "masculinity" works against him while Jade's "feminine" frame again works in Jade-player's favor. The exchange between Double H and Jade also demonstrates a deference to her unique abilities and feminine attributes from an older, more experienced man. Similarly, in battle situations when Jade-player can direct some of Double H's actions (such as pressing a key or button to make him deploy certain attacks), Double H responds with "Yes sir!," ostensibly following her "order." This also operates to legitimize Jade's character—despite Double H's own masculinity, he has no issue with deferring to her command and showing his appreciation for her knowledge and skill. The value of Jade's physique is evident elsewhere; for example, Jade-player is able to shimmy across a narrow ledge, leaving Pey'j (and his large boar-like frame) behind, as he exclaims, "whoa, count me out Jade!" Yet it is not just her physique that is relied upon—the whole narrative journey is based around Jade's character as one who will help others. For example, after crossing the narrow ledge, Jade-player then has to work out how to lower a platform for Pey'j to cross and join her, where he thanks her again for her assistance. Through the other characters' acceptance and appreciation of her skills, we are therefore presented with a less stereotypically gendered narrative for Jade's character.

In neither example of rescue does Jade reject the praise and thanks of her comrades, merely responding in cut-scenes by telling Double H that she is not sure how they will get out and replying to Pey'j teasingly: "Mmmm, shut-up! You're makin' me hungry! I'm gonna regret saving you . . . " Friman has argued that the gendering of female characters in videogames can operate through their behavior "by having them act in an overly empathic or panicky manner—in other words in a stereotypically feminine manner" (2015, 19), yet through these exchanges and Jade's reactions to the capture of her friends, we can see that, while concerned, she is not hyperfeminized. Her casual exchange with Pey'j is instead "banter"-like, again emphasizing comedic, familial camaraderie (elsewhere, after rescuing Pey'j *again*, she calls him an "old fart") rather than an overtly emotional "feminine" response. However, Jade is not *un*emotional: when Pey'j is captured and feared dead, there is a cut-scene during which Jade says, in a sad voice with downturned eyes, "all I know is how much he meant to me," over sentimental, slow music. When Pey'j then makes contact, she says, "Hey, that's my uncle . . . PEY'J!! PEY'J!! IS THAT YOU??" in excited tones with raised eyebrows and triumphant music in the background, and we are left in no doubt as to the love between these characters and the apparent relief that Jade experiences, thus demonstrating her clear affection.

Booting and Shooting: Skills and Profession

There are "stereotypes of the female body as weak, fragile, and delicate" (Adams et al. 2005, 26) and the stereotypical female character is seen to embody the supposedly "feminine" traits of being pretty, dainty, weaker, and sexualized. In contrast, we have already seen how Jade-player is able to use her slight frame as an asset: a source of stealth. Yet her body is also used as a source of defensive strength.

Stereotypical feminine behavior would suggest a strong focus on more domestic activities, based around the home and caring for others. Obviously, these stereotypes are highly problematic and outdated, deeply rooted within hegemonic patriarchy, which operates to both consign and constrict women to specific "roles," while also undervaluing those roles and the labor involved. Jade is presented as a caregiver within the game, as the opening sequence to the game shows her to be fostering the children of those who have been captured during the alien invasion. This role as caregiver is also evident in the fact that Jade-player is responsible for the health of Pey'j and Double H at various points within the game—when their health bars deteriorate through injury from battle, Jade-player must give them energy—they cannot "heal" themselves. Energy is exchanged through the consumption of food, and so from this perspective, Jade is giving them food or feeding them to help them heal. Once again, this is a stereotypically feminine act of nurturing through attendance to domestic tasks. Yet, when her lighthouse home is attacked and the children are threatened, the player can perform Jade's fighting skills for the first time. In this embodiment of the fierce mother archetype, Jade-player is able to employ nurturing and caregiving *through* strength and aggression, blending stereotypically feminine qualities with stereotypically masculine acts.

While fighting is usually an attribute consigned to the realm of the "masculine," Jade is proficient in a form of martial arts and utilizes her Daï-jo combat staff to engage in fights with the alien forces. Although at times she has aid from her comrades, she is often the lone fighter against multiple alien entities. Through the player's use of the keyboard/controller, Jade-player is able to engage in coordinated attacks against her enemies. Jade's abilities allow her to wield her staff in a variety of attack moves; Jade-player can collect energy in the Daï-jo, which stores it temporarily, before releasing a super-attack function that inflicts increased damage on surrounding enemies. If Pey'j or Double H are in the same fight as her, the avatar-gamer can instruct them to carry out their "super-action," which, according to the "Beyond Good and Evil Wiki" (n.d.) "execute[s] a ground pound, which will launch enemies into the air. Jade can then use her Daï-jo to slow down time, aim, and thrust foes in a certain direction." The range of attacks and Jade's coordinated deployment of them indicate skill and prowess. Of course, this is not an uncomplicated reading—Jade's efficiency at fighting is brought into being in part through the player's proficiency at the game itself, again demonstrating the intra-dependence of avatar and gamer in this posthuman subjectivity. Yet the skill is implied, and the weapon itself ("Daï-jo" means "great staff") signifies Jade's apparent ability to both defend herself and, through the narrative of the game, to save others.

Beyond fighting aliens and her underground task of exposing the Alpha Section's corruption and DomZ infiltration, Jade also owns her own photojournalism company, Jade Reporting. Jade's skill with a camera and in her profession are notable because, rather than just operating as background story, they become an integral part of the gameplay and progression. Friman notes that while some videogames attribute backgrounds or professions that hint at expertise or power to female characters, this does not equate to actually allowing them to act those out—these need to be reinforced through in-game relationships and actions. Her research found that many supposed female character "experts" actually failed to embody or act in their expert position until prompted to do so by a male character (2015, 14). This therefore reinforces the "passive female" trope, failing to promote strong and active female characters. From this perspective, Jade's actual ability to act as expert and earn money for her skills puts her in a more pro-active "masculine" role, as "[p]aid work away from the home therefore acquires masculine connotations, whereas feminine connotations are reserved for running a household and caring for a family" (van der Tuin 2018, 15). Yet, initially, the reason that Jade-player needs to engage with photography at the very start of the game is to earn money to get the power at her lighthouse home back on, in order to protect the household and the orphans she looks after. Moreover, Jade's continued work is in order to help find those who have disappeared and been captured by the DomZ invaders, and her work is therefore motivated by care, compassion, and social justice, rather than by financial gain. Her work is therefore placed in reference to others in a wider network, positioning her as (posthumanistly) egalitarian rather than (humanistly) elitist.

Where masculinity has specific connotations of "what is active and free, the rational consciousness, mind, culture, self-determination, responsibility, and being" (van der Tuin 2018, 15), Jade's character is closely aligned with these supposedly masculine ideals. Interestingly, this corresponds with Ness's research that shows in film, unlike other heroines:

> [F]emale reporters were not as easily subjugated by the camera's gaze, since women in the genre are often responsible for investigating the action. [. . .] They also often underwent a form of masculization, with the female reporters adopting male-associated names and modes of dress designed to downplay their femininity. (1997, 72)

This analysis may well be applicable to Jade: she operates as investigator, and with her aforementioned aesthetic, Jade adopts certain masculine forms of dress and downplays her femininity through banter. Jade therefore embodies tomboyish "resistance against a normative femininity" (Holland and Harpin 2015, 307); however, she does not resist femininity in its entirety, as she still draws on "feminine" traits such as caregiving, nurturing, protection, and stealth by utilizing her feminine frame to great effect where her male counterparts are unable to follow.

We might therefore consider that Jade embodies certain aspects of posthumanism's postdualistic agenda, as she borrows traits from both realms, blending them to such a degree that they are intertwined and entangled. Her caregiving is related to her strength, her profession to her desire for justice, her stealthy accomplishments working alongside the strength of others, and her relationships based on familial love and amicable collegiality, while not veering into sexualized discrimination or gendered subservience. Through the close integration of masculine and feminine stereotypes, Jade remixes different values, traits, behaviors, and aesthetics to accommodate a gender performance that deterritorializes her actions from a gendered "norm" and reterritorializes them in a postdualistic embodiment and narrative.

CONCLUSION

Little has been written on *Beyond Good and Evil* to date, and this chapter therefore not only contributes to research surrounding the intersections of gender studies and posthuman theory but applies that to a lesser-known media product. Despite being a videogame from 2003, the game demonstrates a gendered postdualism that can be considered posthuman. The character of Jade embodies a variety of what might stereotypically be considered both feminine and masculine traits, thereby positioning her as a "tomboy" figure. Jade is an empathetic caregiver, with a slight physique that is used to her advantage in order to progress through the game. She subverts the expectation that small equates to weak, and instead embeds small with an active power signifying stealth and access. Coupled with her feminine facial features that often express emotive responses in cut-scenes, she does not wholly disrupt "feminine" gender norms. However, her strength, skill with a Daï-jo combat stick, and profession as a photographer demonstrate a variety of active abilities that position her in a more "masculine" field of reference. One of the key things that allows Jade to disrupt certain gendered binaries is the way in which the game as a whole does not focus on her gender as an impetus for plot progression. She is neither seen as a damsel in distress nor a romantic figure or sexualized object. Through other characters' intra-actions with Jade, her abilities, skills, and personality are seen as valued, whether through praise, deference, or shared "banter" as equals. This emphasizes Jade's ability to combine a variety of feminine and masculine traits that allow her to disrupt their binary categorizations, incorporating both to thereby embody a posthuman remixing of these emergent behaviors.

Barad has argued that "[a]gency is not about choice in any liberal humanist sense; rather, it is about the possibilities and accountability entailed in reconfiguring material-discursive apparatuses of bodily production, including the boundary articulations and exclusions that are marked by those practices" (2007, 214). From this perspective, Jade is not considered to be "choosing" one gendered performance over another, but through Jade's actions and intra-actions, the material-discursive apparatus of gender is rearticulated in a postdualistic way. Lyttleton-Smith has suggested that Barad's approach to agential-realism "offers an onto-epistemology that situates emergent, observable phenomena (under which category gender is located) as necessarily produced through the 'intra-action' of the material and the discursive" (2015,

83). Here, gender is configured through material relations and discursive, performative actions. Jade's intra-actions draw on observable material-discursive actions situated within both feminine and masculine gender performances, allowing an alternative, postdualist gender identity to arise. Chang claims that "the posthuman subject is always a test, a border crossing, and a horizon of possibility" (2012, 86). Through the material-discursive configuration of the tomboy, the posthuman subject is able to test post-gender performances. Characters such as Jade, and our ability to play with and as her in a less obviously gendered, humanistic world than our own, allow us to embrace the tomboy as a hopeful horizon of postdualistic possibility. With *Beyond Good and Evil 2* apparently "well underway" (Ubisoft 2020) let us hope for further posthuman prospects and promises for the future.

NOTES

1. Throughout this analysis I draw on both cut-scenes as well as in-game action. I therefore use "Jade-player" to demonstrate playable moments, rather than cut-scenes during which the player watches but cannot adjust the action. Jade-player is also used in order to demonstrate the intra-action of the avatar-gamer posthuman subjectivity (see, e.g., Wilde 2018).

2. Whilst it is beyond the scope of this chapter to fully articulate issues of race and intersectionality as they apply to Jade, it is worth mentioning that her race is also presented as somewhat ambiguous, allowing for multiple readings. (see for example Chris Kohler, "'Jade Is Black?!': Racial Ambiguity in Games," Wired, 2007).

BIBLIOGRAPHY

Adams, Natalie, Alison Schmitke, and Amy Franklin. 2005. "Tomboys, Dykes, and Girly Girls: Interrogating the Subjectivities of Adolescent Female Athletes." *Women's Studies Quarterly* 33 (1/2): 17–34.

Ancel, Michel. 2003. *Beyond Good and Evil.* Ubisoft. Videogame.

Barad, Karen. 2007. *Meeting the Universe Halfway: Quantum Physics and the Entanglement of Matter and Meaning*. Durham: Duke University Press.

Beasley, Berrin, and Tracy Collins Standley. 2002. "Shirts vs. Skins: Clothing as an Indicator of Gender Role Stereotyping in Video Games." *Mass Communication & Society* 5 (3): 279–293.

Beyond Good and Evil Wiki. n.d. "Daï-jo." Accessed October 8, 2020. https://beyondgoodandevil.fandom.com/wiki/Da%C3%AF-jo.

Braidotti, Rosi. 2013. *The Posthuman*. Cambridge: Polity Press.

Bratta, Phil. 2015. "The Public Pants: A Visual Rhetoric of Gendered and Classed Imperialism." *Visual Culture & Gender* 10: 20–8.

Buikema, Rosemarie. 2018. "The Arena of Imaginings: Sarah Bartmann and the Ethics of Representation." In *Doing Gender in Media, Art and Culture: A Comprehensive Guide to Gender Studies,* edited by Rosemarie Buikema, Liedeke Plate, and Kathrin Thiele, 81–93. Abington: Routledge.

Butler, Judith. 1990. *Gender Trouble.* London: Routledge.

Carr, C. Lynn. 1998. "Tomboy Resistance and Conformity: Agency in Social Psychological Gender Theory." *Gender and Society* 12 (12): 528–53.

Chang, Edmond Y. 2012. "Technoqueer: Re/Con/Figuring Posthuman Narratives." Doctoral Thesis: University of Washington. https://digital.lib.washington.edu /researchworks/bitstream/handle/1773/22631/Chang_washington_0250E_11129 .pdf?sequence=1&isAllowed=y.

Craig, Traci, and Jessica LaCroix. 2001. "Tomboy as Protective Identity." *Journal of Lesbian* Studies 15 (4): 450–65.

Creed, Barbara. 1995. "Lesbian Bodies: Tribades, Tomboys and Tarts." In *Sexy Bodies: The Strange Carnalities of Feminism*, edited by Elizabeth Grosz and Elspeth Probyn, 86–103. Abington: Routledge.

Derrida, Jacques. (1972) 1981. *Positions.* (Trans. Alan Bass). Chicago: The University of Chicago Press.

Descartes, Rene. (1637) 1924. *Discourse on the Method.* New York: Cosimo Classics.

Downs, Edward, and Stacey L. Smith. 2010. "Keeping Abreast of Hypersexuality: A Video Game Character Content Analysis." *Sex Roles* 62 (11): 721–33.

Eklund, Lisa. 2011. "Doing Gender in Cyberspace: The Performance of Gender by Female *World of Warcraft* Players." *Convergence* 17 (3): 323–42.

Ferrando, Francesca. 2016. "Humans Have Always Been Posthuman: A Spiritual Genealogy of the Posthuman." In *Critical Posthumanism and Planetary Futures,* edited by Debashish Banerji and Makarand R. Paranjape, 243–56. New Delhi: Springer.

Ferrando, Francesca. 2019. *Philosophical Posthumanism*. London: Bloomsbury.

Friman, Usva. 2015. "From Pixel Babes to Active Agents: How to Fix the Lack of Diversity in Female Digital Game Characters." *Well Played: A Journal on Video Games, Values, and Meaning* 4 (3): 11–25.

Gane, Nicholas. 2016. "Posthuman." *Theory, Culture, & Society* 23 (2/3): 431–4.

Graham, Elaine. 2002. *Representations of the Post/Human*. Manchester: Manchester University Press.

Halberstam, Judith, and Ira Livingston. 1995. *Posthuman Bodies*. Indianapolis: Indiana University Press.

Haenfler, Ross. 2013. *Subcultures: The Basics*. London: Routledge.

Haraway, Donna. 2016. *A Cyborg Manifesto*. Minnesota: University of Minnesota Press.

Hartley, John. 2002. *Communication, Cultural and Media Studies: The Key Concepts*. Abington: Routledge.

Hayles, N. Katherine. 1999. *How We Became Posthuman*. London: The University of Chicago Press.

Holland, Samantha, and Julie Harpin. 2015. "Who is the 'Girly' Girl? Tomboys, Hyper-Femininity and Gender." *Journal of Gender Studies* 24 (3): 293–309.

Hoofd, Ingrid. 2018. "Malala and the Politics of Feminist New Media Activism." In *Doing Gender in Media, Art and Culture: A Comprehensive Guide to Gender Studies,* edited by Rosemarie Buikema, Liedeke Plate, and Kathrin Thiele, 222–32. Abington: Routledge.

Jansz, Jeroen, and Raynel G. Martis. 2017. "The Lara Phenomenon: Powerful Female Characters in Video Games." *Sex Roles* 56: 141–8.

Jones, Owain. 1999. "Tomboy Tales: The Rural, Nature and the Gender of Childhood." *Gender, Place and Culture* 6 (2): 117–36.

Kant, Immanuel. 1784. "An Answer to the Question: What is Enlightenment?" http://donelan.faculty.writing.ucsb.edu/enlight.html.

Kohler, Chris. 2007. "'Jade Is Black?!': Racial Ambiguity in Games." *Wired.* February 18, 2007. https://www.wired.com/2007/02/jades-black-rac/.

Kroker, Arthur. 2012. *Body Drift: Butler, Hayles, Haraway*. Minneapolis: University of Minnesota Press.

Lyttleton-Smith, Jennifer. 2015. "Becoming Gendered Bodies: A Posthuman Analysis of How Gender is Produced in an Early Childhood Classroom." Doctoral Thesis: Cardiff University. http://orca.cf.ac.uk/86260/2/Jennifer%20Lyttleton-Smith%20Final%20Thesis.pdf.

Mulvey, Laura. 1999. "Visual Pleasure and Narrative Cinema." In *Film Theory and Criticism: Introductory Readings,* edited by Leo Braudy and Marshall Cohen, 833–44. New York: Oxford University Press.

Ness, Richard. 1997. *From Headline Hunter to Superman: A Journalism Filmography*. Lanham: Scarecrow Press.

Pepperell, Robert. 2003. *The Posthuman Condition: Consciousness Beyond the Brain*. Bristol: Intellect.

Pinckard, Jane, and Clara Fernández-Vara. 2015. "Introduction: Special Issue on Diversity in Games." *Well Played: A Journal on Video Games, Values, and Meaning* 4 (3): 1–20.

Proehl, Kristen. 2018. *Battling Girlhood: Sympathy, Social Justice, and the Tomboy Figure in American Literature*. Milton: Taylor & Francis Group.

Royse, Pam, Joon Lee, Baasanjav Undrahbuyan, Mark Hopson, and Mia Consalvo. 2007. "Women and Games: Technologies of the Gendered Self." *New Media & Society* 9 (4): 555–76.

Sarkeesian, Anita. 2015. "Jade: Positive Female Characters in Video Games." *Feminist Frequency*. May 11, 2015. https://feministfrequency.com/video/jade-beyond-good-evil/.

Schilt, Kristin, and Laurel Westbrook. 2009. "Doing Gender, Doing Heteronormativity: 'Gender Normals,' Transgender People, and the Social Maintenance of Heterosexuality." *Gender and Society* 23 (4): 440–64.

Skerski, Jamie. 2011. "Tomboy Chic: Re-Fashioning Gender Rebellion." *Journal of Lesbian Studies* 15 (4): 466–79.

Sundén, Jenny. 2012. "Desires at Play: On Closeness and Epistemological Uncertainty." *Games and Culture* 7 (2): 164–84.

Taylor, T. L. 2006. *Play Between Worlds: Exploring Online Gaming Culture*. Cambridge: MIT Press.

Thorne, Barrie. 1993. *Gender Play: Girls and Boys in School*. New York: Routledge.

Toffoletti, Kim. 2007. *Cyborgs and Barbie Dolls*. London: I.B. Taurus.

Ubisoft. 2020. "Space Monkey Program: The Road Ahead." July 12, 2020. https://beyondgoodandevil.ubisoft.com/en-us/news/ignt22183-Space-Monkey-Program:-The-Road-Ahead.

van der Tuin, Iris. 2018. "The Arena of Feminism: Simone de Beauvoir and the History of Feminism." In *Doing Gender in Media, Art and Culture: A Comprehensive Guide to Gender Studies,* edited by Rosemarie Buikema, Liedeke Plate, and Kathrin Thiele, 9–23. Oxon: Routledge.

West, Candace, and Don Zimmerman. 1987. "Doing Gender." *Gender & Society* 1 (2): 125–51.

Wilde, Poppy, and Adrienne Evans. 2019. "Empathy at Play: Embodying Posthuman Subjectivities in Gaming." *Convergence* 25 (5/6): 791–806.

Wilde, Poppy. 2018. "Avatar Affectivity and Affection." *Transformations* 31: 25–43. http://www.transformationsjournal.org/wp-content/uploads/2018/06/Trans31_02_wilde.pdf.

———. 2020. "I, Posthuman: A Deliberately Provocative Title." *International Review of Qualitative Research* 13 (3): 365–80.

Chapter 10

How #Tomboy Instagram Reclaims the Tomboy from White, Middle-Class Straight Women

Holly M. Wells

In October 2015, about one year after the publication of Liz Prince's *Tomboy*, Marisa Meltzer, in an article for *The New York Times*, asked, "Where have all the tomboys gone?" She argued that tomboy heroines are "far harder to find" than in "yesteryear" and quotes Feminist Press publisher Jennifer Baumgardner as saying, "No one brings us these stories. Tomboy doesn't feel present tense to me at all. It feels retro."

What this article, and many others in recent years, are picking up on is the slow demise of the stereotypical white, middle-to upper-middle-class tomboy, a girl who grows up in jeans and baseball caps, wearing her hair in a ponytail while she climbs trees and plays baseball with the (white) boys. This is a girl who would eventually grow out of her tomboy behavior (for "tomboy," some argue, is not an identity, but a behavior) and realize her inner girl—probably right around the time she hit puberty and discovered that the boys on her baseball team were actually pretty cute—who is, unfailingly, a white, cisgender girl of a certain class.

Michelle Abate (2008) argues that the tomboy "code of conduct" is, in fact, a "racialized construct" (xii). She points out that the eighteenth-century image of women as frail resulted in a generation of weak, tired women, for which "tomboyism emerged as an antidote" (xii):

> Calling for sensible clothing, physical exercise and a wholesome diet, this code of conduct was designed to improve the strength and stamina of the nation's future wives and mothers and, by extension, the offspring they produced. In this way, tomboyism was more than simply a new childrearing practice or gender

> expression for the nation's girls; it was a eugenic practice or, at least, a means to help ensure white racial supremacy. (Abate 2008, xii)

Ironically, though, as Abate points out, literary tomboys are drawn with language that evokes brown-ness. They have "brown" skin and "brown" hair, they are "wild and uncivilized," they are referred to as "monkeys" or "little apes" (xii). Even the word, *tomboy*, broken down into *tom* and *boy*, calls to mind racial epithets (Abate 2008, xii). The entire enterprise of literature about tomboys seems to equate them with primitivism, holding them firmly on the boundaries of "male and female, adult and child, heterosexual and homosexual, masculine and feminine" and "blackness and whiteness" (xiii). So, if Meltzer and Baumgardner are right, the "retro" image of the white, hetero tomboy—which carries with it these rich, complex, and somewhat hidden connotations of otherness, of an exoticism that is also inferiority—is perhaps fading from popular culture as new and more diverse voices are beginning to make themselves heard.

While this demise has been occurring, however, another tomboy has arisen in her place. She is white or a girl of color, or both; she comes from the suburbs or the country or the inner city; she may be straight but is more likely to be lesbian or gender nonbinary; and she/they is/are not a little girl anymore. Today's tomboys live on social media. They are young people and adults. They plaster their accounts with positive messages and, especially, visuals representing the gender nonconformity that has likely been with them since they were children.

The research question I investigate with this study deals with whether popular depictions of tomboys accurately reflect the lived experiences and representations of tomboys, particularly adult women.

BACKGROUND

Visual representations of the tomboy have been an interest area of mine for some years now, after I gave a talk on the topic at a local conference. Having grown up a tomboy, I was intrigued to note that the topic was now of interest to young adults who did not remind me of myself at all. My childhood included playing (and watching) football with guys, wearing jeans and Nikes, avoiding bras for as long as I possibly could without drawing attention, and even, at one point, being called "Hal" by my mother. My parents probably assumed I would grow out of it eventually, and, for the most part, I did, although I never embraced the opposite: the "girly" look. To this day, I still feel like an impostor in a dress or skirt. But I never wanted to be a man; I simply did not want to be the kind of woman the magazines told me I had to be. I married (a man) and had children in the usual way, but the ultra-feminine, stay-at-home-mom aesthetic never appealed to me at all: not the mommy-group mom, not the cooking-sewing-crafting mom, not the crunchy-granola-homemade-baby-food mom. I wanted to earn a living, although I bristled when a former employer demanded I wear "professional-looking" dresses or skirts to work. But I did not see myself as androgynous or as challenging gender norms; rather, I just thought of myself as a grown-up tomboy.

In contrast, the audience at this conference comprised almost entirely of female attendees, many of them students, particularly young women (or perhaps nonbinary people) whose dress and appearance suggested androgyny. The data from my study suggested that "tomboy" was now a contested term, that a battle for ownership was going on with what seemed to be an old-fashioned reference; however, seeing that challenge illustrated in living color before me was eye opening, to say the least.

So, to find out more about who represents as "tomboy" now, in 2020, I did close readings of two popular recent books about tomboys: Liz Prince's (2014) graphic memoir *Tomboy* and blogger Lizzie Garrett Mettler's (2012) photo book *Tomboy Style* (based on her now-defunct blog of the same name). I then spent a week sampling Instagram for instances of #tomboy and #tomboystyle hashtagged posts, to find out whether these two books accurately represent modern tomboys. Using qualitative methods of visual analysis, I discovered that Prince's and Mettler's books depict the tomboy as white, cisgender, and middle-to upper-class, which fits well with the historical image of the tomboy in Western culture (examples of which abound in this volume). Instagram users, however, illustrate a tomboy who is sometimes that girl/woman but more often is not; Instagram tomboys are far more diverse.

The structure of this chapter is as follows: first, I summarize the salient literature on tomboys in fields such as psychology, sociology, and literature. Next, I explicate my research methodology and detail my findings. Finally, I discuss some implications of the disparity between white cisgender tomboy representation and social media's alternate reality.

LITERATURE REVIEW

No shortage exists of research on tomboys, particularly on the advantages and disadvantages of identifying as tomboy. All sorts of benefits come with self-identifying as a tomboy: the "masculine" or "androgynous" characteristics that come with being a tomboy seem to increase girls' and women's confidence and success in both college and work environments (Hilgenkamp and Livingston 2002); give them access to traditionally masculine pastimes (Morgan 1998) and male power (Carr 1998); let them "dress comfortably and without restriction" (Legge 2011, 99); allow them to be fashionably "edgy" while still safely fitting a "traditional white, middle-class, heterosexual femininity" (Crepax 2016, 293) that is "a safe version [of gender ambiguity] stripped of any radical message" (Crepax 2016, 295); help to build adaptive flexibility in their behaviors (Martin et al. 2017); give them access in the new technological workplace (Donnelly and Twenge 2016); help them avoid the "secret, hidden, relational and indirect forms of aggression" meted out by female peers (Mannay 2013, 10); allow them a "strong connection to self" and a "comfort in one's body" (Legge 2011, 97); provide an excuse to give work and career greater salience than home life (Geldenhuys et al. 2019); and supply them with assertiveness and self-reliance (Burn et al. 1996).

Of course, tomboy identification is not without its challenges, and some tomboys choose to identify as such for less-than-positive reasons. Girls who appear to be tomboys are viewed as abnormal the older they get; after beginning adolescence, they are often teased or harassed and called names such as "weird," "loser," "frumpy," "manly," or "beast" (Legge 2011, 211). Some girls continue to reject "girly-girl" behaviors and "flirty-fashion" dress in what is ostensibly an effort to distance themselves from those girls who are "dress[ing] to impress the boys" (Renold 2005, 55), but what is actually a visual attempt to look their age, "positioning those that did participate in the flirty-fashion culture as immature in a premature desire for older sexualities" (Renold 2005, 55). Carr (1998), interviewing adult women who identified as tomboys when children, found that "dislike of feminine roles and female role models" was a recurring theme, as well as a "perceived need for emotional and physical protection from men" and the "desire for the attention of male role models" (535). As Carr explains, "[M]ost participants did not feel their mothers were role models they wanted to emulate" (537). They found their mothers lacking in intelligence and ambition, helpless, overworked, and unrewarded (538). Several of the other participants were incest survivors and rejected femininity for protection via "a retreat to the perceived safety of masculinity" (539). Evidently, the choice to identify as a tomboy can be a positive way to express non-traditional gender behaviors, a method of self-preservation, or a reaction to gender shame.

There does not seem to be a great deal of space in adulthood for self-identification as a tomboy or for tomboyish behaviors, however. Even studies of women ages 70 and over whose physical fitness is good and who attribute that to their being "tomboys" as young girls place that identity firmly in the past (Cousins 1997, 230).

In a study of women between the ages of 18 and 60, Hilgenkamp and Livingston (2002) found that the higher a woman rated herself on a scale of tomboy identification, the more likely she was to say she was successful in her chosen career, but this correlation did not hold for questions of whether she could jog for twenty minutes straight or pass a college course. The traits correlated with confidence in career choice included "ambitious," "make decisions easily," "have leadership abilities," "independent," "self-reliant," "self-sufficient," "willing to take a stand," and "analytical" (Hilgenkamp and Livingston 2002, 746–747). The authors describe these as "agentic masculine qualities (a.k.a. tomboy identities)" and suggest that "young girls should be allowed and perhaps encouraged to develop" these qualities to make them "more resilient and successful individuals" (Hilgenkamp and Livingston 2002, 748). What is troubling here is the identification of tomboy as a masculine identity; this leaves little room for self-identifying females to exhibit any of these qualities as adults without it being said that whatever successes they attain are due to their acting "like men."[1]

In recent years, adult tomboys have been working to (re)claim the tomboy identity beyond its childhood origins and limitations. For instance, in the r/AskWomen subreddit, a thread asking the question, "Women that are still 'tomboys,' how has this affected your life?" received ninety-eight comments last year, describing lives rich with both feminine-coded and masculine-coded hobbies and lifestyles, difficult relationships with parents (most often mothers), a fraught relationship with makeup and fashion, dealing with men who say, "I like you because you're not like other girls," and even a few late realizations that they were lesbian.

Butch[2] author "Titus Androgynous," writing for *DapperQ* in 2011, relates another difficulty for the adult tomboy: negotiating the grey area between not-girly and boy. As a kid, they "developed a wicked side arm pitch, I could pop-a-wheelie and make really long skid marks on my bike, and I could burp the loudest and longest of anyone on my block" (Androgynous 2011). But everything changed when they were mistaken for a boy: "I remember feeling embarrassed when I was actually mistaken for one. I wasn't trying to be anything other than what I was, and I would think, 'Can't they see who I am?'" Discovering that there was a word for what they were, "tomboy," brought relief, at least until "you were expected to grow out of it." "Being a tomboy was okay. Being a butch, and all that implied, was not." In other words, "tomboy" worked while they were a child, but upon becoming an adult, this term seemed no longer to fit what they knew they were: a lesbian.

Obviously, then, the gap for research on adult tomboys is more like a yawning chasm. This chapter focuses solely on visual self-portrayals of adult tomboys, with a particular focus on style because it is arguably the most readily identifiable attribute of adult gender nonconformity and because gender nonconformity becomes part of observers' initial impressions.

Research suggests that people form accurate first impressions of others incredibly quickly. For example, Gosling, Gaddis, and Vazire (2007) found that observers could correctly identify such personality traits as extraversion, agreeability, conscientiousness, and openness (as self-identified by Facebook user/subjects) just from a Facebook photo. Chan et al. (2011) found that both men and women are very good at accurately distinguishing a person's traits from those of others they know, and that women seem to have an advantage in forming "more accurately generalized impressions of others across different targets that have a broad and diverse set of personality characteristics" (2011, 119). So, women, particularly, seem to have a skill for accurate first impressions and for norming people into categories based on appearance.

Although it seems to be human nature to quickly categorize others based on appearance, this ability does not always have positive results. Observers with biases against LGBTQ+ people, for example, might judge an androgynous or masculine-appearing woman negatively, whether or not she is/they are LGBTQ+. Studies suggest that learning a person has a different sexual orientation from the one an observer initially thought matters little: even when presented with knowledge that is contrary to a first impression, observers tend to keep their first impression as truth. In one study, "[p]articipants generally identified the person's sexual orientation based on how they looked—even if it contradicted the facts presented to them" (Society for Personality and Social Psychology 2014). Is it any wonder, then, that "tomboy" women seem to be using social media to reclaim, or create, a positive image for tomboys in all their various forms?

METHODOLOGY

Data Sets

Working from an intersectional feminist standpoint, the present study uses a qualitative methodology to compare two sets of visual texts: one set is collected from two books, *Tomboy: A Memoir* by Liz Prince (a graphic novel) and *Tomboy Style: Beyond the Boundaries of Fashion* by Lizzie Garrett Mettler (a photo book with limited text). These books were chosen based on their popularity in a search for visual books about tomboys.

The other data set is a selection of 1,412 individual posts collected from Instagram between January 23 and January 31, 2020, at various times of day, featuring either of the hashtags #tomboy or #tomboystyle. The #tomboystyle hashtag was chosen because after #tomboy, it is by far the most frequently appearing tomboy-related hashtag on Instagram (keywordtool.io).

Comparing published works on the theme of tomboys to social media posts on tomboys yields insight into my research questions: how do adult tomboys represent themselves in 2020, and how do those representations compare with popular nonfiction representations of tomboys? Working from an assumption that adult tomboys are not all white, cisgender girls/women, I wanted to show the diversity of real-life tomboys. Table 10.1 shows the top five hashtags related to "tomboy" as listed by the Web-based app keywordtool.io.

Instagram Collection Methodology

Without hiring a coding expert, it can be difficult to collect data using Instagram's API (Application Programming Interface) (this is even more difficult post-June 2020, as Facebook has recently disabled the Legacy Instagram API). As a substitute method, I chose to screen-capture images from my Chrome browser. However, this, too, proved difficult after several days, as Instagram simply stopped cooperating and I was forced to use other services, such as Pinsta.me (which also went down two days into using it) and Webstagram (which apparently discontinued its Instagram service in April 2020), to grab visuals from the Web. In spite of these minor difficulties, data collection was not negatively impacted.

Images were collected in groups of three (this is the number of Instagram posts that fit comfortably across a 32" monitor so that, when screen-capped, they retain good resolution with legible text), the exceptions being times when only one or two new images appeared in a row with older, already-captured images. Each post was captured along with all accompanying text that was immediately visible. Occasionally, so many hashtags had been added to the post that not all of them appeared unless I clicked on the post to load it individually (which I did not do, for I was more interested in the visuals than the additional hashtags). Screen captures were made on a MacBook Pro using the Command+Shift+4 method and saved as JPEG files.

Recognizing the difficulty inherent in determining "what constitutes a coherent dataset on a platform such as Instagram" (Ging and Garvey 2017, 5), I decided to collect data over a period of eight days in January 2020, collecting at different times of day to allow for data from users around the world. On each day, new images using either or both hashtags were collected. If any images were later found to be duplicates, they were deleted.

Table 10.1

Hashtags	*Posts*
#tomboystyle	943,360
#tomboylook	284,465
#tomboymodel	183,966
#tomboyfashion	272,878
#tomboyargentina	1,154

Coding Method

Because as a critical researcher I am working from a transactional and subjectivist epistemology (Guba and Lincoln 1994), I employ a methodology that allows for the data to carry on a reflexive dialogue with me through thematic decomposition analysis (Stenner 1993). This form of thematic discourse analysis "identifies patterns (themes, stories) within data, and theorizes language as constitutive of meaning and meaning as social" (Braun and Clarke 2006, 8). Following Braun and Clarke (2006), I do not argue that themes "reside within" the data; rather, I agree that "[i]f themes 'reside' anywhere, they reside in our heads" as researchers (Ely et al. 1997, qtd. in Braun and Clarke 2006, 7). Any meaning that may come from the identified themes is socially constructed, not intrinsic; subjective, not objective/realist; and transactional, not absolute. This method is particularly appropriate for an intersectional feminist discussion of tomboy representation because of the socially constructed nature of gender performance, race, class, sexuality, ability, and other aspects of physical appearance.

First, I looked specifically at (cartoon) images of adult tomboys in Prince's graphic memoir, including images of herself as an adult, a woman named Harley, and a woman named Maggie. There were three such character images. I also coded the photograph of the author from the back cover. I then examined eighty-eight photographs of what Lizzie Garrett Mettler considers tomboys. Finally, I reviewed a randomly selected subset of 150 (roughly 10 percent) of the 1,412 Instagram images coded #tomboy or #tomboystyle.

Using NVIVO 12 software, I coded all eighty-eight images from the *Tomboy Style* book, the four images of adult tomboys in *Tomboy: A Memoir*, and the 150-image subset from Instagram. Coding images in NVIVO involves drawing a selection rectangle around a given item for coding and then dragging it to a node (or creating a new one if none exists that adequately describes the item). For example, in the "facial expression" category, a smile showing the subject's teeth was coded "smiling with teeth." I performed coding on the images from the two books first on notebook paper, and then in an Excel spreadsheet, which I imported into NVIVO. Because the Instagram data were already electronic, I began by coding them in NVIVO. As I progressed, I found I needed more nodes than existed in the book data. For example, only three Black women appeared in the book data, none of whom was wearing natural African hair. The Instagram data, on the other hand, contained several instances of subjects with natural afros, braids, or twists, which did not seem to fit well with the existing nodes for hairstyles. Thus, the process of coding and creating nodes and categories was "iterative, comparative, interactive, and abductive" (Charmaz 2013, 294).

The first round of coding, which covered the data from both books, proceeded from sixteen basic categories, based on initial observation: accessories, apparent race or skin color, vices (smoking/drinking), body types, bottoms (clothing), eye contact, facewear (glasses/shades), facial expression, footwear, hair color, hair style, makeup, model's pose, outerwear, photo setting, and tops (clothing). Each of these categories contained several nodes. Additional nodes were added to each category as second round coding began on the Instagram data in NVIVO 12.

As the second round was completed and initial analysis of the results began, it was decided that several categories did not have numbers significant enough to further analyze. These categories were dropped from the final round: bottoms (too few photos showed subject's lower half), footwear (as previous), model's pose, outerwear, and vices. An additional category was added for Instagram images that were also advertisements, but it was also dropped from the final analysis.

Analysis Method and Results

This study uses a grounded theory method of analysis (Charmaz 2013) involving multiple layers of coding, comparison of codes, establishment and revision of categories, treatment of the major categories as concepts, and comparison of concepts (Charmaz 2013, 295). As Charmaz (2013) notes, "[T]he purpose of grounded theory is to construct middle-range theory from data" (296). As such, the goal of this analysis was to establish some preliminary theories about the differences in the ways static texts such as trade books represent tomboys and the ways tomboys represent themselves on dynamic social media such as Instagram.

For each data set, I noted frequently appearing visual themes. A theme, according to Braun and Clarke, "captures something important about the data in relation to the research question, and represents some level of *patterned* response or meaning within the data set (Braun and Clarke 2006, 10). Because I wanted to offer a "rich thematic description of [the] entire data set" (Braun and Clarke 2006, 11), I worked inductively, attempting to code data without "trying to fit it into a pre-existing coding frame, or [my] analytic preconceptions" (Braun and Clarke 2006, 12). In addition, I used a semantic approach to identifying themes, taking them from "within the explicit or surface meanings of the data" (Braun and Clarke 2006, 13) and not reading into what is there. This process moves from description to interpretation through abductive reasoning, from simply organizing the data to offering hypotheses as to what the patterns may signify.

In order to accomplish this "semantic approach" to visual themes, I employ a methodology I have used in previous works in visual rhetoric (e.g., Wells

2012; Wells, 2020) that is built on the work of Kress and van Leeuwen (1996, 2006), Finnegan (2001), and Smith (2007). Obviously, visuals are not words; however, they can be seen to present something like verbal propositions. The theoretical framework for this methodology is the assumption that visuals can sometimes represent arguments, and that they do so enthymematically, with the understanding that the enthymeme is a syllogism with propositions that are probabilities or signs (Smith 2007). Using this approach, I can identify not only visual themes but also possible visual arguments, with the caveat that the enthymemes can never be "proven" or "disproven," only shown to be "likely" based on cultural endoxa (the beliefs of a consensus of wise people in a given culture). Put another way, seeing an image as (possibly) visually representing commonly accepted cultural understandings gives us the ability to "put words to the pictures." Moreover, when themes recur in multiple images, this repetition can itself be considered a form of visual argument (Fahnestock 1999, particularly Chapter 5 on ploche and polyptoton).

Table 10.1 illustrates the categories and nodes after the second round of coding. The percentages shown are of overall occurrence in the individual data set. For example, "tattoos and body art" occurs in 37 percent of the Instagram data and in 0 percent of the book data. The Likelihood of Occurrence translates as "This node is [x] times more likely to occur in [y] data set." For instance, "1.1 BK" may be read "Hats were 1.1 times more likely to occur in the books than in the Instagram data." (If I could not determine a node in a given image, I did not code it.)

A basic population comparison was performed in Microsoft Excel to determine which nodes occurred in large enough numbers to be interesting. For nodes involving individual subjects, the total population of both data sets n=291. For nodes involving the entire image and not individual subjects, the total number of images in both data sets n=242. At each node, the total number of occurrences of that node was divided by the appropriate population total n (either 291 or 242) to determine the percentage of occurrence in the total data set. A median function was performed on these results and found to be 11.34 percent; therefore, all nodes occurring less than 11.34 percent of the time were dropped from the final round of mathematical analysis.

Next, it was determined that Instagram data comprised 54.98 percent of the total population and book images the other 45.02 percent. To determine the lift of each node in a given data set, the percentage of occurrence of that node was divided by the percentage of the total population. This was performed on all the data, but only lift totals from nodes that occurred at least 11.34 percent of the time in the entire data set were brought forward for the next level of analysis. The other nodes were not analyzed further.

These lift totals were then copied to a separate sheet and analyzed for median (1.004), mean (1.005), and standard deviation (0.446). It was determined that lift totals of 1.22 and above were significant for the purposes of this project. This procedure left 18 nodes in 5 categories (see Table 10.2).

A further step was then taken to review the remaining categories and nodes to see whether they might fit into broader themes (see Table 10.3). These themes include "what a tomboy's body looks like," "how a tomboy's hair looks," "how tomboys engage with their audience," "what tomboys wear," and "where tomboys are when they are photographed or photograph themselves."

What a Tomboy's Body Looks Like

In the category of body type, three nodes emerge as interesting: average, slim/athletic, and androgynous. During coding, I defined an average build as appearing roughly to be between women's sizes medium and extra-large, inclusive. I defined slim as appearing roughly to be size small or extra-small, and athletic to be a woman of roughly that size with visible muscular definition or obvious strength. An androgynous body type appeared to be boyish or dubious as to binary gender; many Instagram users were helpful enough to hashtag their images #androgynous or #nonbinary. The main difference between slim/athletic and androgynous, then, is that the former still appears female in binary coding (e.g., has breasts, hips, slimmer shoulders), whereas the latter lacks some or all of the traits of a binary female-appearing person.

Table 10.2

NODE	SIGNIFICANCE	DATA SET	CATEGORY
Neutral w/parted lips	1.22	BK	Facial expression
Bangs	1.26	BK	Hairstyle
Offer gaze	1.34	BK	Gaze
Light brown/blonde	1.37	BK	Hair color
Outdoor setting	1.52	BK	Photo setting
Button-down or collared shirt	1.55	BK	Top
Medium length hair	1.55	BK	Hairstyle
Average build	1.58	BK	Body type
Sweater or cardigan top	1.6	BK	Top
Slim/athletic	1.67	BK	Body type
Athletic top	1.93	BK	Top
T-shirt top	1.35	IG	Top
Indoor setting	1.48	IG	Photo setting
Black hair color	1.63	IG	Hair color
Androgynous	1.79	IG	Body type
Hoodie	1.8	IG	Top
Selfie gaze	1.8	IG	Gaze
Tattoos	1.82	IG	Accessories

Table 10.3

THEME	*CATEGORY*	*NODE*	*SIGNIFICANT IN DATA SET*
What a tomboy's body looks like			
	Body type		
		Average	Books
		Slim or athletic	Books
		Androgynous	Instagram
How a tomboy's hair looks			
	Hair style		
		Bangs on forehead	Books
		Medium-length cut	Books
	Hair color		
		Light brown or blonde	Books
		Black	Instagram
How tomboys engage with their audience			
	Gaze		
		Demand	Instagram
		Offer	Books
	Facial expression		
		Neutral with parted lips	Books
What tomboys wear			
	Clothing: Tops		
		Button-down or collared shirt	Books
		Sweater or cardigan	Books
		Athletic	Books
		T-shirt	Instagram
		Hoodie	Instagram
	Accessories		
		Tattoos and body art	Instagram
Where tomboys are when they are photographed or photograph themselves			
	Photo setting		
		Indoors	Instagram
		Outdoors	Books

In the images from the *Tomboy: A Memoir* and *Tomboy Style* books, adult tomboys were much more likely (1.58 times) to appear of average build than the subjects in the Instagram data set. They were also 1.67 times more likely to appear slim or of athletic build. On the other hand, the Instagram photos were much more likely to feature an androgynous body type.

How a Tomboy's Hair Looks

This theme comprises two categories: hair style and hair color. In the hair style category, two nodes stood out: wearing bangs on the forehead, and having a medium-length cut. Both these nodes appeared more often in the books than on Instagram (1.26 and 1.55 times more likely, respectively). Bangs bring to mind hairstyles often worn by little children, especially girls, who may have long hair in the back but bangs to keep their hair from constantly getting into their eyes. Medium-length haircuts (reaching to the shoulder but not much further; just enough to pull into a hair band, but not a ponytail) seem to be popular in all eras, from the 1920s onward.

In the hair color category, light brown or blonde hair figured prominently in the books, appearing 1.37 times more often than on Instagram. Conversely, black hair appeared 1.63 times more often on Instagram. Lighter hair is associated primarily with white people, although anyone can dye one's hair blonde; black hair occurs most often in Asian and Black people, although some white and Hispanic people have black hair and some dye their hair black. Because many of the *Tomboy Style* photographs (as well as all the drawings and some of the Instagram photos) appeared in monochrome, it was often difficult to decide whether a subject's dark hair was black or brown; I usually assigned the node based on whether the subject appeared to have Caucasian/European background or not.

How Tomboys Engage with Their Audience

The engagement theme deals with how a photo or drawing subject engages with the viewer. An image in which the subject's eyes do not meet the viewer's makes the viewer the subject of that gaze, and "the represented participant is the object of the viewer's dispassionate scrutiny" (Kress and van Leeuwen 2006, 119). In other words, the person in the photo or drawing carries on her/their life with no assumption or acknowledgment of an audience whatsoever. Kress and van Leeuwen (1996, 2006) refer to this as *offer gaze*. The offer gaze featured 1.34 times more often in the books than it did in the Instagram data set.

The image in which a subject's eyes do meet the viewer's, however, creates something of a relationship between subject and viewer, even if it is somewhat contrived or imagined. The gaze of a subject acknowledges a viewer's presence in a way the offer gaze does not. It "creates a visual form of direct address," an "image act" (Kress and van Leeuwen 2006, 117). That act is referred to as a *demand gaze* (2006, 118), so called because the eye contact between represented subject and viewer demands the viewer's attention: "Exactly what kind of relation is then signified by other means, for instance by the facial expression of the represented participants" (2006, 118). The demand gaze appeared more often on Instagram (1.11 times more likely), but this difference was not considered significant for the purposes of this study.

As I began coding the Instagram data, I realized that having only demand and offer gazes as nodes was insufficient. I needed a third node for those self-portraits taken in front of mirrors, in which the subject is looking, not at the viewer, but at herself/themselves on the smartphone screen. Aptly, I named this *selfie gaze.* Although self-portraits first appeared in the 1830s, the first usage of the word "selfie" to refer especially to a self-portrait taken with a smartphone was recorded in an Australian online forum in 2002.[3] Whereas technically, this gaze could easily fit into the *offer* node, it seemed to me to warrant its own node, since it straddles the line between the demand of subject eye contact with viewer and the objectification that occurs without it. Most subjects in photos featuring offer gaze could arguably be seen to be oblivious to their represented audience, whereas the individual "taking a selfie" clearly is acknowledging an audience in the act of pointing the smartphone at a mirror. These complex images include the subject herself/themselves, the smartphone, the subject's eye contact with the subject's self on the smartphone screen, and the entire interaction reflected in the mirror. Selfie gaze was 1.8 times more likely to occur in the Instagram set than in the books (it did not occur at all in the books).

I broke the facial expression category into 7 nodes: frown, neutral, neutral with parted lips, smile with teeth showing, smile without teeth showing, pursed lips/"duck face"/pulling a face, and masked. However, the only node with a significant different was neutral with parted lips, which I defined during coding as an expression in which there was no visible smile and no furrowing of the brow (which would have indicated a frown), but the lips were parted (sometimes showing teeth, sometimes not). I chose to code this expression because it occurred frequently in the *Tomboy Style* book and reminded me of the expression Victoria's Secret supermodels often wear (i.e., "sexy"). Neutral with parted lips was 1.22 times more likely to occur in the books than in the Instagram data set.

What Tomboys Wear

When I first began this project, the aspect of tomboys that was most interesting to me was clothing. Other chapters in this volume cover the childhood tomboy; I was more concerned with what an adult tomboy looks like in the wild, knowing only that, as an adult tomboy myself, I perform "tomboy" mostly by wearing trouser suits and mannish-looking oxford shoes to work (fashion magazines often refer to this style as "borrowing from the boys"). However, I was aware that, as a cisgender female, my "tomboy" performance differs from those of LGBTQ+ tomboys, having followed the #tomboy and #tomboystyle hashtags on Instagram for several years.

My clothing category initially contained many more subcategories and nodes, but because there were so many, most did not have large enough numbers to be interesting for the purposes of this project. However, two categories did feature some notable nodes: clothing/tops and accessories. In the clothing/tops category, these nodes proved significant: button-down or collared shirts, sweaters or cardigans, athletic tops, T-shirts, and hoodies. In the accessories category, the tattoos and body art node also proved significant.

I coded any shirt with a collar (such as a polo shirt) or visible buttons down the front in the button-down and collared shirt node, even if the shirt was worn under another garment, such as a sweater or cardigan. This node first came up when I was coding the *Tomboy Style* book; button-down oxford shirts appeared regularly, especially in the section subtitled "The Prep." In fact, a photo of a woman wearing what is evidently a man's Brooks Brothers shirt I captioned, "In 1954 Brooks Brothers' New York City store set up a counter 'discreetly' in the back [. . .] where women could buy the men's shirts they were already wearing" (Garrett Mettler 2012, 71). This type of top appeared 1.55 times more often in the books than on Instagram. Sweaters and cardigans were also very popular, but more so in the books, appearing 1.6 times as often as in the Instagram set.

I coded any top that was an actual athletic uniform (e.g., softball jersey), sport-specific gear (e.g., equestrian apparel), or being worn to work out (e.g., a Lycra/Spandex workout shirt) in the photo as athletic. Because so many of the *Tomboy Style* subjects were engaged in various sports or workout activities, the athletic top appeared 1.93 times more often here than in the Instagram data.

The other two clothing nodes appear much more frequently in the Instagram data. I coded both long-sleeve and short-sleeve cotton-looking shirts with no collars or cuffs and no other adornment (besides any printing on the front) as T-shirts. Due to the quality of some social media photos, it is often difficult to determine with 100% percent certainty that any item fits a single node, and T-shirts was no exception; however, if there is any overlap, I believe it is likely to be with the sweater node, as some of the tops that appeared to be long-sleeve T-shirts could have been sweaters. The T-shirt node appears in the Instagram data 1.35 times more frequently than in the books.

Last in the clothing category is the hoodie, which I coded as any thick, fleece-looking pullover with an attached hood (whether it was worn covering the head or not). Hoodies have figured in the national conversation on race and crime for quite some time now (Civile and Obhi's 2017 study of police bias toward hoodie wearers is one of many on the topic). The hoodie appears 1.8 times more frequently in the Instagram set than in the books (where it did not appear at all).

In the accessories category, one node stood out from the others: tattoos and body art. I decided that a single set of earrings was not necessarily worth noting, because so many people of all genders have at least one piercing. Therefore, I coded as body art any piercing beyond the basic earlobe piercing, so ear piercings above the lobe, multiple lobe piercings, nose rings, lip or cheek piercings, or any other visible piercing counted toward this node, as did any visible tattoo art. This node was 1.82 times more likely in the Instagram set than in the books, where it did not appear at all.

Where Tomboys Are When Photographed

Coding in this category seemed important to me because I noticed while reading the *Tomboy Style* book that the vast majority of subjects were pictured outdoors, doing active things—often, doing stereotypically *male* things. This seemed to me to fit the stereotype of the tomboy child as a girl who does "boy" things like climbing trees or playing baseball. I was surprised, after round 2 of coding, to find that Instagram tomboys did not seem as interested in being outdoors as the so-called tomboys Lizzie Garrett Mettler curated for her collection.

Any photo that seemed to have lighting or setting one might expect to see indoors was coded as occurring indoors. Outdoor photos were coded as such when outdoor elements were visible in the shot, where lighting suggested sunlight, or when the subject was seated in a car (which seemed to me to lack the privacy of being truly indoors). If I could not determine setting in a given image, I did not code it for setting.

Instagram users in my sample were 1.48 times more likely to be indoors, whereas the subjects of Garrett Mettler's photos and the characters in Prince's book were 1.52 times more likely to be outdoors.

DISCUSSION

What first drew me to this project was reading Prince's memoir and glancing through Garrett Mettler's style guide for tomboys. As I perused the images, I was immediately struck by how little diversity existed in either book; women of color and LGBTQ+ adults were essentially absent, except for one androgynous woman in Garrett Mettler's collection who might qualify as butch to some viewers. Garrett Mettler's images come from professional photographers around the world and include models, socialites, performers, professional athletes, pioneers, royalty, and a few "common folk," but they are nearly all white and appear to represent middle-to upper-middle-class pursuits and lifestyles, judging by the activities represented (horse racing, lots of sailing, college rowing, tennis, and the like). To participate in this club, one should have money and influence, or at least be able to take on the appearance of them.

Prince's memoir is less about class and more about an individual tomboy's story of not fitting into traditional gender roles. She makes frequent mention of having been mistaken for a boy as a child; she also mentions being called "queer" (2014, 42) and getting away with a "kissing spree" (with boys as her target) in second grade because she looked more like a boy than a girl (49–50). But she is careful to point out along that way that, although she wears a baseball cap and hates dresses, she likes boys; she is straight. I see myself in her; this tomboy reminds me of myself as both a child and an adult. So, where, in these two popular books, were the tomboys who looked like the ones I had seen on social media?

The present study merely scratches the surface of this issue of representation. I presently have enough data to continue studying Instagram alone for years (and new data are being produced daily). This examination of tomboy visual representation suggests several interesting (and even surprising) things about "real" tomboys, at least those who use Instagram: they come in all different shapes, including slightly overweight to obese, androgynous, and even male-appearing; they are about as likely to have long hair as tomboys in the two books I analyzed; they are comfortable wearing their hair in all colors, including blue and hot pink, but not necessarily in natural grey (Instagram does not appear to be as popular with middle-aged users who might be more likely to be naturally grey); they are Asian, Black, brown, and white; they demand our attention by looking us directly in the eye; they love casual clothes like T-shirts and hoodies, and body art like piercings and tattoos; and they are just as comfortable showing themselves hanging out indoors as being outside participating in some "boyish" activity (many of which they can do indoors, like weightlifting).

No hard and fast answers can come from studies of visual rhetoric. Every image is open to interpretation; however, we can often determine a likely interpretation based on cultural commonplaces, called *doxa*, or the opinions of the best-educated and most reputable people in a society, *endoxa*. If we "know" as a culture, for example, that "tomboys are girls who dress and act like boys," we can draw certain inferences from images based on this culturally accepted knowledge (the accuracy of which is not being debated but simply accepted as one possible truth). With this understanding, and working from an intersectional feminist standpoint, we can draw several possible conclusions about adult tomboys from the results of the present study.

Based on the books, we may begin with these commonplaces about tomboys:

1. Tomboys are females who are slim, athletic, or average in build.
2. Tomboys may prefer to have their hair cut into bangs to keep it out of their eyes, and they may prefer a medium-length cut to longer or shorter hair.
3. Tomboys are somewhat likely to be blonde or light brown haired.
4. Tomboys are likely to be photographed when they are not posing for a viewer and looking into the viewer's eyes.
5. Adult tomboys prefer masculine clothing such as button-down oxford shirts or collared polo shirts. They also may prefer sweaters or cardigans to less-casual clothing.
6. Adult tomboys have clear, unadorned skin, with only a single tasteful set of earrings if any.
7. Adult tomboys may often be seen in an athletic pursuit.
8. The natural habitat of adult tomboys is in the outdoors.

The findings from the sample of Instagram data suggest otherwise, however:

1. IG (Instagram) tomboys may be slim, athletic, or average, but they may also be slightly overweight, obese, androgynous, or even male-presenting.
2. IG tomboys wear their hair in a variety of styles, including long, short, and medium, with or without bangs, in an afro or in braids or twists.
3. IG tomboys are more likely to have dark hair than light, but they are blonde, brown, bleached, blue, rainbow, hot pink, and many other colors—except possibly natural grey.
4. IG tomboys are likely to look directly into the camera, demanding the attention of their viewers.
5. IG tomboys wear a variety of tops including "masculine" ones, but they seem to prefer casual tops such as T-shirts and hoodies.

6. IG tomboys often decorate their bodies with various types of art such as tattoos and body piercings, in addition to earrings.
7. IG tomboys do not seem to be particularly interested in showing themselves involved in athletic activities; many are content simply to show a head and shoulders portrait of themselves and their hair and clothing.
8. IG tomboys are more likely to represent themselves indoors, whether at work, at home, or in school.

It may be reasonable to argue, then, that Liz Prince's very personal representation of the adult tomboy is certainly not a representation that is broadly applicable, particularly to LGBTQ+ tomboys; and further, that Lizzie Garrett Mettler's curated collection of tomboy style throughout the decades fails to capture the reality of young adult tomboys as they represent themselves on Instagram in 2020. Taking this theorizing a step further, I suggest that "real" adult tomboys are far more diverse than either book allows for (though Prince's memoir can be forgiven, as it is a personal account). I expect that continued analysis of the large data set I have collected from Instagram will only add richness to the themes and categories already constructed.

LIMITATIONS

Coding visual data is a time-consuming project, particularly when using a grounded theory methodology, because the categories are only loosely suggested at the beginning, the nodes arise only through the actual analysis and keep evolving as subsequent layers of analysis occur, and themes do not rise to the top until several layers of analysis have occurred. In addition, visual data has the disadvantage of being impossible to code automatically, as opposed to textual data, which can be searched. The decision to code only about 10 percent of the entire Instagram data set was difficult but necessary given the time constraints of the project. I plan to continue working on these data in the coming months, to find out where the themes and categories lead.

Although an analysis of hashtags included with these 150 images was beyond the scope of this study, I noted anecdotally that many featured hashtags such as #lgbtq, #lesbian, #bi, #nonbinary, #gay, #trans, and so on. Obviously, hashtag data are not included in the books; if a given subject were to be identified as LGBTQ+, it would have to be in the photo caption (and many of the photos were not captioned—captions tended to accompany only famous subjects). Such information about characters in Prince's memoir comes from the context of the book itself, and none of the adult tomboys is explicitly coded as LGBTQ+. A future project using these data may focus solely on concurrence of LGBTQ+ hashtags with #tomboy and #tomboystyle hashtags.

Finally, it would be useful to find additional books about tomboy representation, to see whether different authors tell richer and more complex stories about who adult tomboys are. The current project began when I purchased the Prince and Garrett Mettler texts on Amazon; I plan to continue searching for books that have sold well enough to be considered influential to some extent on the cultural concept of adult tomboys.

NOTES

1. A perfect illustration of this problem is the controversy over Serena Williams' femininity and physique. She is sometimes criticized for being "too masculine"; men on social media often argue that she is so dominant in her sport because she is built like a man, as if muscles alone (i.e., brute force) are what make a champion tennis player.

2. The butch identity has been considered a lesbian "gender" (see, e.g., Halberstam, 1998; Munt, 1998; Levitt and Hiestand, 2005) and usually consists of masculine-presenting attire, hairstyle, and (lack of) makeup. When post-World War II butch-femme communities began to appear in the United States, butch women took on traditional masculine roles in the relationship, while the femme partner upheld an exaggerated feminine image (Levitt and Hiestand, 2005). Feminism's Second Wave challenged these lesbian recreations of patriarchal marriage relationships, pressuring lesbians to move away from these gender representations toward an androgynous aesthetic (Levitt and Hiestand, 2005). It wasn't until the 1980s that lesbian couples began to reclaim the butch/femme presentations in a "desire to remain authentic to an internal sense of gender in the face of social pressure to be feminine" (Levitt and Hiestand, 2005, p. 40).

3. *Oxford English Dictionary*, online ed. (2020), s.v. "selfie."

BIBLIOGRAPHY

Abate, Michelle Ann. 2008. *Tomboys: A Literary and Cultural History.* Philadelphia: Temple University Press.

Ahlqvist, Sheana, May Ling Halim, Faith K. Greulich, Leah E. Lurye, and Diane Ruble. 2013. "The Potential Benefits and Risks of Identifying as a Tomboy: A Social Identity Perspective." *Self and Identity* 12 (5): 563–81.

Andrews, Naomi C.Z., Carol Lynn Martin, Rachel E. Cook, Ryan D. Field, and Dawn E. England. 2019. "Exploring Dual Gender Typicality Among Young Adults in the United States." *International Journal of Behavioral Development* 43 (4): 314–21.

Androgynous, Titus. 2011. "The Tomboy Who Wouldn't Grow Up." *DapperQ: Ungendering Fashion*. https://www.dapperq.com/2011/02/the-tomboy-who-wouldnt-grow-up/.

Atkinson, BM, TV Smulders, and JC Wallenberg. 2017. "An Endocrine Basis for Tomboy Identity: The Second-to-Fourth Digit Ratio (2D:4D) in 'Tomboys.'" *Psychoneuroendocrinology* 79: 9–12.

Azizah, Afifah, and Juneman Abraham. 2018. "Content Analysis and Exploratory Factor Analysis of Relationship Goals Among Young Adults: Converging Data from Instagram and Offline Surveys." *International Journal of Advanced Computer Research* 8 (34): 11–34.

Bailey, J. Michael, Kathleen T. Bechtold, and Sheri A. Berenbaum. 2002. "Who Are Tomboys and Why Should We Study Them?" *Archives of Sexual Behavior* 31 (4): 333–41.

Boepple, Leah, and J. Kevin Thompson. 2016. "A Content Analytic Comparison of Fitspiration and Thinspiration Websites." *International Journal of Eating Disorders* 49: 98–101.

Braun, Virginia, and Victoria Clarke. 2006. "Using Thematic Analysis in Psychology." *Qualitative Research in Psychology* 3 (2): 77–101.

Burn, Shawn Meghan, A. Kathleen O'Neil, and Shirley Nederend. 1996. "Childhood Tomboyism and Adult Androgyny." *Sex Roles* 34 (5–6): 419–28.

Carr, C. Lynn. 1998. "Tomboy Resistance and Conformity: Agency in Social Psychological Gender Theory." *Gender & Society* 12 (5): 528–53.

Carrotte, Elise Rose, Ivanka Pritchard, and Megan Su Cheng Lim. 2017. "'Fitspiration' on Social Media: A Content Analysis of Gendered Images." *Journal of Medical Internet Research* 19 (3): e95.

Chan, Meanne, Katherine H. Rogers, Kate L. Parisotto, and Jeremy C. Biesanz. 2011. "Forming First Impressions: The Role of Gender and Normative Accuracy in Personality Perception." *Journal of Research in Personality* 45: 117–20.

Cherian, Roy, Marisa Westbrook, Danielle Ramo, and Urmimala Sarkar. 2018. "Representations of Codeine Misuse on Instagram: Content Analysis." *JMIR Public Health and Surveillance* 4 (1): e22.

Civile, Ciro, and Sukhvinder Obhi. 2017. "Students Wearing Police Uniforms Exhibit Biased Attention toward Individuals Wearing Hoodies." *Frontiers in Psychology* 8 (62): 1–14.

Cohen, Rachel, Toby Newton-John, and Amy Slater. 2017. "The Relationship Between Facebook and Instagram Appearance-focused Activities and Body Image Concerns in Young Women." *Body Image* 23: 183–87.

Cousins, Sandra O'Brien. 1997. "Elderly Tomboys? Sources of Self-efficacy for Physical Activity in Late Life." *Journal of Aging and Physical Activity* 5: 229–43.

Coyle, Emily F., Megan Fulcher, and Darinka Trübutschek. 2016. "Sissies, Mama's Boys, and Tomboys: Is Children's Gender Nonconformity More Acceptable When Nonconforming Traits Are Positive?" *Archives of Sexual Behavior* 45: 1827–38.

Craig, Traci Y., and Jessica M. LaCroix. 2011. "Tomboy as Protective Identity." *Journal of Lesbian Studies* 15 (4): 450–65.

Crepax, Rosa. 2017. "The Aesthetics of Mainstream Androgyny: A Feminist Analysis of a Fashion Trend." PhD Thesis, University of London.

Donnelly, Kristin, and Jean M. Twenge. 2017. "Masculine and Feminine Traits on the Bem Sex-role Inventory, 1993–2012: A Cross-temporal Meta-analysis." *Sex Roles* 76 (9–10): 556–65.

Fahnestock, Jeanne. 1999. *Rhetorical Figures in Science*. New York: Oxford University Press.

Fardouly, Jasmine, Brydie K. Willburger, and Lenny R. Vartanian. 2018. "Instagram Use and Young Women's Body Image Concerns and Self-objectification: Testing Mediational Pathways." *New Media & Society* 20 (4): 1380–95.

Geldenhuys, Madelyn, Anita Bosch, Shuaib Jeewa, and Ioulia Koutris. 2019. "Gender Traits in Relation to Work Versus Career Salience." *SA Journal of Industrial Psychology* 45: a1588.

Ging, Debbie. 2018. "'Written in These Scars Are the Stories I Can't Explain': A Content Analysis of Pro-ana and Thinspiration Image Sharing on Instagram." *New Media and Society* 20 (3): 1181–200.

Guba, Egon G., and Yvonna S. Lincoln. 1994. "Competing Paradigms in Qualitative Research." In *Handbook of Qualitative Research*, edited by N. K. Denzin and Y. S. Lincoln, 105–17. Thousand Oaks: Sage Publications, Inc.

Highfield, Tim, and Tama Leaver. 2015. "A Methodology for Mapping Instagram Hashtags." *First Monday* 20 (1): 1–11.

Hilgenkamp, Kathryn D., and Mary Margaret Livingston. 2002. "Tomboys, Masculine Characteristics, and Self-ratings of Confidence in Career Success." *Psychological Reports* 90: 743–9.

Hines, Melissa, Susan Golombok, John Rust, Katie J. Johnston, Jean Golding, and the Avon Longitudinal Study of Parents and Children Study Team. 2002. "Testosterone During Pregnancy and Gender Role Behavior of Preschool Children: A Longitudinal, Population Study." *Child Development* 73 (6): 1678–87.

Hu, Yuheng, Lydia Manikonda, and Subbarao Kambhampati. 2014. "What We Instagram: A First analysis of Instagram Photo Content and User Types." *Proceedings of the Eight International AAAI Conference on Weblogs and Social Media*, Ann Arbor, MI, June 1–4: 595–8.

KeywordTool. 2020. Key Tools Limited, Sheung Wan, Hong Kong. Keywordtool.io

Kleemans, Mariska, Serena Daalmans, Ilana Carbaat, and Doeschka Anschütz. 2018. "Picture Perfect: The Direct Effect of Manipulated Instagram Photos on Body Image in Adolescent Girls." *Media Psychology* 21 (1): 93–110.

Legge, Robyn B. 2011. "As the Body Unfolds: Examining Girls' Changing Experiences with the Socially Constructed Labels 'Tomboy' and 'Girly Girl.'" PhD thesis, University of Toronto.

Levitt, Heidi M., and Katherine R. Hiestand. 2005. "Gender Within Lesbian Sexuality: Butch and Femme Perspectives." *Journal of Constructivist Psychology* 18: 39–51.

Mannay, Dawn. 2013. "'If It's Pink, Scrape the Pink Off': Negotiating Acceptable 'Tomboy' Femininity in the Playground." *Women in Society* 5. n.p.

Martin, Carol Lynn, Rachel E. Cook, and Naomi C.Z. Andrews. 2017. "Reviving Androgyny: A Modern Day Perspective on Flexibility of Gender Identity and Behavior." *Sex Roles* 76, (9–10): 592–603.

Martin, Carol Lynn, Matthew D. DiDonato, Laura Clary, Richard A. Fabes, Tyson Kreiger, Francisco Palermo, and Laura Hanis. 2012. "Preschool Children with Gender Normative and Gender Non-Normative Peer Preferences: Psychosocial and Environmental Correlates." *Archives of Sexual Behavior* 41 (4): 831–47.

Martin, Carol Lynn, and Lisa M. Dinella. 2012. "Congruence Between Gender Stereotypes and Activity Preference in Self-identified Tomboys and Non-tomboys." *Archives of Sexual Behavior* 41: 599–610.

McNely, Brian J. 2012. "Shaping Organizational Image-Power Through Images: Case Histories of Instagram." *Proceedings of the 2012 IEEE International Professional Communication Conference*, October 8–10, 2012.

Meltzer, Marisa. "Where Have All the Tomboys Gone?" *The New York Times*. October 13, 2015. https://www.nytimes.com/2015/10/15/fashion/where-have-all-the-tomboys-gone.html.

Morgan, Betsy L. 1998. "A Three Generational Study of Tomboy Behavior." *Sex Roles* 39 (9–10): 787–800.

Paechter, Carrie. 2010. "Tomboys and Girly-girls: Embodied Femininities in Primary Schools." *Discourse: Studies in the Cultural Politics of Education* 31 (2): 221–35.

Pila, Eva, Jonathan M. Mond, Scott Griffiths, Deborah Mitchison, and Stuart B. Murray. 2017. "A Thematic Content Analysis of #Cheatmeal Images on Social Media: Characterizing an Emerging Dietary Trend." *International Journal of Eating Disorders* 50: 698–706.

Renold, Emma. 2005. *Girls, Boys and Junior Sexualities: Exploring Children's Gender and Sexual Relations in the Primary School.* Abingdon, UK: RoutledgeFalmer.

Ronson, Jacqueline. "How Do Girls Become Tomboys?" *Fatherly*. March 19, 2018. https://www.fatherly.com/love-money/where-do-tomboys-come-from-girls/.

Safronova, Valeriya. "Meet CoverGirl's New Cover Boy." *The New York Times*. October 12, 2016. https://www.nytimes.com/2016/10/16/fashion/meet-covergirls-new-cover-boy.html.

Salmon, Catherine A., and Jessica A. Hehman. 2018. "Second to Fourth Digit Ratio (2D:4D), Tomboyism, and Temperament." *Personality and Individual Differences* 123: 13–4.

Skerski, Jamie. 2011. "Tomboy Chic: Re-Fashioning Gender Rebellion." *Journal of Lesbian Studies* 15 (4): 466–79.

Society for Personality and Social Psychology. "Even fact will not change first impressions." *ScienceDaily*. www.sciencedaily.com/releases/2014/02/140214111207.htm.

Stenner, Paul. 1993. "Discoursing Jealousy." *Discourse Analytic Research: Repertoires and Readings of Texts in Action*: 94–132.

Index

Page references for figures and tables are italicized.

#GamerGate, 195
#tomboy, 10, 209–28
#tomboystyle, 10, 211, 214, *215*, 216, 223, 228

Abate, Michelle Ann, 1, 3, 16, 17, 18, 19, 32, 34, 36, 38, 44, 75, 91, 92, 93, 95, 115, 118, 123, 127, 129–30, 131n9, 140–41, 142, 143, 146, 147, 152n5–53, 209–10
abortion, 48
Ahmed, Sara, 63–64
Alcott, Louisa May, 1–2, 17, 18, 19, 20, 21, 24, 25, 26, 27, 39, 131
Aliens:
    film, 151
    Ripley, 151
Amazon:
    books, 97, 100, 228
    videos, 135, *136*, 151
American Tomboys: 1850–1915, 31
Ancel, Michel, 187
And Baby Makes Seven, 37, 48–51
android, 137, 146, 151, 152
Annedroids:
    Eyes, 137
    Hands, 137
    junkyard, 137, 144, 145–46, 149, 153
    Maggie, 154
    Nick, *136*, 137, 144, 145, 149, 151, 154, 155
    PAL, 137, 149, 151
    Sagan, Anne, 135–57
    Shania, 137, 144, 145, 148, 149, 151, 152
    show, 9, 135–57
    Wilbert, 137
Anzaldúa, Gloria, 37
Ashby, Emily, 137, 152, 153
ASPIRES, 2, 146, 154
Atwell, Hayley, 119
Autobiography of a Tomboy, 15

Bad News Bears, The:
    film, 3
    Whurlitzer, Amanda, 3
Bahri, Deepika, 86
Balay, Anne, 142
Ballon Rouge, Le, 53
Bamber, Judie, 69
Barnett, David, 47
Barton, Clara, 25
baseball, 3, 65–66, 161, 209, 224, 225
Beaty, Andrea, 97, 99

beauty, 21, 27, 95, 122, 127, 128, 129, 154, 163, 198
Beauvoir, Simon de, 21
Bechdel Test, 111
Beecher, Catherine, 25
BEM Sex Role Inventory, 93–94
Bend it Like Beckham:
film, 3
Jules, 3
Berlin, 45
Beyond Good and Evil, 9–10, 187–208
Alpha Section, 197, 199, 202
Daï-jo, 199, 202, 204
DomZ, 197, 199–200, 202, 203
Double H, 197, 199–202
Hillys, 196–97, 199
IRIS Network, 197, 199
Jade, 9–10, 187, 194, 196–205
Jade Reporting, 202
Pey'j, 197, 199, 200–202
bicycle, 17, 146, 179, 213
Black, Capitola, 21
Bletchley Park, 124
Boehmer, Elleke, 83
Bordo, Susan, 20
Bradley, Amanda, 4, 5
Brannon, Linda, 75
Brave, 135
Breakfast Club, The, 163
Brecht, Bertolt, 7, 37, 44, 45, 46–48
Brecht in Practice: Theatre, Theory and Performance, 46–47
breeches roles, 34–*35*, 39
Brooks Brothers, 223
Brown, Katy, 27
Brown, Millie Bobby, *166*, 181
Bryn Mawr College, 18
Bustle, 169
Butch Geography, 7, 57–72
Butler, Judith, 113–14, 192, 193

California, 27, 127, 170, 171
Camaro Z28, 177
Campfire Girls, The, 22
Canada:
Canadian Astronaut Corps, 155
Governor General of Canada, 155
television, 9, 135–57
Carlson, Ashley Lynn, 95, 144, 145, 153
Carr, Lynn, 139, 141, 147, 148–49, 150, 153, 187, 193, 194, 211, 212
Cassini, Giovanni Domenico, 152
Centipede, *172*
Chestnutt, Charles, 17
Chicago, 163
Chicago World's Fair, 27
China, *40*
Churchill, Winston, 125
Civil War, 19, 22, 140, 142, 146
Clark, Sheryl, 139, 148
class, 1, 10, 18, 19, 21, 26, 43, 48, 189, 190, 209–28
clothing, 8, 16, 34, 37, 59, 92, 98, 99, 101, 102, 115, 118, 135, 139, 141, 142, 143, 144–45, 149, 153, 155, 161, 162, 163, 164, 165, 167, 168–69, 170, 171, 177, 178, 179, 181, 198, 209–10, 217, 223–24, 225, 226, 227, 228. *See also* costume, dress
Clueless, 163
Cohen, Daniel E., 21
College Fashion, 162
comic book, 3, 111, 113, 130
Common Sense Media, 152
Cornell University, 176
costume, 117, 116, 118, 149, 155, 164, 174, 175, 181. *See also* clothing, dress
Cowan, Gloria, 145
Craig, Traci, 33, 115, 116, 122, 127, 131, 143, 145, 146, 148, 155, 176, 193–94, 198
Croft, Laura, 197
Crowell, Hope J, 144, 153
Culkin, Katie, 23, 24
Currie, Dawn, 141
Curtis, Ariana Randolph Wormeley, 39
Cushman, Charlotte, 24, 27

Damour, Lisa, 6, 32

Dangarembga, Tsitsi, 8, 73–89
DapperQ, 213
Daughters of Genius, 27
Davies, Cristyn, 142–43, 153
Davis, Lisa Selin, 2–3, 5, 6, 159
Dean-Ruzicka, Rachel, 94, 95
Derrida, Jacques, 189
Descartes, René, 189
Despicable Me, 135
Deutch, Howard, 163
Dick Van Dyke Show:
  Moore, Mary Tyler, 2
  show, 2
Dietrich, Marlene, 2
Dig Dug, *172*
Di Liello, Adrianna, 137
DiQuinzio, Patrice, 32
Divergent:
  film, 180
  Prior, Tris, 180
doll, 110
Dora the Explorer, 135
Dowlin, Jadiel, *136*–37
dress, 2, 26, 27, 59, 83, 93, 98, 99, 101, 103, 125, 163, 164, *166*, 210, 211, 225. *See also* clothing, costume
Duffer Brothers, The, 159–83
Dungeons & Dragons, 177

E! News, 181
Eilish, Billie, 6
Elise, Dianne, 76, 77, 178
Emmy Award, *136*
England, 74, 79, 81, 110
Enlightenment, 188
Entertainment Weekly, 181
Everquest, 195
Everything Kids' Science Experiments Book, The, 100–102, 103

Facebook, 214, *215*
Facts of Life, The:
  Polniaczek, Jo, 2
  show, 2

fashion, 2, 27, 91, 137, 144, 145, 153, 162, 168–69, 178, 212, 213, 214, 223
Feige, Kevin, 110
Female Masculinity, 138
femme fatale, 9, 109, 110, 114, 119–29
femme forte, 128
Ferris Bueller's Day Off, 170–71
fishing, 3, 17, 24
Fixer Upper, 97, 99
flapper, 123
Foucault, Michel, 60
Francis, Becky, 138, 147
Freaky Friday, 3
Freeman, Elizabeth, 61, 66, 71
Freemont, Jessie Benton, 27
Freud, Sigmund, 77

Gains, Joanna, 97
Game of Thrones:
  show, 6
  Stark, Arya, 6
gardening, 8, 97, 98–99, 148
Gemmil, Allie, 169
gender fluidity, 102, 103, 137, 167
gender identity, 5, 6, 26, 67, 74–75, 78, 81, 94, 95, 96, 98, 99, 118, 167, 123, 138–39, 140, 149, 162, 167, 192–94, 205
gender performance, 7, 10, 37, 38, 91, 92, 146, 187, 193, 194, 196, 204, 205, 216
Gender Trouble, 113
George, Ivy, *121*
Gerwig, Greta, 130
Ghostbusters, 174, 175
Gilder, Jeannette, 15, 23
Girls of Central High, The, 22
Girl Scouts of the United States of America, 5–6
girly girl, 94, 115, 123, 139, 140, 147, 154, 210, 212, 213
glasses, 101, 217
Godey's Lady's Book, 20
Gonsalves, Allison, 147
Good Place, The:

Shellstrop, Eleanor, 6
show, 6
Graham, Elaine, 191
Grand Theft Auto V, 195
Graves, Gabriella, *121*
Gravity Falls:
Corduroy, Wendy, 6, 181
Pines, Dipper, 181
show, 6, 181
Valentino, Robbie, 181
Great Depression, 44
Gypsy Breynton, 21, 34, 142

Elle magazine, 2
Evans, Chris, 131

hair, 5, 8, 10, 21, 26, 27, 28, 93, 98, 99, 101, 102, 103, 125, 135, *136*, 139, 140, 144, 145, 149, 150, 154, 162–63, 164, 165, 167, 170, 171, *172*, 174, 175, 177, 178, 179, 181, 197, 209, 210, 216, 217, *219–220*, 221, 225, 226, 227, 228
Halberstam, Jack, 26, 59, 61, 64, 67, 69, 75, 77, 80–81, 84, 138, 140, 141, 144, 193, 228
Hall, Joanne, 143
Hampstead, 125
Harding, Natasha, 2
Harper, F. E. W., 17, 18
Harper's Bizarre, 27
Heckerling, Amy, 163
Hepburn, Audrey, 2
Hesper, 23
Hidden Hand, The, 21
Hindsgaul, Sarah, 178, 181
Hirsch, Alex, 181
History of Sexuality: An Introduction, Volume 1, The, 60
Hitler, Adolf, 46, 117, 119
hobbyhorse, 120
Holley, Anne, 135, *136*, 144
Hollywood, 2, 3, 126–27, 152
Hosmer, Harriet, 23–24, 25, 27
Hughes, John, 163, 164, 170, 171
Human Body Activity Book for Kids, 100, 102, 103
Hunger Games, The:
Everdeen, Katniss, 124, 180
film, 124, 142, 144, 149, 180

Instagram, 10, 170, 209, 211, 214–24, *220*, 225, 226, 227
Iscove, Robert, 163

Jacobs, Harriet, 17, 18
Jennings, Rebecca, 123
Jo's Boys, 25
Johnson, J. J., *136*, 152
Julius Caesar, 51
Juno, 3

Kant, Immanuel, 188
Keeling, Kara, 71
Kenny, Correia, 152
Kings College London, 154
Knaier, Michelle L., 96, 101
knight, 110, 120, 125
Kohler, Chris, 205

Lacroix, Jessica, 33, 115, 116, 122, 127, 131, 143, 145, 146, 148, 155, 176, 193–94, 198
Lady Chatterley's Lover, 82
Larcom, Lucy, 25
Last Man Standing:
Baxter, Eve, 6
show, 6
Lawrence, D. H., 82
League of Their Own, A, 3
Lee, Harper, 34
Lego Movie, The:
film, 135
Wyldstyle, 135
Lemke, Jay, 95
Life magazine, 126
lipstick, 120, 125, 128, 167, 198, 120, 125, 128. *See also* makeup
Little House on the Prairie, 2, 34
Little Men, 25

Little Mermaid, The, 142, 144, 150
Little Women:
book, 2, 17, 18, 19, 21, 22, 25, 39, 124, 142, 150
film (2019), 130
March, Jo, 2, 17, 18, 19, 20, 21, 22, 25, 34, 39, 91, 124, 130, 131
Lorde, Audre, 60–61, 63, 68, 69

Mabura, Lily G. N., 80
makeover, 145, 163–69, 176, 178, 181
makeup, 10, 149, 153, 154, 164–65, *166*, 167, 213. 217, 228. *See also* lipstick
male gaze, 27, 196, 199
Manus, Vicki Briault, 80
marriage, 18, 20, 22, 26, 31, 32, 34, 38, 39, 41, 43, 44, 45, 47, 50, 80, 125, 141, 228
Marshall, Garry, 163
Marvel Cinematic Universe (MCU), 9, 109–33
Agent Carter, 109–33

Avengers, The, 2012, 112
Avengers: Endgame, 112, 113, 114, 115–16, 130, 131
Barnes, Bucky, 118
Black Widow, 111, 114
Captain America, 109, 110, 111, 113, 114, 116–19, 130, 131
Captain America: The First Avenger, 111, 114, 115
Captain Britain, 111
Captain Marvel, 109, 111, 114
Captain Marvel, 110, 111
Carter, Peggy, 9, 109–33, *121*
Cully, Agnes, 120, 122, 126
Foster, Dr. Jane, 111
Frost, Whitney, 9, 110, 120–23, *121*, 124, 128, 130
Gamora, 111
Iron Man, 110, 131
Iron Man, 111, 112–14
Isodyne Industries, 122
Nebula, 111
Okoye, 111
Potts, Pepper, 111, 113, 131
Rogers, Steve, 111, 114, 116–19, 130
Scarlet Witch, 111
Shuri, 111
Slane, Obadiah, 113
Stark, Howard, 118
Stark, Tony, 112–14, 131
Strategic Homeland Intervention, Enforcement, and Logistics Division (S. H. I. E. L. D.), 109, 116
Strategic Scientific Reserve (SSR), 109, 115–16, 199, 131
Super Serum, 117
Thanos, 113, 131
Thor, 111
Thor: Love and Thunder, 111
Uncle Bud, 120, *121*, 122, 125, 126
Valkyrie, 111
Van Dyne, Dr. Janet, 111
What If . . . ?, 111
Zero Matter, 126, 127, 129
Marvelous Mrs. Maisel, The:
Myerson, Susie, 6
masquerade, 128
McDaniel, Jamie, 174
McDermott, Shawna, 91–92, 103, 123–24, 142, 143–44, 146, 149, 150
McIntyre, Gina, 180–81
McLeod, Anne Scout, 16, 17
Mean Girls:
film, 124, 142, 144, 149
George, Regina, 124
Meltzer, Marisa, 3, 4, 209, 210
Mettler, Lizzie Garrett, 211, 214, 216, 224, 225, 226, 228
Million Dollar Baby:
film, 3
Fitzgerald, Maggie, 3
mirror, 126, 165, *166*, 167, 178, 222

Miss Congeniality, 163
Modern Motherhood: An American History, 52
Mother Courage and Her Children:
  Mother Courage, 7, 45–47
  play, 37, 44–48
motorcycle, 3
Mouton, Louise Chandler, 26
Mulan:
  film, 135
multi-generational, *136*
Muñoz, José Esteban, 58, 61, 62, 64, 65, 68–69
Murphy, Katherine J., 111, 130
My Girl:
  film, 3
  Sultenfuss, Vada, 3
My Little Pony: Friendship in Magic:
  Rainbow Dash, 135
  show, 135
Myers, Michael, 174, 175

Nancy Drew, 22
Nazism, 44, 46
Nelson, Maggie, 68
Nervous Conditions:
  anorexia, 85–87
  Babamukuru, 74, 76, 77, 79, 80, 81, 82–83, 84–85
  book, 8, 73–89
  Maiguru, 77, 79–80, 81, 82
  Nhamo, 8, 75–76
  Nyasha, 74, 79–87
  Tambu, 8, 73–81, 83, 85, 86, 87
New Jersey, 23, 153
New Woman, *36*, 52, 123
New York City, 25, 116, 127, 223
Nicolás, Susana, 128
Niles, Thomas, 19
Nobel Prize, 148
Nodelman, Perry, 96
NVIVO 12, 216, 217

offer gaze, *219*, 221–22
Oklahoma, 120, 126
Orange is the New Black:
  show, 6
  Washington, Poussey, 6
Orenstein, Peggy, 153
Our Famous Women: Comprising the Lives and Deeds of Famous American Women, 24, 25, 26
Ozick, Cynthia, 21

Paechter, Carrie, 94, 138, 139–40, 145, 148, 149, 152
Parents' Choice Gold Award, *136*
Parton, James, 27
Payette, Julie, 155
Petrie, Donald, 163
Phelps, Elizabeth Stuart, 1, 21, 34
photojournalist, 197, 203
piercing, 224, 225, 227
pink, 98, 99, 145, 149, 153, 163, 164, 165, *166*, 171, *172*–73, 198, 225, 226
Pinsta.me, *215*
Plumb, Pat, 145
Powerpuff Girls, The, 135
pregnancy, 37, 48, 49, 50, 51
Prince, Liz, 209, 211, 216, 224, 225, 227, 228
Princess Diaries, The, 163
Prix Jeunesse International, 152
punk, 155, 162, 163, 167
Punky Bruster, 2

race, 21, 48, 73, 74, 101, 205, 209–28
radio, 120, 122
Rahman, Muzna, 85
rebellion, 4, 18, 19, 22, 24, 28, 74, 76, 82, 85, 86, 123, 124, 135, 141, 153
Red Cross, 25
Reiner, Carl, 2
Reiss, Michael, 95
Reitman, Ivan, 174
Rhodesia, 8, 73–89
Roberts, David, 97
Robinson, Ashley Sufflé, 113
Robinson, Kerry, 142–43, 153
Robinson, Tom, 100

robotics, 9, *136*, 137, 144, 146, 150, 151, 152, 154
Romp, The:
musical, 31
Tomboy, Pricilla, 31
Roseanne:
Conner, Darlene, 2
show, 2
Rosie Revere, Engineer, 97, 99–100, 102
Rosie Revere and the Raucous Riveters, 97
Rosie the Riveter, 34, 119
Runkle, Lucia Gilbert, 25

Sagan, Carl, 152
Sarkeesian, Anita, 195, 198, 199
Savin-Williams, Ritch, C., 176
Sedgewick, Eve, 59
Selvick, Stephanie M., 83
Sentilles, Renée, 15, 16, 18, 19–20, 21, 22, 26, 31, 32, 33, 34, 39, 43, 47, 51, 52, 142
She's All That, 163
Shendruk, Amanda, 130
showgirl, 109, 117, 118, 119
Sicherman, Barbara, 18, 19, 21, 22
Sink, Sadie, 159, 170, *172*
sissy, 75, 118
skateboard, 169, *172*–73, 174, 177, 179
Skelton, Christine, 138
Skerski, Jamie, 151, 153
smoking, 21, 217, 218
social justice, 91, 196, 203
social media, 10, 170, 209–31
Sofia Valdez, Future Prez, 97
Some Kind of Wonderful, 3, 163
Southworth, E. D. E. N., 21
Spade, Dean, 67
Spirit of Seventy-Six, or The Coming Woman, a Prophetic Drama, The:
Carberry, Thomas, *40*, 41, 42
play, 37, 39–44
Wigfall, Judge Susan, 37, 39–*40*, 41, 42, 43, 44
Spivak, Gayatri, 78
Stahl, Lynne, 6, 139, 142, 147
Star Wars: The Rise of Skywalker, 130
Stein, Ben, 170
STEM, 8, 9, 94, 95–6, 97, 101–103, 135–57, 187
Stockton, Kathryn Bond, 34, 59, 68, 71, 142
Stokes, Katie, 100
Stranger Things:
Axel, 167
Benny's Burgers, 160, 163
Buckley, Robin, 181
Byers, Joyce, 168
Byers, Will, 161, 163, 167, 175, 176, 177, 180, 181
Clarke, Scott, 170–72, 180
D'Artagnan, 176–77
Dottie, 167
Eleven, 9, 159, 160–69, *166*, 170, 177, 178, 179, 180, 181
Funshine, 167
Hargrove, Billy, 175–76
Hawkins National Laboratory, 160, 167
Henderson, Dustin, 164, 165, *166*, 170, *172*, 173, 175, 176
Hopper, James, 163, 167, 168
Kali, 163, 167–68
Mayfield, Max, 6, 9, 159, 162, 168, 169–79, 180
Melvald's General Store, 168
Mick, 167
Mind Flayer, 179
Newby, Bob, 177
show, 6, 9, 159–83
Sinclair, Lucas, 163–64, 165, *166*, 170, *172*, 173, 174, 175, 176, 179
Snow Ball, 178
Starcourt Mall, 168
Upside Down, 163, 167
Wheeler, Mike, 161, 163, 164–65, *166*, 167, 168, 170, 175, 176, 177, 181

Wheeler, Nancy, 161, 162, 163, 165, 179
Zoomer, 177
Stranger Things: Worlds Turned Upside Down: The Official Behind-the-Scenes Companion, 180
Stoller, Robert, 138
Stowe, Harriet Beecher, 17, 25
suffrage, 37, 39–44

tattoo, 218, *219*, *220*, 223, 224, 225, 227
Telegraph, The, 180
Third Reich, 44
Thirty Years' War, 37, 45
Thomas, Carey M., 18–19
Time magazine, 131
Title IX, 2
To Kill a Mockingbird, 34
tomboy:
as adult, 26, 116, 209–28
as aggressive, 39, 46, 92, 93, 146, 169, *172*, 177, 196, 202
aging out of, 9, 58, 67, 124, 140–41, 178–79
as androgynous, 10, 39, 97, 101, 102, 137, 139–40, 149, 209–28
as asexual, *36*, 86, 128
as "butch," 57–72, 81, 213, 225, 228
of color, 10, 17–18, 73–89, 209–28
as LGBTQ+, 4–5, 6, 10, 57–72, 80, 83, 94, 95, 96, 149, 153, 175–76, 209–28
as mother, 31–54
as motherless, 147, 154
as postcolonial figure, 73–89
tamed, 9, 21, 25, 84, 123, 124, 126, 127, 129, 131, 141–44, 150
untamed, 9, 25, 116, 125, 143, 151
Tomboy: A Memoir, 209, 211, 214, 216, 221
Tomboy: The Surprising History and Future of Girls Who Dare to Be Different, 6, 159
Tomboy at Work, The, 15
Tomboy Project, The, 92–93, 94
Tomboy Style, 211, 214, 216, 221, 222, 223, 224
Tomboys: A Literary and Cultural History, 1, 91, 115
Tomboys and Bachelor Girls: A Lesbian History of Post-War Britain 1945–1971, 123
Tree-climbing, 15, 16, 17, 21, 26, 64, 140, 141, 193, 209, 224
Turing, Alan, 152

Ubisoft, 187, 196, 205
Uncle Tom's Cabin:
book, 17
Topsy, 17, 18

Uncovering Stranger Things: Essays on Eighties Nostalgia, Cynicism and Innocence in the Series, 162
unicorn, 149
United Kingdom, 73, 95, *136*
United States, 1, 5, 19, 25, 39, 91, 95, *136*, 228
University of Oklahoma, 126
Uwakweh, Pauline Ada, 78

Valley Girl, 175
Vandenberg-Daves, Jodi, 52, 154
Verhage, Florentien, 37
Victoria's Secret, 222
Victorian Era, 16, 17, 19, 20, 25, 32, 34, 39, 50
videogame, 9–10, 177, 187–208
virgin, 109, 116, 131
Vogel, Paula, 37, 48, 48–51

W magazine, 170, 181
Waite, Stacey, 7–8, 57–72
Walker, Peter, 180
Walking Dead, The:

Greene, Maggie, 6
show, 6
Walsh, Karen, M., 174
Waltons, The:
show, 2
Walton, Mary Ellen, 2
Waugh, Amanda, 77, 78, 85
We Are the Gardeners, 97, 98–99, 100, 102
Weaver, Sigourney, 151
Webstagram, *215*
wedding, 81
wedding dress, 125
What Katy Did, 142
Wilcox, Kim, 181
Wilson, Harriet, 17
Wired, 205
Wizard of Oz, The, 155
Wolfhard, Finn, *166*
World Health Organization, 152
World of Warcraft, 195, 198
World War I, 128
World War II, 34, 122, 125, 128, 228
Women in STEM on Television, 95
Women's Army Corps, 34
Women's Medical College, The, 25
Woodfern, Winnie, 21
Words About Pictures, 96
Wright, Bradford, 111
Wright, Derek, 86

Yarbrough, Scott, 128

Zeisler, Andi, 17
Zevy, Lee, 86

About the Editors

Erica Joan Dymond is an assistant professor of English at East Stroudsburg University, with a PhD in English from Lehigh University. She has been a consulting editor for the peer-reviewed, academic journal *The Explicator* since 2011. She has also acted as a manuscript reviewer for the Amazon Breakthrough Novel Award and a peer-reviewer for Focal Press as well as Routledge. Her work has been published in academic journals such as *The Journal of Popular Culture* and *The Explicator*. Likewise, her work appears in academic texts such as *A Cuban Cinema Companion* and *The Encyclopedia of Japanese Horror Films*. She is co-editor of *The Encyclopedia of Sexism in American Films* (Rowman & Littlefield 2019) and the forthcoming *The Encyclopedia of LGBTQIA+ Portrayals in American Films* (Rowman & Littlefield 2022).

Jen Harrison is a freelance writer, editor, and dissertation coach with a PhD in Children's Literature from Aberystwyth University in the UK. Jen specializes in research focusing on ecocriticism, posthumanism, and children's literature and culture. In addition to editing this collection, Jen has recently published monographs exploring posthumanism and the environment in young adult dystopia and *Winnie the Pooh*, as well as articles on *Harry Potter*, *The Hunger Games*, and Neil Gaiman's *The Ocean at the End of the Lane*. She is an editor for the peer-reviewed journal *Jeunesse: Young People, Texts, Cultures*, a reviewer for *The Children's Book Review website*, and CEO of ReadWritePerfect.com academic coaching.

As a young girl, **Holly Wells** wanted nothing more than to be a novelist. Although her fiction writing career fizzled out in her early 30s, Holly's love for the written word led to MA and PhD degrees in English and rhet/comp, respectively. She is now associate professor of English at East Stroudsburg University, where she primarily teaches writing and professional writing courses at the graduate and undergraduate levels. Her published research focuses on intersections of visual rhetoric and gender representation in the sciences and on social media. Research for future projects is concentrating on autoethnography and memoir.

About the Contributors

Lynn Deboeck is an adjunct assistant professor of theatre and gender studies at the University of Utah. Her research interests revolve around pedagogy, directing live performance and the performance and representation of maternity and reproduction in Western theatrical traditions. Her work has appeared in a number of edited collections, including ones published by Bloomsbury Methuen and Routledge, and in journals such as *Frontiers: A Journal of Women's Studies* and *PARtake: The Journal of Performance as Research.*

Rebecca Feasey is senior lecturer in film and media communications at Bath Spa University. She has published a range of work on the representation of gender in popular media culture. She has published in journals such as *Feminist Media Studies* and the *Journal of Gender Studies*. She has written book length studies on masculinity and popular television (EUP 2008), motherhood on the small screen (Anthem 2012), maternal audiences (Peter Lang 2016) and infertility and non-traditional family building in the media (Palgrave Macmillan, 2019).

CE Mackenzie is a PhD candidate in critical and cultural studies at the University of Pittsburgh. With a blend of both academic and creative training, their work explores epistemological possibilities that disrupt, resist, and subvert capital's hold on the imagination. Specifically, they are interested in theories of care, and how by queering our notions of health we might undermine cultural demands for productivity, positivity, and assimilation. Their work has appeared in such spaces as *QED: A Journal in GLBTQ Worldmaking, CutBank Literary Magazine, The Colorado Review,* and *The Toast,* among others.

Cara McClintock-Walsh is a professor of English at Northampton Community College, where she teaches courses in women and gender studies and Irish literature. She is also the coordinator of the honors program and currently holds the Robert J. Kopecek endowed chair in the humanities. She has published articles on Irish literature (in the collection *Postcolonialism and WB Yeats*), modern American literature, and on topics involving gender and representation. Her current scholarship involves unearthing the connections between African American and Irish theater in the early twentieth century. In her spare time, she is mother to two great kids. Her interest in the MCU can be attributed almost wholly to the influence of her fourteen-year-old daughter.

Tatiana Prorokova-Konrad is a postdoctoral researcher at the Department of English and American Studies, University of Vienna, Austria. She holds a PhD in American studies from the University of Marburg, Germany. She was a visiting researcher at the Forest History Society (2019), an Ebeling fellow at the American Antiquarian Society (2018), and a visiting scholar at the University of South Alabama, USA (2016). She is the author of *Docu-Fictions of War: U.S. Interventionism in Film and Literature* (University of Nebraska Press 2019), the editor of *Transportation and the Culture of Climate Change: Accelerating Ride to Global Crisis* (West Virginia University Press 2020) and *Cold War II: Hollywood's Renewed Obsession with Russia* (University Press of Mississippi 2020), and a coeditor of *Cultures of War in Graphic Novels: Violence, Trauma, and Memory* (Rutgers University Press 2018).

Renée M. Sentilles is Henry Eldridge Bourne professor of history at Case Western Reserve University in Cleveland, Ohio. She studies and teaches the social and cultural histories of people in the United States, and predominately writes about the experiences of girls and women in the nineteenth and early twentieth centuries. As well as writing articles and essays, she has produced two historical monographs: *Performing Menken: Adah Isaacs Menken and the Birth of American Celebrity* (Cambridge, 2003) and *American Tomboys, 1850–1915* (Massachusetts 2018).

Poppy Wilde, PhD is a lecturer in media and communication at Birmingham City University. Her work focuses on what it means and how it feels to be posthuman, by exploring how posthuman subjectivities are enabled and embodied. She has conducted autoethnographic projects exploring the lived experience of MMORPG gaming with particular focus on the avatar-gamer as an embodiment of posthuman subjectivity. In her current work she is extending this to explore further insights in gaming, from species hybridity to moral ambiguity, as well as researching critical posthumanism through a variety of different contexts, from zombie studies to storytelling.

www.ingramcontent.com/pod-product-compliance
Lightning Source LLC
Chambersburg PA
CBHW022307280326
41932CB00010B/1009
* 9 7 8 1 7 9 3 6 2 2 9 6 9 *